Cycl
Kettle Valley
Railway

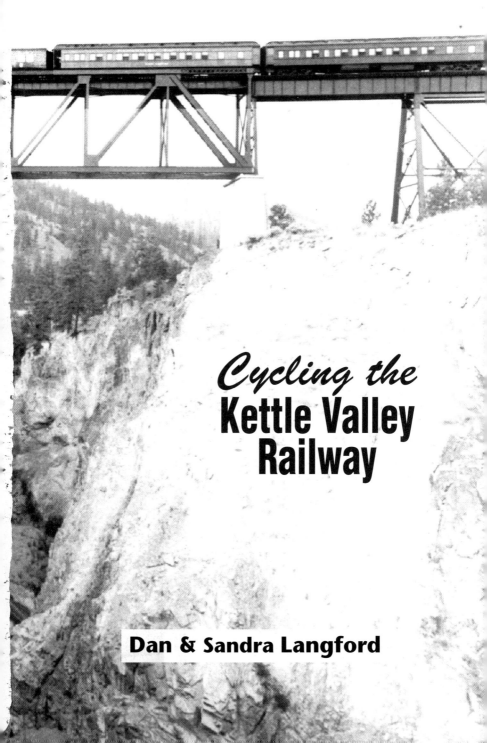

Cycling the
Kettle Valley
Railway

Dan & Sandra Langford

*Front cover: Cycling over the trestle spanning the out fall of Otter Lake
(km 139.2, Princeton Subdivision)
Title page: Trout Creek Bridge km 11.7, Princeton Subdivision (Penticton Museum)*

Maps © Dan Langford, 1994, 1997, 2002.
Photos by Sandra and Dan Langford unless otherwise noted.
Timetables and newspaper clippings courtesy of the Penticton Museum.

We acknowledge the financial support of the Government of Canada through
the Book Publishing Industry Development Program (BPIDP) for our
publishing activities.

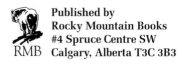

**Published by
Rocky Mountain Books
#4 Spruce Centre SW
RMB Calgary, Alberta T3C 3B3**

National Library of Canada Cataloguing in Publication Data

Langford, Dan, 1959-
  Cycling the Kettle Valley Railway

  ISBN 0-921102-88-7

  1. Bicycle touring--British Columbia--Okanagan-Similkameen--Guide-
books. 2. Bicycle trails--British Columbia--Okanagan-Similkameen--Guide-
books. 3. Okanagan-Similkameen (B.C.)--Guidebooks. 4. Kettle Valley
Railway--Guidebooks. I. Langford, Sandra, 1962- II. Title.
FC3845.O4A3 2002   796.6'4'097115   C2002-910473-4
F1089.O5L36 2002

CONTENTS

PREFACE

In the summer of 1991 our friends were asking about our summer plans-our reply, "Cycling the Kettle Valley Railway." Their response consistently echoed, "Where is that?" Indeed that had been our response when reading a mention of this rail-cycle trip in a magazine. That year we blindly set off at Midway with what little information we could find and biked to Osoyoos. With the rails were still in place from Penticton to Merritt we returned to the abandoned railway numerous times to cycle the railbed as the rails were removed. By the summer of 1993 it became evident that a guidebook was needed to increase awareness of this unbelievable tourist resource and so others could also enjoy this both breath taking and sometimes muscle-aching adventure.

The labour of researching for this guidebook was full of excitement, frustration and a lot of hard work. We spent weeks cycling into the back county with tape recorder, camera and maps and books in hand, at times doing a lot of back tracking and making very little headway. But, as with most backcountry adventures, enjoyment often comes at the expense of hard work.

Every year we continued to return to the railway, many times as part of Robbin McKinney's Great Exploration Tour. With these return visits we were able to get valuable feedback to incorporate into new editions.

While cycling the abandoned rail corridors we were delighted at the number of individuals and tour groups enjoying the rail-trail and utilizing our book as a guide. We met many local cyclists as well as cyclists from all over the world. We are grateful for all the letters, email and phone calls we have received over the past few years. They have been both inspiring and informative. Once again we hope you find with in these pages all that inspired us to cycle these spectacular railways.

Dan and Sandra, 2002 ▄

ACKNOWLEDGEMENTS

Many people and organizations provided support and encouragement in the production of this 3rd edition. Thanks to all those who have written and emailed their suggestions, updates and comments. They were all very important to us in getting all the information of this great trail together. Thanks also for their help and encouragement to: Ken Campbell, Sjeng Derkx, Pierre Dupont, Hanna Heintz, Craig and Karen Henderson (Vista Treks), Léon Lebrun, Robbin McKinney (Great Explorations), Chris Moslin, Steven Rigby, Elaine Robinson, Murphy Shewchuk, Joe Smuin, Brian Springinotic, Fred Thiessen, Walter Volovsek.

And a special thanks to all those who work to build and maintain these wonderful railtrails ▄

INTRODUCTION

The Kettle Valley Railway (KVR) is an abandoned railbed situated in the Southern Interior of British Columbia, weaving its way through the Okanagan-Similkameen region. This area has much to offer including wilderness parks, warm climate, unique towns and cities, and diverse landscapes such as mountains, rivers, canyons, orchards, lakes, sandy beaches and Canada's own desert.

The development of the Kettle Valley Railway was inspired by both the discovery of incredible mineral wealth in B.C.'s southeastern (Kootenay) mountains, as well as the fear of American domination of this region. The purpose of the KVR was to divert the Kootenay riches to the province's own seaport in Vancouver, rather than cross the border by U.S. rails.

Through the determination and ability of Andrew McCulloch, the chief engineer, the dream of a "coast-to-Kootenay" line was fulfilled, and the Kettle Valley Railway was realized. His ability to engineer the KVR through such unforgiving terrain as Myra Canyon and the Coquihalla Pass, accounted for much of the railway's reputation as an engineering marvel. These challenges were handled so skilfully by McCulloch that the railway was soon dubbed "McCulloch's Wonder." Today, you will find many commemorative plaques along this corridor recognizing McCulloch's work on the KVR.

While cycling this corridor, we find ourselves surrounded by the history of this unique railway. One example is the tunnels and trestles of Myra Canyon, reminding us of the engineering complexities and sheer labour required to see this railway to completion. While the trestles and tunnels are a sure reminder to the cyclist of the origin of this trail, you soon forget while cycling along a tree-lined railbed of green grass that 80 years ago locomotives laden with silver, copper, iron, coal and lumber began thundering over newly laid tracks.

Abandoned railway corridors hold unparalleled opportunities as recreational trails, and the KVR is no exception. This corridor is one of the most dynamic routes in the area, with some truly impressive scenery and spectacular views. The easy grade in most sections makes it suitable for either casual family cycling or easy day riding. The over 800 kilometres of travel routes make it challenging for the more adventuresome. Utilizing the numerous unique accommodations and camping facilities along this route allows for weekend or extended trips.

This book provides you with a practical guide to cycling the Kettle Valley Railway. You will find detailed maps, historical information, safety tips and a kilometre by kilometre trail guide to each of the KVR subdivisions. Other useful information provided to assist you in planning your trip is the listing of local accommodations, tour operators and services. Many groups and individuals have become active in the management of the KVR trail corridor. As a result of growing public interest and government support, we are beginning to see the conversion of the abandoned Kettle Valley Railway into a multi-use corridor that beckons the backcountry cyclist ▬

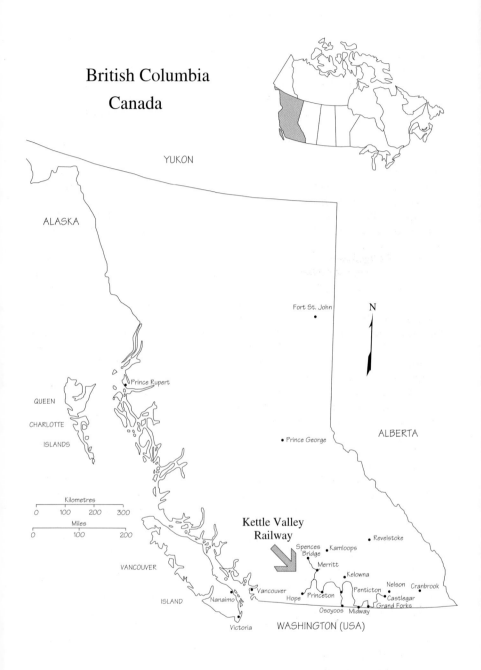

British Columbia
Canada

YUKON

ALASKA

Fort St. John

N

Prince Rupert

QUEEN

CHARLOTTE

ISLANDS

ALBERTA

Prince George

Kilometres

0   100   200   300

Miles

0   100   200

Kettle Valley
Railway

Revelstoke

Spences   Kamloops
Bridge
        Merritt

VANCOUVER   Kelowna
                                                    Nelson   Cranbrook
                          Vancouver   Penticton
ISLAND   Princeton   Castlegar
        Nanaimo   Hope   Grand Forks
                                    Osoyoos   Midway
Victoria   WASHINGTON (USA)

GEOGRAPHY

British Columbia is the westernmost province of Canada covering 952,263 square kilometres of spectacular mountains, glaciers, plains, rivers, valleys, lakes, coastline and islands. British Columbia's varied landscape was created by a complex series of geological events, the first of which was the movement of land masses over the earth's surface creating mountains upon collision as well as surface volcanic eruptions at points of separation. The movement of these plates in a direction parallel to each other created the mountains and deep valleys of B.C., which have one common characteristic: each range lies with its axis parallel to the province's coastline. Rivers therefore predominantly flow in a north or south direction, each separated by one or more of the mountain ranges. A second geological event was the ice age. Evidence of the powerful erosive effects of the glaciers can be best seen in the Okanagan Valley where these glaciers crawled their way up the valleys between mountain ranges, widening the valley, grinding against rocks, and leaving glacial silt and melt water as they retreated.

These unusual geographic features have blessed this province with a wide variety of climates and scenic wonders without equal in the world. However, it has also restricted the nature of human mobility in an eastern or western direction. This has been a dominant influence in the development of British Columbia, including that of the Kettle Valley Railway. With the beginning of the KVR's construction, after years of political and corporate struggle, attention was often focused on these geographical obstacles that needed to be overcome, some of which were almost without parallel in the history of Canadian railway construction.

The route of the Kettle Valley Railway lies mainly in the Southern Interior Plateau, known as the Okanagan-Similkameen region, which is bordered on either side by mountains. To the east of the Interior Plateau is the Purcell Range of the Columbia Mountains, while to the west are the Cascade Mountains, which mark the eastern border of the area known as Southwestern British Columbia.

The Kettle Valley Railway consists of five subdivisions that make their way across 500 kilometres of mountains and valleys from the Kootenays to the coast. The Carmi Subdivision begins at an elevation of 580 metres in the town of Midway, situated in the Midway Range of the Columbia Mountains. Progressing northwest along the railbed, you climb through the Beaverdell Range of the Columbia Mountains to reach the railway's summit in the Okanagan Highlands, at an elevation of 1270 metres. The railbed then descends from the Highlands down into the Okanagan Valley of the Interior Plateau reaching Penticton at an elevation of 341 metres.

Penticton is a junction point along the KVR. The Osoyoos Subdivision progresses south from Penticton. The railbed follows the Okanagan River Valley at a relatively level grade to reach the terminus in Osoyoos at an elevation of 281 metres.

The Princeton Subdivision progresses in a northwest direction from Penticton. The KVR climbs out of the Okanagan Valley, then follows the Trout Creek Valley as it winds its way through the Cascade Mountain foothills of

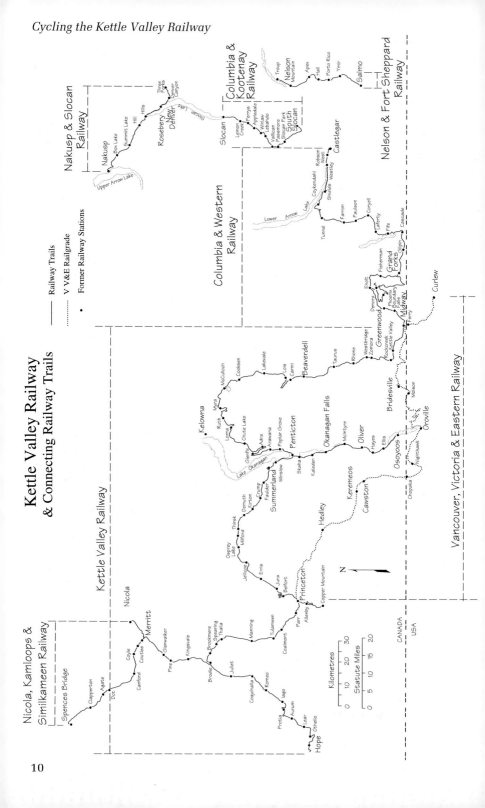

Cycling the Kettle Valley Railway

Kettle Valley Railway
& Connecting Railway Trails

Railway Trails
V V&E Railgrade
● Former Railway Stations

the Interior Plateau. After reaching the summit at Osprey Lake at an elevation of 1098 metres, the railbed descends to an elevation of 648 metres in Princeton. The Tulameen River Valley is followed out of Princeton, and the railbed climbs, reaching an elevation of 962 metres at Brookmere. Just past Brookmere are two subdivisions, one going north and the other south. The Merritt Subdivision progresses north from Brookmere. The railbed follows the Coldwater River Valley on a gentle downhill grade to reach Merritt at an elevation of 567 metres.

The Coquihalla Subdivision progresses southwest from Brodie, following the Coquihalla River Valley through the impressive Cascade Mountains to arrive at Hope. Beginning at an elevation of 962 metres in Brookmere, the railbed climbs to 1115 metres at the summit at Coquihalla, then descends to an elevation of only 44 metres at Hope. The KVR line across the Cascade Mountains to the east of Hope was known as the most difficult and expensive piece of trackage ever built in the history of railroads.

Cycling the length of this distinctive railway enables cyclists to experience the impressive qualities that a rail-trail corridor can offer. The KVR corridor is particularly unique with its numerous trestles, bridges, tunnels, 2.2% grades, and even a couple of switchbacks and a spiral tunnel that have all been incorporated to tackle the geography of this area of British Columbia. You can certainly appreciate why geography was one reason that demanded this was to be a railway like no other ━

CLIMATE

The climate of British Columbia can be summarized in one word—varied. One of the greatest influences on the climate is the geography. The mountains have a major effect on the weather, as the moist ocean air makes its way east across this varied landscape. For the most part, the western slopes of the Columbia Mountains and the Cascade Mountains tend to receive more precipitation, with a more arid and drier climate in the Interior Plateau. This variation becomes quite evident while cycling, for you can find snow at higher elevations, and farther down the trail bask in the sun.

The Carmi Subdivision follows along the mountains and valleys of the Kootenays, before beginning its descent into the Interior Plateau. The climate of the Kootenays is influenced by both continental and ocean air. The Kootenays have some of the same climactic characteristics as the Interior Plateau, with the exception in the higher elevations. Winters tend to be cold and dry except at higher elevations, which may have heavy rainfall in the summer and heavy winter snowfall from mid-November to April. Summers are hot, dry and low on humidity, though again, it is not uncommon for higher elevations to have an occasional July snow flurry.

Both the Princeton Subdivision and the Merritt Subdivision lie within the Southern Interior Plateau. The climate of this region is generally mild, warm and arid. Most of the summer days are dry and hot; the winters colder and somewhat wetter. However, with its proximity to the Cascade Mountains, even the occasional summer rain shower can quickly fall upon you with little advance warning.

11

The Osoyoos Subdivision also lies within the Southern Interior Plateau, but more importantly, it lies within the Okanagan Valley. This valley has some very distinct and unique features, such as the area between Oliver and Osoyoos that is considered Canada's only true desert and only climatic zone of its type in Canada. With an average rainfall of only 20 centimetres and temperatures ranging up to 46°C, summer days are sunny and warm, with desert nights refreshingly cool.

Snow in late May near Ruth, km 146.8, Carmi Subdivision.

The climate of the Coquihalla Subdivision is influenced by the rugged forest-covered, snow capped Cascade Mountains, and the proximity to the ocean. For about six months of every year, heavy snowfall was an extreme obstacle that often closed the Coquihalla Subdivision to rail service. It was a never ending battle for the men and their equipment to clear the tracks. Summer also presented its own problems with heavy rainfall and many washouts. It is reported that precipitation is heavier here than anywhere else in the province, with snow depths of over 12.7 metres not uncommon.

When making plans to cycle one or more subdivisions, prepare for the weather in that region. It is invaluable to the enjoyment of your trip to know the region through which you are travelling, and to be aware that weather can change rapidly in this land of mountains and valleys. For example, if cycling the Carmi Subdivision in May, you can have snow on the ground at Chute Lake, yet temperatures of 30°C in Penticton

FLORA AND FAUNA

There is a large variety of plants and animals along the route of the KVR, such as the lush coastal growth around Hope or the more broken forests and arid land of the Interior Plateau. Because of the Pacific's moist westerly winds and the north-south mountain walls that block them, the differences in both the vegetation and animal life can be quite profound.

The Carmi Subdivision lies among the dense conifer forests of the Kootenays, with occasional open meadow areas and marshlands. The forested landscape of the Kootenays is home to a variety of wildlife—squirrels, rabbits, deer, elk, moose, bear, beaver. Sightings are common. As you descend from the summit at Myra, the heavier forested areas begin to give way to the more broken forest and semi-arid landscape of the Interior Plateau.

The Princeton and Merritt subdivisions of the Interior Plateau have more open and dry sites. The most common tree in this more semi-arid area is the ponderosa pine. Because there are more sunny openings between trees, there is room for a more varied undergrowth. Wildflowers thrive and scatter these interior forests with a wide array of colour. The rich grasslands of this region occupy the climatic zone between the desert sagebrush and the pine forested areas. Local conditions and microclimates can also create grasslands. These grasslands were never the rolling carpet of the great plains but, as in Merritt, ranching has flourished. Wildlife, including bears, moose, deer, coyotes, ground hogs and yellow-bellied marmots—to name a few, are plentiful throughout this area of the Interior Plateau.

The Osoyoos Subdivision is similar to the semi-arid drylands of the Interior Plateau, except for some distinct flora and fauna found within the desert conditions south of Oliver. This desert land is the most northern home to some typical desert wildlife such as the five-toed kangaroo rat, pocket and grasshopper mice, burrowing owls, sage cottontail rabbits, calliope hummingbirds, turkey vultures and the largest concentration of birds of prey in the country. One might also chance a rare glimpse at the turtles and rattlesnakes that wander these parts. Some typical desert plants include the sagebrush, poison ivy and the prickly pear cactus. Also commonly found in this area are plants that actually avoid living in the desert by lining the streams and sending deep roots down to the underground water table. Irrigation also changes the desert landscape to one of beautiful orchards and vineyards. However, the desert again shows its true face where artificial watering ends.

Another unique region of the Osoyoos Subdivision worth special mention is Vaseux Lake, which lies within the Vaseux-Bighorn National Wildlife Area, a sanctuary for birds and wildlife. It is home to over 200 species of birds at different times of the year. Rare trumpeter swans and other waterfowl winter on the lake, and large numbers of Canada geese nest here yearly. On the eastern slopes above the lake you will often see the herd of California bighorn sheep that range here.

Wildlife is abundant along the KVR.

Much of the Coquihalla Subdivision enjoys a moist coastal climate. These rain forests are exceptionally damp with lush woods filled with a heavy undergrowth of ferns and mosses. Flowers of the shady forest tend to be shorter, more widespread, and have white blossoms as they are not attracting bees, but often de-

Myra Canyon. Notice new guard rails upgraded by the Myra Canyon Trestle Restoration Society.

pend upon ants or beetles for propagation. As light trickles through the trees and the moisture hangs in the air, you find this to be a magical place, especially while travelling the railbed from Othello toward Hope. While standing quietly, you will notice the eery quiet of these rain forests. Birds are often well above the heavy growth and most forest mammals prefer brushy woods broken by clearings. However, Hope boasts of having more than 200 species of birds and several breeds of mammals including deer, bear, coyote, cougar and mountain goat ▃

HAZARDS OF THE TRAIL

Trestles

Some trestles have been removed, and others must be detoured because of unsafe conditions. However, for the cyclist the true hazard of the trestles is self-created. There have been serious falls from the Myra Canyon trestles owing to cyclists riding instead of walking across trestles.

In September 1992, a 22 year-old cyclist, while crossing a trestle, fell from her bike to the rocks 25 metres below. Again in June 1993, a 20 year-old cyclist riding her mountain bike fell from a trestle to the rocks six metres below. She was semiconscious when a helicopter arrived at the scene to transport her to hospital. Witnesses stated the cyclist was riding slowly; however, once losing her balance, she had no time to react. Accidents like these can be avoided by walking instead of riding your bike across a trestle.

The Myra Canyon Trestle Restoration Society has installed permanent decking and hand rails on the trestles through Myra Canyon. This area of the KVR has been a main focus owing to the large volume of people exploring the canyon and the serious accidents mentioned above. Most other trestle crossings of the KVR are now in the process of being planked. Regardless of being planked or not, be smart; stop and walk your bike across all trestles and bridges.

Tunnels

Except for the Coquihalla Subdivision, only one tunnel—the spiral tunnel at Adra in the Carmi Subdivision—is presently barricaded due to unsafe conditions. Most of the KVR tunnels have some loose rockfall within them. In order to avoid accidents, we suggest you walk your bike through the tunnels because of both the decreased visibility and the unknown cycling surface. Total darkness can actually be experienced in some tunnels. The KVR steam engines have left the tunnel walls black from soot and with little reflective quality. Even a flashlight at times gives little reprieve from the blackness. Be careful where you step. With fallen rocks in places, you could easily trip or twist your ankle. If you have a lantern, that is ideal. It is also a good idea to keep your helmet on in case of rockfall from above. Livestock can also be another hazard in tunnels. Cows go into tunnels to get out of the heat of the sun. As you're walking, it can be quite unnerving to hear or see something lurking in the darkness.

Reliability of the Trail

The reliability of the KVR corridor may change from season to season and year to year. Sections of the trail can be hard to cycle after a heavy rain or a late spring thaw. New rock slides or washouts may have occurred, or there could be changes from erosion or construction. Be aware that this is a backcountry corridor with backcountry problems. However, with the planned future development of most sections, you may also find some pleasant changes en route.

Multi-use of the Trail

Throughout the KVR corridor you will meet other people using the trail. Although some areas are inaccessible to motorized traffic, other areas are not. In fact, some portions of the trail are kept weed-free and are pleasant to cycle because of the occasional vehicle traffic. Horses and hikers are also found using these trails, especially above Kelowna and Penticton. Some trail sections get fairly well chewed up due to frequent use by large horse parties, especially if conditions have been wet. Be cautious and courteous when passing horses as they can be easily spooked.

Horses are often met when cycling the railbed.

A more hazardous encounter is that of logging trucks. Many sections of the KVR are used by the forestry industry, which has created major washboarding along some stretches. If you meet up with a logging truck, stay well off the trail and away from corners. A heavily laden truck has little manoeuvrability and no way of suddenly stopping. When a truck passes, watch for sweepers (extra long logs that overhang the back of the truck by as much as six metres). On a steep road with sharp curves, these logs can sweep you right over the edge.

Being Prepared for Your Journey

Two cyclists can be on the same trip; to one it is exhilarating, and to the other it is a horrible disaster. The difference most often lies in how prepared the cyclist was for the expected and unexpected parts of the trip. Proper equipment is the first consideration. Bring what you need, what you may need and also what you hope not to need. This last group includes things like a first aid kit or even your bike helmet. Although you don't plan to fall from your bike, even a slight blow to the head from a rock or tree stump could result in a serious head injury. Proper gear helps to ensure your trip is not disastrous.

Being prepared includes not only planning, but also being physically and mentally prepared for your venture. This will enable you to deal more effectively with whatever you might encounter. As a result, things such as delays or weather changes are not likely to ruin your trip. It is also important to know how to repair your bike in case of breakdown. The repair equipment won't work by itself!

Judging the distance you can cycle is another factor in preparing for your trip. The average fully packed cyclist manages about 10 kilometres an hour, a little faster on downhill runs, and a little slower on some of the steeper detour roads. You must also take into account your down time, such as food and rest breaks, and also time spent exploring. A good day's cycle will usually average about 70 kilometres. Be sure to plan your trip keeping in mind the ability levels of your entire group.

Private Property
At the time of writing this updated edition, almost all of the right-of-ways previously owned by CPR and other railway companies have purchased by the Government of British Columbia or donated to The Trans Canada Trail Foundation. It is the hope of all involved with rail-trails that there will be expedient development of these corridors into official multi-use trails. Until then, when cycling the sections that are private property, one should obtain prior permission. The public corridors owned by the B.C. government can be freely travelled without fear of trespassing.

Sections of the right-of-ways that have been sold or leased to private interests do exist. The majority of these occur on spurs or older abandoned lines. Pieces have also been sold or leased within the boundaries of Penticton. Since this is an ever-changing feature of these right-of-ways, it is sometimes difficult to determine ownership. Complicating the matter are adjacent landowners erecting fences and placing no trespassing signs on sections of the railbed with no real legal claim to the right-of-way. It becomes a case of trespassing at your own risk.

One other factor to consider is that the KVR bisects a number of Indian reservations. The Indian reservations around Penticton and Merritt have all regained ownership of the right-of-way through their land, and should be respected as such. Although cycling along some of these sections does still occur, one should contact the appropriate band and also be aware that cycling through private property is a venture at your own risk.

No matter who owns the land, please respect the property you cross and close all gates. Even though the adjacent landowners may have taken the unilateral action of running a fence across the right-of-way, it is best to let the issues that led to this action be worked out by the proper authorities. The main reason for the action taken by landowners is owing to the fear that unrestricted travel through their land invites vandalism, noise, fires and garbage. We who wish to preserve these corridors for public use must help relieve these fears, and not add to them ▬

Ownership of the abandoned railway corridors (Spring, 2002)

Carmi Subdivision	B.C. government
Osoyoos Subdivision	
km 0.0 - km 7.1	Penticton Indian Band
km 7.1 - Okanagan Falls	CPR
Okanagan Falls to Osoyoos	B.C. government & local municipalities, with pieces sold or leased to private interests
Princeton Subdivision	B.C. government & 1.6kms Penticton Indian Band
Merritt Subdivision	B.C. government & Coldwater Indian Band
Coquihalla Subdivision	Trans Mountain Pipeline (B.C. Gas) & B.C. government
Copper Mountain Subdivision	B.C. government with pieces sold to private interests
VV&E Railway	Mostly private
NK&S Railway	B.C. government & 3 local Indian Bands
Columbia & Western Railway	CPR
Castlegar to Grand Forks	Trans Canada Trail Foundation
Grand Forks to Midway	B.C. government
Nelson &Fort Sheppard Railway	B.C. Government & BNR & 1 private interest
Columbia& Kootenay Railway	
South Slocan to Slocan	Trans Canada Trail Foundation
Nakusp & Slocan Railway	B.C.Government

DRINKING WATER

It is recommended not to drink from any water source without some method of purification. Often it is inconceivable that a clear, cold, rushing mountain stream is too polluted to drink. The problem is most often the presence of the organism Giardia. Millions of North Americans are suspected of having giardiasis, however, many of these may only be carriers. Carriers remain perfectly healthy showing no signs of the disease, yet can excrete Giardia cysts through their feces for months or even years. Other animals that can carry or contract Giardia include cattle, horses, dogs, rabbits, coyotes, deer and beaver (the common name of giardiasis is Beaver Fever). Symptoms that appear after seven to 14 days of incubation are weight loss, diarrhea, cramps, bloating, nasty burps, anorexia and vomiting.

To prevent your own case of the "bad-water blues," some form of water treatment is required. One method is to boil water for a minimum of 10 minutes to kill all bacteria, viruses and parasites. A second method is to use iodine tablets. Be sure to carefully follow the directions on the bottle for maximum effectiveness. One drawback to this method is a noticeable iodine taste to the water, which can be camouflaged by adding flavoured juice crystals. The third method of water treatment is to use a water filtration system. This system is strongly recommended for frequent or extended backcountry trips. With any water treatment method it is recommended to still use the cleanest water available to minimize possible contamination.

HYPOTHERMIA

Hypothermia is a condition that results from the body's core temperature dropping to a point where your body can no longer generate heat on its own. This danger is not restricted to only high altitudes or winter conditions. With a combination of rain and wind, a person who is exhausted and unprepared can quickly fall victim. Your best defence against hypothermia is to be familiar with the symptoms, prevention and management, and to take them seriously. Deaths from hypothermia are not uncommon.

Symptoms start with a feeling of coldness, but as the body core temperature drops, uncontrolled shivering begins in an attempt to warm the body. Symptoms then progress to poor muscle coordination, weakness, lethargy, impaired judgement, and finally to unconsciousness and death unless action is taken.

The prevention of hypothermia begins with being prepared and knowledgable about the contributing factors. Foremost is wet clothing from either rain or perspiration. To stay dry from rain, we simply utilize proper raingear. Unfortunately, though most people have the proper gear, they don't stop to put it on. To help prevent perspiration wetness while cycling, take layers of clothes off as needed; then to help prevent subsequent chilling, throw back on an extra layer once stopped. A combination of clothing that works very effectively together while cycling is that of polypropylene undergarments (absorbs perspiration away from your skin) and breathable Gortex outerwear (allows perspiration through the fabric while keeping wind and rain out). Be sure you also have some method of keeping equipment and extra clothes dry, such as enclosing them in a plastic bag. There can be nothing more discouraging and potentially dangerous than to stop at your camp to find your sleeping bag wet. You should always ensure you have warm, dry clothes available upon reaching your final destination.

Exhaustion is a second contributing factor that will hasten a victim's advancement toward hypothermia, as your body requires extra energy to help keep itself warm. To prevent exhaustion, avoid getting overfatigued by stopping and resting for short periods, though not long enough to get chilled. You should also take this rest time to eat small amounts of high calorie foods to help meet your body's extra requirements.

Managing hypothermia begins firstly with reducing further heat loss. Get out of the wind or wear a windproof shell, protect your head and back of neck from heat loss, and get dry clothes on. Secondly, begin core

Proper raingear is a must for any long distance cycle.

rewarming. Because the body is not adequately producing enough heat on its own, things like hot drinks (with sugar) or attempting light exercise such as walking, can generate heat within the body to raise the core temperature. Methods used to provide heat to only the outer skin, such as skin to skin warming, or sitting by a hot fire, can be helpful in the beginning stages but since it does not directly warm the inner core, it can be dangerous to someone profoundly hypothermic. This peripheral or outer skin warming causes vasodilation, and with a severely hypothermic victim, it can cause further cardiovascular collapse. Peripheral warming should therefore be delayed until the core temperature can be raised.

Remember that the combination of wind, wetness and a state of exhaustion are all precipitating factors to hypothermia. By taking the time to prevent these and quickly responding to initial hypothermic symptoms, you can prevent yourself or your travel companion from falling victim. As a final note, in an advanced state of hypothermia, all necessary steps must be made to get medical help as this is a medical emergency ⛟

HYPERTHERMIA

Hyperthermia, or heat stroke, is a condition that results when the body's core temperature is abnormally elevated and the body can no longer adequately cool itself. The advancement toward hyperthermia begins with a state of heat exhaustion, a condition we have probably all experienced to varying degrees. The symptoms of heat exhaustion are: headache, dizziness, faintness, loss of appetite, nausea, and a cool and clammy skin. The management for heat exhaustion is to remove yourself from the heat to a cooler environment and drink plenty of fluids. If unable to get out of the heat, some relief comes from wearing a head covering (the styrofoam filling of a cycling helmet works great), drinking plenty of fluids to replenish perspiration loss, wearing loose fitting clothes to allow air flow, and getting your clothes and hair wet to generate heat loss through evaporation. These actions can also help to prevent the more serious and sometimes fatal condition of hyperthermia.

If you are unable to adequately cool yourself at the stage of heat exhaustion, you may rapidly progress to hyperthermia. The symptoms of hyperthermia are an extremely elevated core temperature, warm/dry skin, visual disturbances, rapid respiration, bounding pulse, depressed level of consciousness, and possibly advancing to unconsciousness, hypotension, shock or death unless action is taken. Management necessitates you cool the person by sponging or immersing in cool water (being careful not to cool too rapidly as it may induce shivering), giving cool fluids and getting medical help as soon as possible.

Other problems that are precipitated by prolonged exposure to the sun and heat are heat cramps and sunburns. Heat cramps are muscle spasms of the arms, legs and occasionally the abdomen, resulting from an excessive loss of sodium. During times of high temperatures and heavy perspiration, sodium loss can be prevented and managed by increasing your intake of both water and sodium.

Sunburn can be easily prevented by covering your skin with clothing or sunscreen (SPF 15 or greater). The best lotions contain PABA, are non-greasy, and do not wash off easily with sweating or even swimming. Be sure to cover all exposed skin including the often forgotten back of the neck and ears. The management of sunburn begins with avoiding further sun exposure and applying cool wet compresses to the burned area. Bland creams or lotions may be helpful in first degree burns, but second degree burns, characterized by blister formations, are best managed by prolonged application of cool wet compresses or immersion in cool water and seeking medical attention if the area burned is extensive ▬

WILDLIFE HAZARDS

Bears
Both black bears and grizzly bears presently range throughout most of the Southern Interior of British Columbia. In the majority of encounters, bears avoid confrontation. In fact, if given enough warning of your approach, they will quickly vacate the area, and you may never even realize a bear was near. The long straight stretches and slow easy curves of the KVR right-of-way increases the distance at which you can see down the trail and the distance at which a bear will be aware of your approach. However, moving quickly and quietly while cycling may increase the possibility of a chance encounter. Your best protection from injury is to first try to prevent an encounter, and second, to be knowledgable about bears and the appropriate actions you should take if encountering one.

Prevention of a chance encounter begins with warning the bear of your approach. Unlike people, scent and sound are a bear's primary early warning senses. Making your presence known with the use of bells or talking will help give advance notice to any wildlife that may be on your path. However, you need to make louder noise in dense forest, as sound will not carry as far. Flowing water or wind in the forest can also muffle any noise within a short distance. Yodelling, singing or the occasional whistle blast are effective sounds that will carry a greater distance than bells or talking. The bear must be able to hear the noise while still far enough away to not feel threatened by your presence, and have enough time to leave. Although making noise is contrary to the peace we may be seeking, it may give peace of mind to know a sudden encounter with an irritated bear can be avoided.

The most dangerous bear is a garbage addicted one. Most injuries are related to garbage scavenging bears that have become conditioned to people, a more frequent occurrence as civilization encroaches farther into the backcountry. Improperly stored food and unclean campsites are contributing factors to bear encounters. When backcountry camping, always store food, garbage, and perfumed items far away from your tent and in a location inaccessible to a bear. To properly store these items, place them in air tight containers or bags to prevent excessive odours. Then store your food bag by tying it high between two trees at least 90 metres from your tent.

Prevention of injury comes from knowing the appropriate action to take when encountering a bear, and sometimes simply a little luck. A bear's actions can be somewhat understood and predicted by the existing circumstances, unfortunately all of which you may not be aware. For example, black bears and grizzly bears often react differently, as will a mother with cubs. Identifying the type of bear can at times be difficult. The colouring of both bears can range from black to blond, and the distinctive lighter coloured snout of the black bear may not be quite so evident. The grizzly bear has a distinctive hump between the shoulders, but the black bear may also appear to have a hump if its head is lower than the rest of its body. The grizzly bear is known as the more aggressive of the bears, and a mother grizzly with cubs, just as any other mammal, can be the most dangerous. If you do not know the type of bear you have encountered, assume it is the more aggressive grizzly bear.

As the KVR corridor travels through bear country, here are some steps in managing encounters with a bear:

- If the bear shows little response to your presence, try to slowly vacate the area without sudden or fast moves.
- If the bear looks directly at you panting heavily or snorting, stand your ground, again making no sudden moves. Trying to run will entice a chase, and at a speed of 13 metres/second, a bear could easily outrun you. Climbing a tree is one option, but remember black bears can climb trees better than most humans. Grizzly bears can climb, much in the same way as a human, to a height of 10 metres or reach three metres to pull you out of the tree.
- If the bear begins to charge, stand your ground. Avoid direct eye contact, but keep a close watch on the bear's movements. Although this is not easily done, most charges are false charges. The bear is attempting to determine whether you are a threat, and to let you know you are unwelcome. After false charging, usually more than once, the bear will probably vacate the area once satisfied.
- If the charge leads to an attack or you feel an attack is imminent, the accepted procedure is to play dead. Position yourself to protect your neck, face and abdomen by clasping the back of your neck with your hands, tucking your head in, laying face to the ground with your knees pulled up and keeping still. The bear may bat at you a few times to ensure you are dead and no longer a threat. Once satisfied, the bear will usually leave the area. Do not move until you are sure the bear is gone. If you fight, run or further aggravate the bear, the attack will usually continue and may lead to a severe or fatal mauling.
- The most serious of encounters is that of predation. Although it is extremely rare for a bear to prey on humans, incidents do occur. If you are being dragged through the bush after being attacked in your tent while sleeping or stalked while on the trail, you can be most certain you have been attacked as an act of predation. In this case your only chance of survival is at some point to escape.

Black bears are generally considered the more tolerant member of the bear family. If you are certain that the bear you have encountered is a black bear, further steps may be followed. Since a black bear can be easily intimidated, it can be particularly effective to show mild aggression such as throwing rocks or making loud noises by yelling or banging pots. This will usually cause the less aggressive black bear to leave or stop an attack. However, this is not recommended for a mother and cubs as it will often aggravate the bear and provoke an attack, as is true for the grizzly bear.

Remember, bear encounters are rare, but your best safety factor is your knowledge of what to do. Be sure to take steps to prevent an encounter, and be both prepared and knowledgable about bears and what action to take when encountering a bear. An excellent reference on this subject is "Bear Attacks—Their Causes and Avoidance," by Stephen Herrero.

Cougar

Cougars are known occasionally to follow people apparently out of curiosity. However cougar attacks on humans are extremely rare, but as cougar number increase and habitat dwindles the more likely your are to encounter a cougar. Adult male cougars average around 64 kg., females about 46 kg. The young stay with their mother up to two years. Daughters often settle near their mother, but sons travel widely in the search of new home ranges, It is during this time of travel that cougars are most likely to encounter humans. Few of the many thousands of people who travel along the rail bed are likely to see, much less confront, a cougar. Yet it is wise to know how to deal with such an incident as your action can either help or hinder a quick retreat by the lion. If you should encounter one;

- Stop, stand tall and don't run. Pick up small children immediately. Running and rapid movements may trigger an attack. A cougars instinct is to chase.
- Face the cougar, talk to it firmly and slowly back away. Always leave the animal an escape route.
- Try to appear larger than the cougar , getting above it. (e.g. stepping up onto a stump). If wearing a jacket, hold it open to further increase your size.
- Do not take your eyes off the animal, especially if it is near a kill or with kittens. Never corner the animal or offer it food.
- If the animal does not flee and shows signs of aggression (crouches with ears back, teeth bared, hissing, tail twitching, and hind feet pumping in preparation to jump), be more assertive. Shout, wave your arms and throw rocks. The idea is to convince the cougar that you are not prey, but a potential danger.
- If the cougar attacks, fight back aggressively and try to stay on your feet. Cougars have been driven away by people who have fought back using anything within reach, including sticks, rocks, shovels, back packs, and clothing - even with just bare hands. Generally, if you are aggressive enough, a cougar will flee, realizing it has made a mistake.

Moose

Moose are found in many areas along the railway, especially in paralleling marshlands. Moose can be particularly dangerous during rutting season in mid-September, when provoked to aggression, or when alarming a mother with her calf. A cow moose will often initially escort the young one to a safe distance, then may return charging just as any other aggravated moose. While the majority of charges are false charges, it would be prudent to quickly clear the area and give the moose adequate room.

Snakes

During the building of the railway, rattlesnakes were one of the many hazards KVR construction workers faced. Rock blasting jolted many rattlesnakes from their rock hiding places, and many workers suffered the bite of an irritated rattler. Rattlesnakes are still found in rocks above Naramata, in fact, rattlers are abundant from Naramata to Osoyoos.

Like most wild animals, rattlesnakes tend to leave the area if they perceive you are coming. Although they have no sense of hearing and have poor sight, they are very sensitive to the smallest of vibrations and therefore will respond to approaching feet or tires. Encountering a snake while cycling on the railbed is rare, but does happen. A snake crossing your path and sensing the bike's vibration, will usually attempt to take cover with the rattler emitting a shrill high pitched hiss as it rushes away.

Because rattlers are cold blooded, they prefer temperatures between 26°C and 32°C, and will not be found hunting when ground temperatures are below 18°C. Rattlers are usually most active just before sunrise and just after sunset, when their prey of small mammals is also more active. During the heat of the day, snakes often take refuge under rocks and beneath overhanging foliage, so it is wise to avoid turning over large rocks and to be cautious when stepping into thick vegetation.

If bitten by a rattlesnake, try to stay calm. Remember that the snake has bitten you out of fright, and having been surprised and striking out in defense, may have injected little or no venom. Rattlesnakes also have a relatively low toxicity venom compared to other snakes, so if the bite cannot be treated it may only result in symptoms of dizziness, vomiting and a fever lasting up to 48 hours. First aid treatments such as cut-suck therapy are considered useless if not dangerous. Snake bite kits that involve a suction device to apply to the bite are available, but their effectiveness is questionable and should under no circumstances be used as an alternative to seeking medical attention.

Following a snake bite, the need for prompt action necessitates that the victim remains calm, relaxed and avoids any strenuous activity. An increased metabolic rate may cause the venom to spread and be absorbed dangerously fast. Foremost, seek medical attention as soon as possible.

Deer

At first you may not believe that deer could be considered a hazard, but after cycling the Kettle Valley Railway you may reconsider. Flushing deer out of the side bush is a continual nuisance that will jolt any cyclist while enjoying a peaceful ride. This quiet mode of travel allows the cyclist to sneak up on the deer. Once aware of your presence, it may bolt across the path in front of you. Sometimes the surprise or nearness of collision is enough to cause a fall. Deer are usually found in small herds. By surprising one, you may find others crossing your path a short distance down the trail. Making noise such as ringing a bell or talking, may better warn a deer of your presence, allowing it to vacate the area ahead of your arrival.

Hunters

Autumn is a beautiful and peaceful time of the year to cycle the KVR. However, it is also hunting season, which can create a hazard for cyclists in the wilderness. Hunters can be found anywhere along the length of this trail as they often use the KVR as an access route to the backcountry and to the great amount of game that are found roaming the countryside. Although the majority of hunters are responsible and cautious, accidents can and do occur with sometimes fatal consequences. If cycling during hunting season, it is necessary to wear bright colours and to make your presence known. Also, be on the watch for carrion (animal remains) from a hunter's kill, as it can attract bears and other wildlife that may attack without provocation in protection of their food source.

Mosquitoes, Ticks and Bees

The severity of insect problems varies from person to person, place to place, or even year to year. Mosquitoes, the most common nuisance, are most effectively dealt with by repellents containing DEET. Citronella repellents are also effective but for very short periods only, the advantage being they are nicer to smell, non-greasy, and can be sprayed on clothing without concern. Mosquito coils also work well if used in your tent or under a tarp.

Ticks can be a nuisance in areas where herds of large animals live. They are found on the tips of tall grasses and other vegetation and will grasp on to your skin or clothing as you brush by. Ticks will then crawl to a spot usually on your buttocks or back, and burrow into your skin to suck blood. Check yourself at least once a day for ticks if you are travelling through tall brush or grass.

Tick season is spring and summer (up to six weeks after snow has melted). Ticks commonly carry the disease Rocky Mountain Spotted Fever (RMSF). If bit, the symptoms that develop in three to 10 days are: severe head and muscle ache, fever and a measles-like rash that often starts on the feet or hands, then spreads. A tick must remain attached to the skin for about two to six hours before transmitting RMSF, so remove the tick as soon as possible. It is very important to remove the entire body because an embedded tick, even part of one, can still transmit the disease. The tick can be removed by grasping the body with tweezers and gently rolling upward. DEET type bug repellent is reputed to be effective against ticks, but if you are bitten and unable to remove the entire tick yourself, be sure to quickly get medical attention.

Bees and wasps also emerge in summer months, and anyone with an allergy to insect stings should carry medication with them at all times. Bee sting kits are available and are recommended if you are potentially susceptible ▃

EQUIPMENT

As with any short or long distance backcountry venture, it can be one of immense pleasure or one of exhausting agony, depending on the amount of care taken in planning. An important part of the planning is the equipment checklist. This checklist will vary, depending on when you are going, where you are going and for how long you are going. You may already have a list of what equipment you find beneficial. The following is a suggested checklist for this particular cycling trip.

Bicycle

The KVR and abandoned railway trails are not particularly demanding on what type of bicycle is used. The factor that demands attention is the surface of the grade when choosing a bike. The surface will vary from hard packed fine crush to loose ballast (large angular shaped rocks used to keep railway ties in place) and sand. Weather will also play a factor in the surface condition. Wet weather will consolidate the surface making it a harder surface to ride on (within limits). Long periods of dry hot weather will make the surface powdery and loose. Areas that receive vehicle traffic will also develop washboards (regularly spaced ridges in the road surface).

Tire size becomes a critical factor in the enjoyment of the ride. Hard narrow tires will sink into and slide on the fine sand and loose ballast increasing the peddling effort and affecting control of the bike. Larger tires at lower tire pressures will float over loose sand and ballast and not disturb the surface. Large tires with low pressures will also reduce the high frequency vibrations transmitted to the handlebars and seat of the bike caused by washboards and ballast on the trail. Fork and full suspension bikes will not necessarily remove these high frequency vibrations. Handle bar suspension systems such as softride and seat post suspensions can help isolate the rider from some of these vibrations of the road.

For day tripping almost any bike with tires wider then 38 mm (1.5 inches) will work for the majority of the rail beds.. For longer trips, especially carrying loads the tire size should be 50 mm (1.95 inches) or greater. Tire pressures kept below 200 KPa (30 psi) will also increase comfort and control in riding the rail bed.

Bicycle Repair Equipment
- tire repair kit (ensure glue has not dried out)
- tire levers
- Allen keys (those that fit your bike)
- wrenches (those that fit your bike)
- head set wrench
- spoke wrench
- screwdrivers
- chain breaker
- chainlinks

- oil
- *tube
- *spokes
- *freewheel removal tool
  (to replace damaged spokes)
- *crank puller
- *crescent wrench
- *cone wrenches
- *grease
- *needle nosed pliers

(*Items may be required for long unsupported trips.)

Equipment for Day Trips

- mountain bike in good working order with large tires
- cyclometer (cycle computer, so you know where you are)
- compass
- bell/whistle
- fanny pack/rear pannier
- CSA approved cycling helmet
- bicycle repair kit
- tire pump
- map(s)
- first–aid/survival kit
- stiff-soled shoes (suitable for hiking)
- cycling gloves
- windshell
- raingear
- second set of day clothes
- other clothing depending on weather, e.g., warm jacket
- sunscreen/sunglasses/sweatband/swimsuit
- mosquito repellent
- matches
- knife
- flashlight/lantern (for the tunnels)
- toilet paper and hand shovel
- water bottles (water included)
- food (some extra in case of delays)
- camera
- and foremost ... this book!

Extra Equipment for Overnight Trips
- extra clothing (polypropylene underclothing, pile jacket/pants, head covering, wools socks, extra day clothes and night wear)
- tarp (to provide shelter in sudden downpours)
- additional food (don't forget high calorie snack food)
- water purification system
- panniers
- sleeping bag (may be needed at some lodgings)
- personal items (towel, toothbrush, biodegradable soap, etc.)
- waterproof bags to keep equipment dry (garbage bags work great)

Extra Equipment for Tenting
- extra tarp (to keep rain off bikes and equipment in camp)
- tent (poles, pegs, ground sheet and fly)
- rope (for hanging food between trees)
- foam pad or air mattress
- air mattress patch kit
- stove, windscreen
- extra fuel
- cooking utensils
- can opener
- dish scrubber
- towel and biodegradable soap
- panniers (front and rear)
- candles
- spare flashlight batteries
- additional food

Cell Phones
Cell phones are finding their way on the KVR in panniers more and more these days and questions of just where and how well they work is being asked more often. With a good analog phone, coverage can get close to 50 % of the trails in this book. Although most digital phones revert to analog when in an analog only coverage area, few excel as an analog phone as a analog only phone will. Digital coverage is limited to around Kelowna, Penticton, Osoyoos, and Hope. Cell phone coverage along the trail is noted in the trail log, though this is dependent on the phone you have and is continually changing as phone companies change equipment and change coverage ▰

A passenger train crosses the impressive frame trestle over West Fork Canyon Creek. This hand-crafted wooden trestle was later replaced in the 1930s with a steel bridge. (Penticton Museum)

HISTORY OF THE KETTLE VALLEY RAILWAY

In 1885 the Canadian Pacific Railway completed a Trans Canada rail line from the Atlantic to the Pacific oceans. The line across British Columbia ran far to the north, through Kicking Horse Pass, Revelstoke and Kamloops. As a result, the Southern Interior of British Columbia was almost completely isolated, with the only modes of transportation being somewhat slow and roundabout, either by steamer on Okanagan Lake or by stage to Keremeos, each then connecting to rail.

With the discovery of silver near Nelson in 1887, the potential wealth in the Kootenays was realized. The natural geography of this area enabled easy U.S. access along the north-south valleys, but it was more difficult for these riches to be transported across the province to the western Canadian centre in Vancouver.

Over the next few years, both Canadian and American railway companies surveyed possible railway routes into the Kootenays. In 1900, CPR tracks arrived from the east to the town of Midway. Between Midway and Hope lay nearly 500 kilometres of rugged mountains, so CPR's commitment to develop any farther west along this route was shaky. However, contracts for development into the Southern Interior of British Columbia were approved to an American rival, Great Northern Railway (GNR). This made the situation critical for Canadian Pacific Railway, if it was to protect its existing investment in southern B.C.

It was only through the combined efforts of J. J. Warren and Thomas Shaughnessy that the CPR was convinced to commit to the construction of a line from the Kootenays to the coast. Early in 1910, J. J. Warren became president and general manager of the Kettle Valley Railway, and shortly after, Andrew McCulloch became chief engineer. Final surveys continued under McCulloch's supervision, and construction began by 1910. This section of line would run from Midway and across the Southern Interior to Merritt, thereby connecting to the CPR main line.

The construction of this line did not come without problems. During the first year, progress moved slowly owing to a shortage of both needed materials and labour. Improvement came in 1912 when the Canadian government lifted the restrictions it had placed on workers coming into Canada from other countries. As a result, despite the sagging economic conditions of the time, the line from Midway to Merritt was half completed by 1913. Construction also commenced on the Coquihalla Subdivision.

There was a growing rivalry over the years between the KVR and the VV&E (Vancouver, Victoria and Eastern Railway, a subsidiary of the GNR), as both railways competed for access routes from the Kootenays to the coast. This rivalry resulted in battles between workers and legal battles in court. However, with the economic slump of 1913 and prospect of world war growing, increased urgency redeveloped for the completion of the entire line including that of the Coquihalla Subdivision. As a result, the VV&E and the KVR tempered their rivalry and agreed to share some trackage. The "Coquihalla Agreement" allowed the KVR to build their tracks through the narrow canyon of the Coquihalla, and permitted the VV&E use of these

Trestle on Carmi Subdivision. In the early 1900s the Kettle Valley Railway became a lifeline linking the communities of the Southern Interior of British Columbia. (Penticton Museum)

KETTLE VALLEY RAILWAY CO.

—

TIME **1** TABLE

TAKING EFFECT AT 24.01 O'CLOCK

SUNDAY, MAY 30, 1915

GOVERNED BY PACIFIC TIME

FOR THE INFORMATION AND GOVERNMENT OF EMPLOYES ONLY

Miles from Brookmere	Telegraph and Telephone Offices	COQUIHALLA SUBDIVISION STATIONS	Telegraph Calls	Car Capacity Sidings
.0	DN	BROOKMERE ......ZK	BR	......
		4.0		
4.0		BRODIE ......ZY		Nil
		Jct. Merritt Sub.		
		5.8		
9.8		JULIET ......Z		35
		8.2		
18.0		COQUIHALLA ......ZY		70
		6.1		
24.1		ROMEO		39
		5.5		
29.6		IAGO ......Z		45
		4.8		
34.4		PORTIA ......ZY		46
		5.4		
39.8		JESSICA ......Z		46
		5.4		
45.2		LEAR ......Z		49
		3.7		
48.9		OTHELLO		70
		5.4		
54.3	D	HOPE ......ZY	KV	47
		2.3		
56.6		ODLUM ......R		Nil
		Rule 41 applies		
		Rule 93A applies		

Courtesy of Penticton Museum.

tracks by paying an annual rental fee. The "Tulameen Agreement" permitted KVR to use the VV&E tracks from Princeton to Brookmere.

In only a few years the KVR became a reality. The last spike of the Carmi Subdivision was driven on October 2, 1914. On May 31, 1915, the entire line from Midway to Merritt officially opened enabling trains to reach Vancouver by connecting to the CPR main line via Merritt. On September 28, 1915, the line opened from Brodie to the Coquihalla Station. The completion of the remaining Coquihalla line was delayed by a record snowfall of 20.4 metres in December, providing a taste of what future winters in the Coquihalla Pass would hold for the Kettle Valley Railway. However, by July 31, 1916, the Coquihalla Subdivision officially opened through to Hope, decreasing the journey to the coast.

The 61 kilometres between Hope and Coquihalla originally had 43 bridges, 12 tunnels and 15 snowsheds. Because this line was constructed during the First World War, there was a restriction of needed manpower and supplies such as explosives and building materials. Therefore, the average cost per kilometre was inflated to $84,525, five times the Canadian average during the same time period.

In the early 1920s many CPR officials suggested abandoning the Coquihalla Subdivision because of the difficulty in keeping the line open through the winter season. As a result, the KVR started a major upgrading program of the Merritt Subdivision in 1922, in anticipation of a permanent diversion to the CPR main line via Merritt. However, on January 28, 1929, a major accident occurred on the CPR main line, forcing a detour over the KVR for a three week period. The incident made the CPR management recognize the value of the KVR as a bypass route.

One of the branch lines built by the KVR was to the Copper Mountain Mine, just south of Princeton. Operations began during World War I because of the wartime demand for copper, but the mine operated for little more than a month before closing in December 1920 owing to depressed postwar copper prices. The mine and railway reopened in August 1925, providing the railway with substantial business until the Depression, forcing it to again close in 1930. Both the mine and railway would lay idle until the demand for copper increased.

A second branch line was the Osoyoos Subdivision, which transported fruit from the Okanagan Valley south of Penticton. March 1923 marked the opening of a section of the branch line from Hayes to Okanagan Falls. The fruit was then transported by barge across Skaha Lake to Penticton. In August 1931, a rail line was constructed from Penticton to Okanagan Falls, thereby eliminating the barge service.

On January 1, 1931, CPR absorbed operations of the KVR, becoming the Kettle Valley Division. Unfortunately for the CPR, this was also at the beginning of a long period of economic depression, which starved the railway of needed traffic and revenue. With the closing of Copper Mountain, an overly hot summer in the Okanagan destroying fruit crops, and numerous forest fires ravaging the Southern Interior, operation costs climbed while at the same time revenue decreased. By 1933, many improvement programs were reduced along with severe cuts in operational expenses.

Train wreck east of Iago at Coquihalla Pass. Construction problems were the norm rather than the exception. Many railway employees were killed or injured during its years of operation. (Penticton Museum)

In September 1939, Canada entered the Second World War. Almost overnight the Depression of the 1930s gave way to a new decade dominated by the industry and commerce of war. Demand for copper, lead, coal and lumber reached new heights. With the West Coast now a significant industrial centre, Kootenay mineral traffic travelled westward. As the demand for fruit in Great Britain increased, the branch line south of Penticton was extended from Hayes to Osoyoos in December 1944, thereby completing the Osoyoos Subdivision. At one point, more than 14,000 railcars of fruit left the Okanagan annually.

In 1947, with wartime restrictions and rationing over, the CPR announced that it would undertake an ambitious program to upgrade the KVR to standards equivalent to that of the company's main line. In early 1949, oil tanks were erected at some stations, beginning the introduction of diesel-electric locomotives and the heavy movement of through freight traffic. This gave the Kettle Valley Division the earned title of "The Second Mainline."

November 1949 marked the opening of the Hope-Princeton Highway, the first of many events that changed the future for the KVR. A general drift away from using the railway for fruit shipments and for passenger service occurred, as preference for the use of the new highway grew. In 1952 the CPR announced an improved passenger schedule but to no avail. However, even with this loss, the KVR remained a busy railway during the 1950s with numerous freight trains leaving Penticton for the coast, as output of the Kootenay mines rolled westward in increasing tonnages.

November 23, 1959, marked a second significant event, which changed the destiny of railroading in Southern British Columbia. Several washouts along the Coquihalla Subdivision resulted in temporary closure of the lines; trains were subsequently diverted via Merritt. Although this in itself was not an unusual event, the CPR decided not to repair or reopen the Coquihalla Subdivision. On January 9, 1961, CPR announced the permanent closure of the line and the last spike was removed October 24, 1962.

HOPE LINE SLIDES ARE CLEARED AWAY

K.V.R. Trains Which Have Been Operating Via Spences Bridge Return to Cut-off

Penticton Herald, November 16, 1916.

Along with the announced closure of the Coquihalla line was the planned rerouting of trains. The traffic from the Kootenays, which encompassed the majority of the KVR traffic, was sent north over the Lake Windermere Subdivision to Golden, and only local Okanagan traffic was sent to the coast over the KVR via Merritt. When the rerouting took effect in September 1961, more than 80% of the KVR's freight traffic vanished in a single day. On July 1, 1962, the Kettle Valley Division was abolished.

The Kettle Valley Railway was built in an age when all freight and passenger movement was by rail. The highways and airplanes of a new age stripped the KVR of its passenger, mail and high revenue traffic. The remaining bulk commodities required longer and heavier trains to remain competitive. As a result, forestry products became practically the only commodity carried on the former KVR.

By 1973, trains stopped running west of Beaverdell, and in 1978 these tracks were removed as were the tracks from the Osoyoos Subdivision in 1979. This left only the tracks from Okanagan Falls to Myra Canyon, which were preserved in an effort to maintain it as a tourist railway. Unfortunately, due to overwhelming economic difficulties, the idea was given up and the tracks removed. Announcement of the closing of the Penticton Station came in 1980, and by 1989 the last train left Merritt. In June 1990, the National Transportation Agency authorized the abandonment of the remaining line. Tracks were subsequently removed between Merritt and Penticton, except for the short section between Winslow and Faulder. These tracks remained in place for the Kettle Valley Steam Railway.

The Kettle Valley Railway will always have a special place in the hearts of those who experienced her influence. For an entire generation, it was the lifeline to the Southern Interior of British Columbia. It has been said that, due to the incredible costs of construction, operation and maintenance, the KVR never made a penny profit for the CPR. However, it has also been said that, for the people of Southern British Columbia, the untold benefit of this determined railway was the development of this region. With our past history influencing to a great extent both our present and our future, the value of this line will continue ◄═

Cycling through Myra Canyon has become increasingly popular, and why not with such incredible scenery, not to mention the historic trestles and tunnels (km 139 Carmi Subdivision).

CYCLING THE KETTLE VALLEY RAILWAY

The Kettle Valley Railway has been an integral part of British Columbia since its beginning. With its abandonment and subsequent track removal, the opportunity now exists for the right-of-way to remain an important corridor for recreational use. The abandoned railbed of the KVR is highly suitable for backcountry cycling, perhaps becoming one of the fastest growing outdoor activities in North America.

The KVR is one of the most dynamic bike routes in the area, with nearly 600 kilometres of trail, much of which remain largely intact and open to use. Abandoned railway right-of-ways are often used by recreationists without any special improvement or upkeep. However, you may occasionally find that the reliability of the trail has changed due to such things as erosion, rock slides, fencing, construction or logging. For the true backcountry cyclist, these minor inconveniences simply add to the ultimate challenge and adventure of the trip. But if you'd rather not perform a little unplanned technical manoeuvring or detouring, you'll be pleased that many groups and individuals are committed to pursuing the restoration of this trail. Ultimately, this will ensure the availability of the corridor for years to come.

Much of the attraction of the Kettle Valley Railway is that it is a true wilderness trail, winding through B.C.'s backcountry and interconnecting various centres. The route offers some truly impressive scenery and spectacular views as you venture through a great variety of environs such as mountains, forests, lakes, desert, orchards and vineyards, not to mention the unique opportunity to guide your bike across the towering trestles and bridges, or inch your way through the darkness of tunnels.

Directly along the corridor you can also find some very unique and historic lodgings. For example, you can stay in Beaverdell at the oldest operating hotel in B.C., cook your supper by lantern light on a wood stove at McCulloch, enjoy some backcountry luxury in a rustic log cabin at Chute Lake or stay in Coalmont at an historic hotel built in 1912. Now how's that for an interesting accommodation package? But don't forget you will also find numerous scenic campsites straight off the trail.

Another great attraction to this trail is that almost all centres en route can be interconnected by bus or car, enabling you to easily return to the trailhead or make circle routes. For a pleasant four to five day circle route, park your car at Midway, cycle to Osoyoos, then bus back to Midway. Services also exist for you to fly to Penticton, then rent a mountain bike or utilize Via Rail service that travels from Jasper into B.C., stopping at locations close to the rail-trail such as Ashcroft or Hope.

Cycling the Kettle Valley Railway offers you a holiday of backcountry cycling that is quite remarkable and unparalleled. The route interconnects many unique centres of the Southern Interior of British Columbia, leading the cyclist to impressive views, beautiful scenery and fascinating places to explore. Cycling this trail is truly a dynamic and challenging venture that unfolds over the expanse of place and time ▰

Text Legend

Throughout this guide, picture keys are used as a quick reference to information about the trail, both historical and current. All measurements are in metric.

†1274Elevation. Metres above sea level.

Station. Most stations along the railways simply consisted of small section houses housing sectionmen and their families. Sectionmen were responsible for patrolling a section of the railway. All that remains of these section houses are the square concrete foundations.

Water Tower. The majority of water towers on the KVR were tall octagonal structures sitting on octagonal concrete foundations. On the top was a sphere that slid up and down a pole to indicate the amount of water in the tower. The large eight-sided concrete foundations of these towers are easily found along the KVR. A few of the towers were not much more than large tanks on poles. In this case, a circle of pile footings can usually be found.

Siding. Most of the stations had sidings that are evident where the railbed becomes wider.

Spur.

Wye. For turning around engines and snowplows.

Road Crossing.

)(55x10 Bridge. The numbers indicate the length and the greatest height of the trestle or bridge in metres. A single number indicates the length.

Bridge Out. Any numbers following the symbol indicate the length and height of the missing trestle or bridge.

84 Tunnel. The number indicates the length of the tunnel in metres.

Λ Camping.

ΛᴮBackcountry Campsite. No facilities.

Lodging. Hotel, Motel, Inn

ᴮ Bed and Breakfast

⊼ Picnicking.

†ᴮ Backcountry Water. Water source is a stream or lake and may need to be purified.

Restaurant or Snack Bar.

Grocery store.

Bike Shop.

Hiking Trail.

Bike Trail

Ⲧ Winery.

Ⅽ Phone.

ⵏ Information Plaque.

1.0 Uphill Grade. The least liked symbol of the bunch. Of course, if you are going in the opposite direction this may be your favourite. A grade symbol is found at each station, the number indicates the average percent grade to the next station. Percent grade is the altitude gain (or loss) of the railway over a specified length, expressed in percent. An uphill grade of 1.0% would mean that the railway rises 1 metre for every 100 metres of length. Grades less then 1.0% will hardly be noticeable.

2.1Downhill Grade. Sit back and enjoy the scenery. Just as with the uphill symbol, the number indicates the average percent downhill grade between stations. Grades approaching 2.0% are great coasting grades.

Level Grade. The average grade between stations is less than 0.1%.

→;→ Detour Off. The rail bed becomes impassable, a detour off the railway onto a road or trail at this point is necessary. Re access the rail bed at the Detour On symbol.

←;← Detour On. After detouring off the rail bed, it is at this point you get back on the railway. If following the rail bed from the other direction the symbols mean the reverse.

⇢;⇢ Possible Detour Off. The rail bed is marginally passable and may require a detour.

Possible Detour On. If you detoured when the rail bed became marginally passable, this is where you reaccess the rail bed.

Water. Good place to stock up on water.

Cell Phone Coverage. Symbol is found only at the stations and indicates a good analog signal can usually be found along the trail here.

Fringe Area Cell Phone Coverage.

Map Legend (Large Scale Maps)

++++++++ KVR, C&W Railbed–Passable (each crosstie represents 200m)	24.9 Distance Marker (kilometres)
++++++++ KVR, C&W Railbed –Not Passable	14.2 Station–Distance Marker (kilometres)
+++++++ KVR, C&W Road built on Railbed	Tunnel
+++++++ VV&E, Railbed–Passable	Trestle, Bridge
+++++++ VV&E, Railbed–Not Passable	Campsite
+++++++ VV&E, Road built on Railbed	Campsite, Backcountry
Active Railway	Lodging
Highway	Picnic Site
Street	Winery
— — — Gravel Road –Main	Mine
— — — Single Lane –2wd	River, Creek
--------- Single Lane –4wd	Contour Line –200m interval
·············· Trail–Single Track	Index Contour Line
	Indian Reservation Boundary

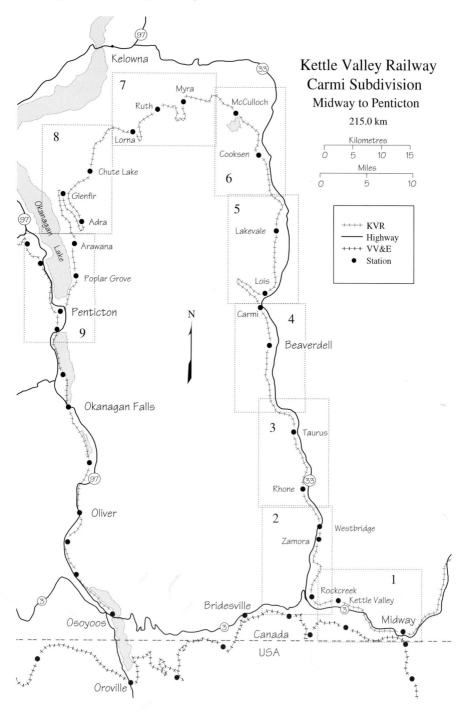

Kelowna

Kettle Valley Railway
Carmi Subdivision
Midway to Penticton

215.0 km

7

Myra

Ruth

McCulloch

8

Lorna

Cooksen

Chute Lake

6

Glenfir

5

Adra

Lakevale

Arawana

Poplar Grove

Lois

Penticton

Carmi

4

9

Beaverdell

N

Okanagan Falls

3

Taurus

Rhone

2

Oliver

Zamora

Westbridge

1

Rockcreek

Kettle Valley

Bridesville

Canada

Midway

Osoyoos

USA

Oroville

Kilometres
0   5   10   15

Miles
0   5   10

++++	KVR
———	Highway
++++	VV&E
●	Station

Okanagan Lake

CARMI SUBDIVISION
Midway to Penticton, 215 kilometres

The section of the KVR between Midway and Penticton is known as the Carmi Subdivision, offering 215 kilometres of delightful cycling on a well-travelled trail and a relatively level terrain. However, the distance can challenge your legs and your endurance. So, pack your panniers, pump up your tires and get ready for an exhilarating three to four day cycle trip. Oh, and if you came for the views, you won't be disappointed.

Start this trip by pedalling your fat tires along the packed gravel, beginning at the Midway Station. The rail bed follows the valley of the Kettle River, passing through the towns, villages and scenic farmland of the Kootenay Boundary Country. Unfortunately, some sections have been fenced owing to ranching or farming, thus entailing a little detouring, bush whacking and cow patty dodging. Nevertheless, this is an easy, enjoyable ride as the trail climbs gently but steadily into the Okanagan Highlands.

When you reach the near abandoned town of Carmi and the remains of the Carmi Mine, you'll want to park your bike as this historic site beckons you to explore its remains. Continuing on the packed gravel trail, you pass through this pine forested back country on a gentle uphill grade to reach Hydraulic Lake. Near McCulloch Station, on the shore of Hydraulic Lake, is McCulloch Lake Resort, with camping, cabins, four-plex chalet and a restaurant full of railway nostalgia.

A near level grade lies between McCulloch and Myra, so if you want to put the pedal to the metal and work up a sweat, you can click off the kilometres, stopping short of the canyon. At Myra Canyon the views abound, and as you cross over the many trestles and through the tunnels, you are again reminded that you're cycling in the tracks of an incredible railway.

Once out of the canyon, your ease of pedalling soon makes you aware of the gentle downhill grade. With gravity as your ally, the next thing you know, you're at Chute Lake. The lodge located here is a beautiful log building set next to the lake. You'll almost believe it's a mirage after such a remote stretch of back country. Cyclists are more than welcome, be it for a piece of Doreen's famous home-made pie, or a few days of R&R.

Leaving Chute Lake, the downhill grade significantly increases as you descend into Penticton. The trail is generally in good shape for a multi-use trail, i.e., hikers, cyclists, motorized vehicles, horses and cows! Some logging roads intersect the rail bed at various points; if tempted to follow, be ready for a wicked descent. Don't be in too much of a hurry, or you will miss the impressive views of the Okanagan Valley. Once you've reached Penticton, you'll wonder why you went so fast.

The end of the trail awaits you in the attractive city of Penticton, nestled between Okanagan and Skaha lakes. Penticton was named by the Indians, meaning: a place to stay forever, and that's just what you may want to do. All conveniences are found here, and it is a great spot for a refreshing dip on a hot day. Who could pass that up after having just cycled 215 km? ᗰ

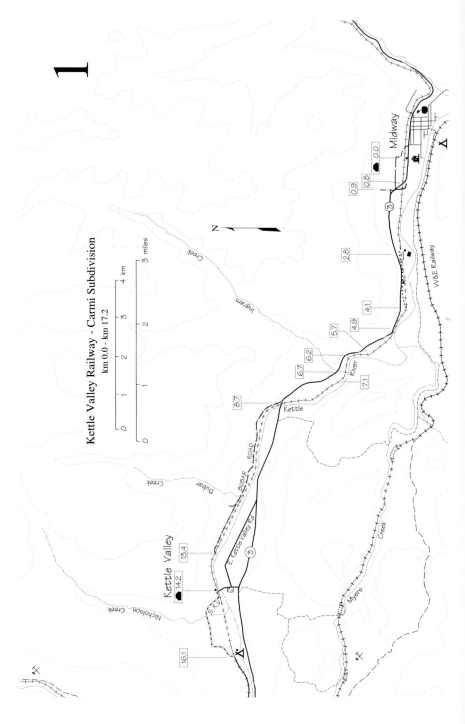

Kettle Valley Railway - Carmi Subdivision
km 0.0 - km 17.2

Midway was a busy town during the railway boom. Today, the original KVR station is a museum.

km
0.0
Midway Station |580 ⬤ 🍴 🏠 Y 🏕 ⛽ ⌂ 🍴 🚿 🚐 🚗 🎣₀.₁

Midway is a town named for the fact that it is halfway the distance across British Columbia. This was a town of much activity during the railway boom as it was a junction point for railways both going and coming from the east and west, and also south from across the border.

The original Midway Station was declared a heritage site and purchased by the Kettle River Museum. The station was then moved a few hundred metres southwest of the original site onto land owned by the Village of Midway. The large sugar maple now northeast of the station was planted from seed by Mrs. Nichols, wife of KVR agent Henry Nichols, to shade the station from the summer sun. Today, the railway station still serves the public as a museum where much of the history of the KVR can be found. The rail grade in front of the Midway Station is wide and clear.

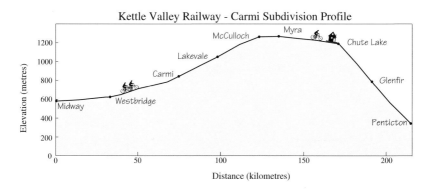

43

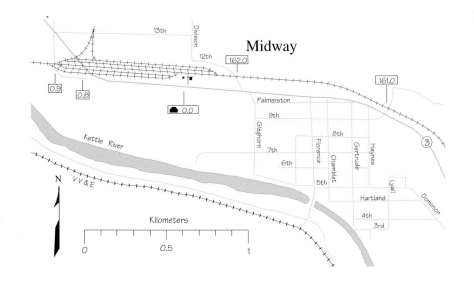

Midway Museum
(Highway 3, Midway, 250-449-2413)

The Battle of Midway

It was in November 1905, in the tiny town of Midway, British Columbia, that the battle between railway rivals James J. Hill of the Great Northern Railway (GNR) and William Van Horne and Thomas Shaughnessy of the Canadian Pacific Railway (CPR) was to come to physical blows.

The rivalry between these two railways began before the construction of the CPR transcontinental line to Vancouver. Hill and Van Horne, then directors of the CPR, disagreed on the route the CPR would take to the western shores of Canada. Hill, a Canadian by birth, wanted the line south through the United States and north to Winnipeg, thus avoiding the costly construction through the rocky Canadian Shield north of Lake Superior. But Van Horne, ironically an American, wanted an all-Canadian route. The majority of CPR directors supported Van Horne's all-Canadian route, infuriating Hill. Hill left the CPR and Canada, swearing revenge against Van Horne and the CPR.

In the years that followed, Hill, with the GNR, attempted to gain control of railways into Canada. He was out-manoeuvred each time by Van Horne, who would not allow an American railway into Canada. In retaliation, Hill drove tracks from Seattle to Vancouver only to be stopped 20 miles short owing to a lack of funding for a bridge over the Fraser River.

His next assault was the successful venture with the Kaslo and Slocan Railway (K&S) in 1895, building a line over the mountains to reach the silver mines of Sandon.

At Sandon, there was a conflict regarding the ownership of land on which the Nakusp & Slocan Railway (N&S) had built their CPR station. In retaliation the K&S men tore down the CPR station and freight shed.

Skirmishes and legal battles between the two railways were common place. In 1899, Shaughnessy, another American by birth, succeeded Van Horne as president of the CPR and continued on with the fight to restrict Hill from getting a foothold into Canada. Of course, this did not stop the CPR from teaming up with Daniel Corbin to drive a rail spike deep into the heart of Hill's Spokane railway monopoly, building a railway from Spokane to the CPR main line and diverting rail traffic bound for the Eastern United States over the CPR main line. Corbin had lost his own railway, the Spokane Falls and Northern Railway to J. J. Hill years earlier. Hill did not take this lying down and put his financial backing into the floundering Vancouver, Victoria and Eastern Railway (VV&E).

The VV&E was chartered in 1896 by William Templeton, mayor of Vancouver, in order to build the coast-to-Kootenay railway to ensure that the riches of the Kootenays would find their way to Vancouver and not into the boxcars of J. J. Hill's GNR. Although there was a general distrust of Hill's promise to build the "coast-to-Kootenay" line, Hill was granted an amendment to the VV&E's charter allowing it to divert through the U.S. in order to complete the line to the coast. The CPR responded immediately by dispatching its surveyors to survey a completely Canadian route from the coast to the Kootenays.

As the grade for the VV&E pushed through west of Midway, it inadvertently crossed a small parcel of land granted to the CPR. On September 30, 1905, the CPR erected a fence across the grade, claiming the VV&E was trespassing. Hill managed to get an expropriation order for the parcel of land, which the CPR immediately claimed invalid and not for the parcel in question. On November 7, 1905, Hill massed an army of workers to the disputed property. The CPR responded at once, by ordering all available railway workers to Midway. Hill, hearing of CPR's move, dispatched additional troops to Midway. On November 9, the brigade of CPR workers armed with shovels, picks and axes massed against the formidable VV&E. Tracks were torn up, shovels and picks clanged against one another, and shots were fired. Miraculously no one was killed. Nightfall put an end to the day's hostilities. The next morning the CPR workers found the disputed area barbwired. Not wishing to contend with the barbwire without wire cutters, the CPR workers headed for the saloons in Ferry, just across the border. There the hostilities ended with the VV&E and CPR workers standing shoulder to shoulder at the bar. In court the CPR was found to be correct, and Hill had to get an expropriation order for the right parcel of land.

The KVR winds along the shoreline of the Kettle River, km 13.4.

The first trestle of the KVR crosses the Kettle River to Kettle River Provincial Park, km 24.9.

West of Midway on the VV&E line is the site at which GN crossed over CPR land in 1905. This incident resulted in the CPR and J. J. Hill's Great Northern Railway fighting the Battle of Midway. The disputed area is five kilometres west of Midway across the Kettle River on the old grade of the VV&E.

0.8   Highway #3 ⵁ
The Highway was realigned in 2000. In the process of realignment the KVR grade becomes indistinct at this point. The rail bed continues straight west paralleling the south side of the power lines.

0.9   Old Highway #3 ⵁ

2.8   Pope and Talbot Ltd.—Midway Sawmill ⊢➔ⵆ
In 1905, the Midway and Vernon Railway (M&V) constructed a grade from the Midway to Rock Creek in an attempt to secure government grants. The C&W at that time, in order to secure right of way, continued its line from Midway to km 4.0. With the failure of the M&V, the KVR continued westward to Rock Creek utilizing the already constructed grade of the M&V. At this point the original M&V grade is about 30 metres to the north, paralleling the KVR grade. At km 4.0 the KVR shifts onto the original M&V grade.
The KVR grade that lies next to the Midway Sawmill has been removed or blocked by fences. The trail around the sawmill at this point skirts the sawmill property by utilizing the old Midway and Vernon railway grade until it reaches the sawmill administration office where by the trail shifts slightly further north to bypass the administration office. The single track trail reconnects to the original KVR grade at km 4.1. This bypass of the original grade will add approximately 100 metres to your odometer reading.

4.1   Trail reconnects to rail grade ⊢⟵ⵆ

4.9   Gate / Texas gate
KVR grade, after this point to km 8.7, runs through cow and horse pastures and can be a little rough in places.

5.7   Gate

6.2   Gate

6.7   Gate

7.1   Gate

8.7   Gate - Highway #3 - Ingram bridge / Burbar Road ⊢➔ⵇ
KVR crosses under Ingram bridge of Highway #3. The rail bed becomes impassable due to rock slides and heavy growth of weeds, while farther down the line, the grade has been ploughed under. Plans are in the works to reconstruct the trail though this problem area.

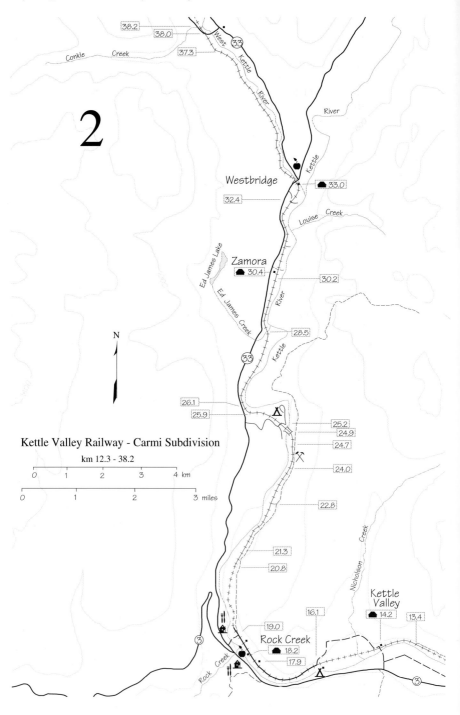

2

Westbridge

Zamora

N

Kettle Valley Railway - Carmi Subdivision

km 12.3 - 38.2

Kettle
Valley

Rock Creek

After crossing under the Highway #3 bridge, detour to the east on to Bubar Road. Small sections of the right-of-way can be seen paralleling the river from Bubar Road. Bubar Road connects with the KVR at km 13.4. The detour is 4.2 kilometres.

An alternative to using Bubar Road is to detour west on Highway #3. Turn on to Kettle Valley East Road, and at the elementary school turn north on to Kettle Valley South Road, crossing over the Kettle River. The road then intersects the KVR just on the other side of the river at km 14.3. The rail bed appears on the right as a one-lane road.

13.4   Bubar Road connects with KVR ⊢←⌐

14.2   Kettle Valley Station |595 ⬛ 🚲 0.2
The name "Kettle" originates from the large whirlpools found along the Kettle River.

14.3   Kettle Valley South Road ⼁ ⊢→⌐
West of the intersection of Kettle Valley Road South, the right-of-way becomes a farmer's field. Though the farm, the rail bed has been ploughed under. Detour north on to Kettle Valley South Road to km 16.1. The detour is 2.7 kilometres.
In the fall of 2001 the one lane bridge spanning the Kettle River just south of this intersection was removed and replaced. Sections of this old one lane bridge were used to replace the missing railway bridge crossing Wilkinson Creek at km 81.2

16.1   Jim Blaine Memorial Park ⟁ ⊢←⌐
Overnight camping, sports ground and playground. Past the campground the KVR rail bed becomes part of the Kettle Valley South Road.

17.9   Abandoned sawmill

18.2   Rock Creek Station |603 ⬛ 🏛 ⛽ 🏕 🍴 ● (🚲 0.2
Named after the community of Rock Creek that already existed here when the KVR came through. The community of Rock Creek was born when gold was discovered in the small creek that enters the Kettle River here. Rock Creek Park (day use only) is across the Kettle River and 300 metres south on Highway #3.

18.9   Rock Creek Road ⼁

19.0   Detour ⊢→⌐
The road branches from the rail bed to the east, and parallels the KVR. The rail bed itself is overgrown and not easily passable. Detour by following the road that narrows and ends at some residential properties. Reaccess the KVR on the west. The detour is 2.3 kilometres.

20.8   Rough access ⊢⇐⌐
The rail bed can be accessed here though it is a little rough.

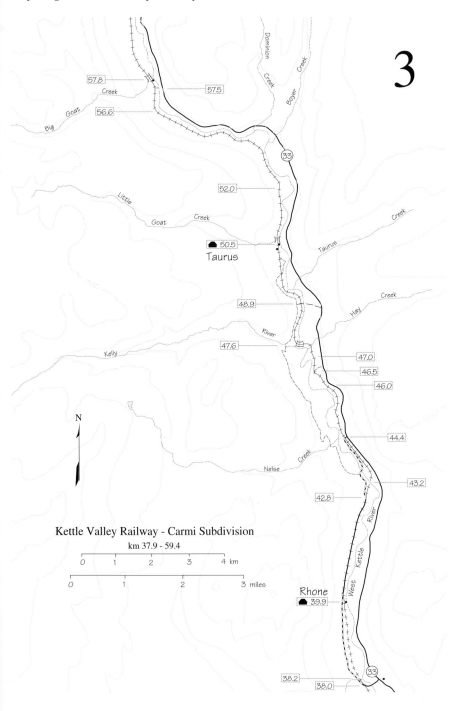

3

57.8

57.5

Creek

56.6

Goat

Big

Dominion Creek

Boyer Creek

33

Little

52.0

Goat Creek

Creek

50.5

Taurus

Taurus

Creek

48.9

Hay Creek

River

47.6

Kelly

47.0

46.5

46.0

N

44.4

Nelse Creek

43.2

42.8

Kettle Valley Railway - Carmi Subdivision

km 37.9 - 59.4

| 0 | 1 | 2 | 3 | 4 km |

| 0 | 1 | 2 | 3 miles |

West Kettle River

Rhone

39.9

33

38.2

38.0

21.3   Detour reconnects with KVR ⫯←⫰

22.8   Gate

24.0   Gate

24.7   Road connects to KVR ⫯

24.9   Kettle River)(72 ▌ ⊼

A through truss bridge crosses the Kettle River entering Kettle River Provincial Park. On the west side of the river is a refreshing picnic site, complete with sandy beach and swimming hole. The KVR bisects the Kettle River Provincial Park, which offers overnight camping to the north of the right-of-way and picnicking to the south.

25.2   Park road to overnight campground ⫯ ▌ ⋀

25.9   Rock slide

A small rock slide from a cut in the out-cropping rock covers the rail bed. A short walkable trail winds through the rock slide.

26.1   Gate

From here to Zamora the KVR runs through farm fields and is gated at km 26.1, 27.0, 28.5 and 29.3. Please be courteous and close all gates behind you.

28.5   Ed James Creek / Gate

The creek has washed away the rail bed and added a technical challenge to the route. Easily walked over.

30.2   Gate

30.4   Zamora Station ¡624 ◼ ⫯ ⫯ ⫘

Named after the Spanish province of Zamora. The section house site is just prior to crossing Zamora Road. Zamora Road provides access to Highway #3.

32.4   Dez Mazes Road ⫯

After Dez Mazes Road to Westbridge, the trail on the KVR winds though some tree growth.

33.0   Westbridge Station ¡625 ◼ ▌ ⫰ ⫯ ▌ ● (⫯0.4

The remains of the section house are found just before crossing Highway #33. Evidence of the water tower was erased when the highway was relocated. Westbridge General Store is located on the highway across the river. The rail bed leaving Westbridge is a well-packed single lane gravel road.

33.1   Highway #33 and Westbridge Road ⫯

34.7   Possible back country campsite ⋀

The open grassland around Zanmora, km 29.6.

Fording West Kettle River, km 43.2.

37.3   Cattle guard

38.0   Blythe-Rhone Road ⵟ ┝➔⌐

Detour west (left) on Blythe-Rhone Road to Rhone, as the bridge that crosses Conkle Creek is out. Following the crossing of Conkle Creek, the right-of-way is weedy and bisected by numerous fences. Follow the paved Blythe-Rhone Road 2.7 kilometres at which point the road runs atop the original railway grade.

38.2   Conkle Creek ⵜ14

Paul Lautard.

39.9   Rhone Station—KVR cyclists rest stop ℹ️*652* ▬ ⌐ 🚲*0.8* ┝←⌐

Named after the Rhone Valley in France. The foundation of the Rhone section house is found 200 metres south of the intersection of the Blythe-Rhone Road and the KVR. On the west side of the road is Paul Lautard's cyclists rest stop. Over the past few years Paul has built a rest stop for weary cyclist which now includes a large shelter, out house, water source, and a caboose which serves as a temporary shelter from inclement weather. Leaving Paul's rest stop the next 2.7 kilometres north the Blythe-Rhone Road runs a top the original grade of the KVR.

42.8   KVR and Blythe-Rhone Road depart ┝⇒⌐

The bridge crossing the West Kettle River at km 43.2 has been removed. The more adventuresome may want to continue on the KVR and wade or boulder hop the West Kettle River. Otherwise continue to follow the Blythe-Rhone Road across the river. From the road bridge crossing the river, the abutments of the old railway bridge are visible 400 metres downstream. 0.9 kilometres past the bridge, the Blythe-Rhone Road again crosses the railway, before intersecting with Highway #33.

43.2   West Kettle River—Little Dipper Campground ⛺ ⛺ 🅱️ ⵜ30

The original railway bridge over the West Kettle River was removed and is being used as a bridge for the Blythe-Rhone Road seven kilometres downstream. Although the bridge is missing, the river can be forded during low water levels. About 100 metres north of the missing bridge along the river is a parking lot/rough campsite off Blythe Rhone Road. This point also is probably the best point to ford the river. Across Blythe Rhone Road is Little Dipper Campground.

44.4   Blythe-Rhone Road ⵟ ┝⇐⌐

Take the KVR on a beautiful and scenic ride to Taurus. This section also has many spots along the river that lend themselves to back country camping.

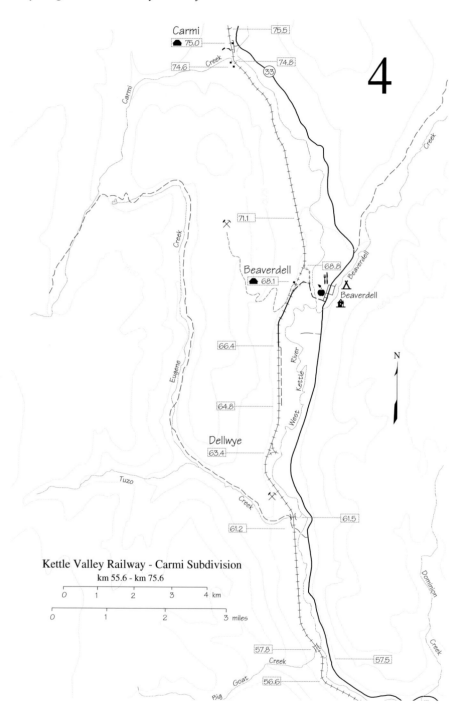

Carmi
75.0
75.5
74.6
Creek
74.8
33

4

Creek

71.1

Beaverdell
68.1
68.8
Beaverdell
Beaverdell

66.4

N

64.8

Kettle River

West Kettle River

Dellwye
63.4

Eugene Creek

Tuzo Creek

61.2
61.5

Kettle Valley Railway - Carmi Subdivision
km 55.6 - km 75.6

0   1   2   3   4 km

0   1   2   3 miles

57.8
Creek
57.5
Goat
56.6
Big
Dominion Creek

46.0   Slide area that is easily passed over

46.5   Access road to Highway #33 ⍏

47.0   Rhone Canyon (Bull Creek Canyon)
Here the West Kettle River cuts a deep gorge through a rocky obstruction in the valley. The original surveys for the KVR suggested that a tunnel be forged through the ridge on the west side of the river. McCulloch, not wanting to waste time and money on tunnel construction, relocated the survey to cross the West Kettle River and hug the east wall of the canyon, thereby avoiding the tunnel. This required two bridges across the West Kettle River.

47.3   Swimming hole

47.6   West Kettle River Δᴮ 🍶ʙ)(33

48.9   Pope & Talbot Forest Service Road ⍏
Highway #33 access.

50.5   Taurus Station ℹ714 🚗 🍶ʙ ⌇ 🚲0.4
Originally named Bull Creek Station, the station was renamed Taurus, after the astrological sign of the bull, to avoid confusion with another CPR station named Bull River. The site of Taurus Station is marked by the large octagonal cement foundation of the water tower and the cement foundation of the section house.

50.6   Little Goat Creek 🍶ʙ)(

52.0   Moose crossing
This marshy area is a particularly good spot to find moose.

56.6   Rainbow trout wild hatchery Δᴮ 🍶ʙ ⍟

57.5   Short trail to the river 🚶

57.8   Water tower—Big Goat Creek 🍶 🍶ʙ)(
On the south side of Big Goat Creek lies the remains of a water tower and a small shed. The only evidence left of this water tower are pieces of foundation and supporting cables coming out of the ground. A small red KVR shed is back in the bushes to the east, and a small trestle crosses over Big Goat Creek.
Logging traffic has reduced spots of the rail bed to washboard.

61.2   Tuzo-Eugene Forest Service Road ⍏

61.5   Tuzo Creek 🍶ʙ)(14
Tuzo Creek was named as a memorial to the sacrifice of J. A. Tuzo, an assistant engineer on the KVR, who was among the first Canadians to be killed in World War I.

Beaverdell Hotel, no doubt one of the busiest hotels during the railway boom, is now the oldest operating hotel in British Columbia, km 68.1.

Tuzo Creek Bridge, km 61.5.

63.4   **Dellwye** Y

A wye was built here to turn around snow plows that were used between here and Penticton. The name was formed from a combination of Beaverdell and wye. Although grassy, the wye is a well-defined cut into the trees.

64.8   KVR parallels Beaverdell Station Road

66.4   Beaverdell Station Road �

From here, the Beaverdell Station Road uses the rail grade for the next 1.8 kilometres. The road passes a sawmill and an abandoned mill that once processed ore from the Highland Silver Mine. The Silver Mine is 500 metres above Beaverdell on Wallace Mountain.

68.1   Beaverdell Station   i787 ▬ ⌇ Λ ⚐ Ӆ ‖ ● ⅃ (⚓0.9 ⌇→⌇

Evidence of both the station and right-of-way are lost in the middle of what are now large tailing ponds. The station was situated at the point where the Beaverdell Station Road turns east toward Beaverdell. Detour following Beaverdell Station Road east for 300 metres. Just past Kettle Valley Welding Limited, turn north on to a one-lane trail that leads around the east side of the tailing ponds. The trail turns on to the rail bed 0.8 kilometres from Beaverdell Station Road.

   If you continue down Beaverdell Station Road to Beaverdell you ride over West Kettle River on the railway bridge that was used to carry the KVR over Wilkinson Creek at km 81.2. Located at Beaverdell is the oldest operating hotel in British Columbia, the Beaverdell Hotel. You will find lodging, campgrounds, restaurants and groceries here. This interesting community makes a great stopover point and is the last place before Penticton for stocking up on food and supplies.

68.8   North end of tailing ponds ⌇←⌇⌇

The one-lane trail that leads around the tailing ponds connects to the right-of-way.

71.1   KVR crosses the open valley bottom of the West Kettle River

74.6   Carmi Mine ✕

Jim Dale staked the Carmi mine in 1896 and named the area after his Illinois home town. Prospering from the gold mine and a 10 stamp mill, the town boasted two hotels, a jail, hospital, two stores and gas stations. With the closing of the mine in 1939, residents moved on. Today all that remains is a near ghost town.

   Mine buildings west of the rail bed were dismantled in 2000. The mine itself was a few hundred metres up the hill.

74.8   Carmi Creek

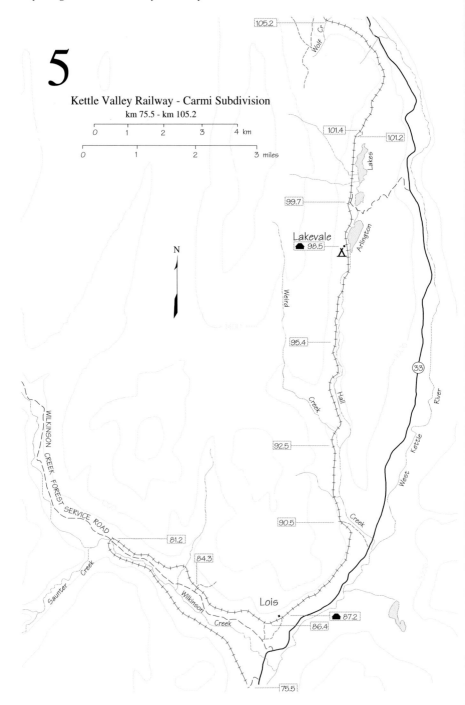

5

Kettle Valley Railway - Carmi Subdivision
km 75.5 - km 105.2

105.2

Wolf Cr.

101.4

101.2

Lakes

99.7

Lakevale
98.5

Arlington

Weird

95.4

Hall

Creek

33

Kettle River

West

92.5

90.5

Creek

WILKINSON CREEK FOREST SERVICE ROAD

81.2

84.3

Wilkinson

Lois

Creek

87.2

86.4

Saunter Creek

75.5

N

75.0 Carmi Station ¡847 🚃 🏠 ⌇ ᨔ0.9

Pine trees now grow from the middle of the section house foundation, and across the rail bed is the water tower foundation. The present–day residents of Carmi live in houses to the east of the rail bed.

75.5 Carmi Creek Forest Service Road ⵙ

Highway #33 can be accessed down this road.

If for some reason you wish to bypass this beautiful loop up Wilkinson Creek you can turn east, down Carmi Creek Forest Service Road and then turn north on Highway #33 and cross Wilkinson Creek. Once across the bridge, turn west on to Wilkinson Creek Forest Service Road. Follow this road for 500 metres and you will find on your right a grass 4x4 path that reconnects you to the KVR. This 4x4 path forks about 150 metres from the start, with the left branch being the most direct route to the KVR and the other branch rejoining the KVR at Lois. Both paths gain 100 metres in altitude in less than a kilometre. The detour is 2.4 to 2.8 kilometres depending on the path chosen Beware, there is a small road prior to the correct path leading up from Wilkinson Creek FSR. This road runs out in about 1.5 km and does not connect to the KVR.

81.2 Wilkinson Creek—Wilkinson Creek Forest Service Road ⵙ ☒ 🏠)(24

The original bridge over this creek was removed shortly after the rail line was abandoned. This bridge is now in use at Beaverdell as a road bridge crossing the West Kettle River. Sections of the one lane road bridge removed in 2001 across the Kettle River at Kettle Valley (km 14.3) was used to replace this missing bridge. Just across the creek, the KVR crosses Wilkinson Creek Forest Service Road. The KVR grade to Lois appears much steeper then it really is, as the river valley falls and the rail bed climbs. Beware, it is quite common to mistaken the forestry road as the rail grade. The rail grade continues straight across the road in line with the bridge.

84.3 Access road to Wilkinson Creek Forest Service Road ⵙ

86.4 4x4 path ⵙ

4x4 path from Wilkinson Creek Forest Service Road intersects the KVR.

87.2 Lois Station ¡955 🚃 ⌇ ⵙ ᨔ0.9

A small shed, the concrete foundation of the station house, and a rock retaining wall are what remain of Lois Station. The second 4x4 path from the Wilkinson Creek Forest Service Road intersects here.

90.5 Small access road to Highway #33 ⵙ

92.5 Rock slide

A small rock slide is easily negotiated. It was in this section that an eastbound freight ran into a rock slide that blocked the line from April 12-18, 1925.

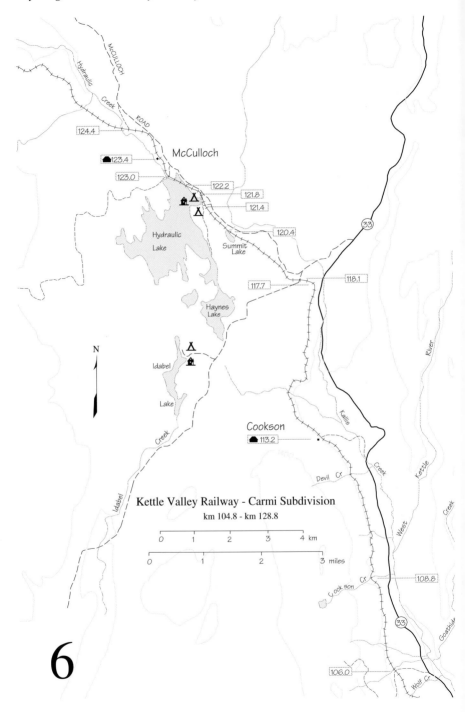

McCulloch

124.4

123.4

123.0

122.2

121.8

121.4

120.4

Hydraulic
Lake

Summit
Lake

117.7

118.1

Haynes
Lake

N

Idabel

Lake

Cookson

113.2

Kettle Valley Railway - Carmi Subdivision
km 104.8 - km 128.8

| 0 | 1 | 2 | 3 | 4 km |

| 0 | 1 | 2 | 3 miles |

108.8

106.0

6

95.4 Creek wash covering KVR

98.5 **Lakevale Station** ⅰ1053 ⛰ 👤 ⌇ 🏕 🏠ᴮ ⅰ 🚲0.9

The remains of the station house and water tower's concrete foundations are found here. This station was originally named Arlington, after the lakes of the same name, but was later changed because a station of the same name was on the Esquimalt & Nanaimo (E&N) rail line.

On the shore of Arlington Lakes is Arlington Lakes Campground, a forestry campground across from Lakevale Station.

99.7 Arlington Lakes Road ⚔

101.2 Grass and trees—road ⟜⇒⦙

The next 160 metres runs through a rock cut that is overgrown. The single track through this section can be quite wet. Following the road to the east (right) will avoid this spot.

101.4 Other side of grass and trees ⦙⇐⦙

105.2 Wolf Creek

The KVR crosses Wolf Creek on a large fill.

106.0 Small access road to Highway #33 ⚔

108.8 Cookson Creek ⚒

A large fill replaced the previous trestle in 1942. The fill has washed away and a small road that itself is washing away skirts around the missing fill. Remains of the original trestle can still be seen far below.

113.2 **Cookson Station** ⅰ1184 ⛰ ⌇ ⅰ 🚲0.7

Cookson was named after a local pioneer and rancher. A small red shack remains 100 metres down the railway from the location of Cookson Station.

117.7 Scenic views of West Kettle River Valley

118.1 Okanagan Falls Forest Service Road 🏕 🏠

4.2 kilometres west on Okanagan Falls Forest Service Road is Idabel Lake Resort.

120.4 Summit Lake

The land surrounding Summit Lake is private property and must be respected as such. This includes the gazebo on the north end of the lake.

121.4 Hydraulic Lake Campground 🏕 🏠ᴮ 👤

Forestry campground within the trees and along the shore of Hydraulic Lake.

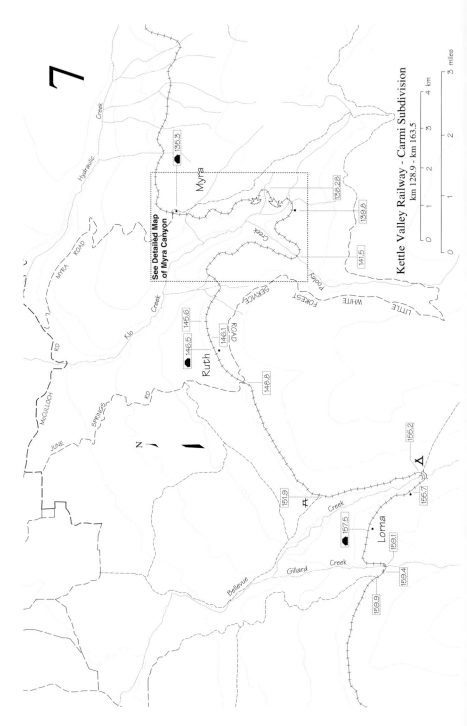

Kettle Valley Railway - Carmi Subdivision
km 128.9 - km 163.5

Lunch at Arlington Lake, km 98.5.

McCulloch Lake Resort, km 121.8.

This 132 metre-long frame trestle marks the summit of the Carmi Subdivision at an elevation of 1274 metres at km 138.22.

121.8   McCulloch Lake Resort and Campground **⚕ ⚒ ▮**

Open year round, the resort has quaint little cabins, a four-plex log chalet, restaurant, and a camping area on the shore of Hydraulic Lake. The facility includes showers, fishing, boating, X-country skiing and canoeing.

Past McCulloch Lake Resort the KVR can become marginally passable depending on the season and the weather. This section can be bypassed using McCulloch Road and reaccessing the KVR at km 122.2

122.2   Access road to McCulloch Road **ᛏ**

Cutting the corner of Hydraulic Lake with a causeway, the KVR creates a lagoon to the north. Beware, the road over the earthen dam at the end of Hydraulic Lake has been mistaken as the KVR.

123.0   Access road to McCulloch Road **ᛏ**

123.4   McCulloch Station �ᵢ1265 **◼ ▮ Ƴ 〗 ◊ ⚬**

On May 31, 1915, at a Penticton banquet in celebration of the opening of the Midway to Merritt line, it was announced that the station at Hydraulic Lake would be renamed McCulloch to honour the Kettle Valley Railway's remarkable engineer, Andrew McCulloch.

Foundations can still be seen. Past the station, the rail bed is used by logging trucks. Evidence of logging is visible all along the KVR to Myra Station.

124.4   Access road to McCulloch Road **ᛏ**

135.2   Myra Forest Service Road **ᛏ**

Used as an access road from Kelowna for day trips into Myra Canyon. This is not an easy road to cycle because of steep grades and loose rock. It is 8.5 kilometres down to McCulloch Road.

135.3   Myra Station ᵢ1270 **◼ 〗 ⫽ ▮ ⚲0.2**

Myra was named after the daughter of engineer J. L. Newman. The cement foundations from the section house and water tower are found here. Just past the station, the railway enters a canyon where it hangs on the sides of cliffs, crosses numerous trestles and travels through two tunnels. The area between Myra and Ruth is now commonly known as Myra Canyon. This canyon forced the railway to wind into the canyon on a wide detour.

During the upgrading of the railway in 1929 two of the trestles in Myra Canyon were replaced with steel and the remaining wooden trestles refitted with new lumber. When the wooden trestles were originally constructed, each timber was cut and bored by hand. No shims were permitted, the fitting had to be exact.

Today the Myra Canyon Trestle Restoration Society is the group largely responsible for the upgrading and maintenance of the KVR corridor through Myra Canyon. The changes in Myra Canyon were to enable this corridor to meet the British Columbia provincial standards for park status. Some of the work involved covering the original trestles with

Enjoying both the view and the luxury of McCulloch Lake Resort, km 121.8.

decking and the installation of handrails. Now upgraded, Myra Canyon, just as the Quintette Tunnels at Othello, has been added to British Columbia's long list of provincial parks.

135.8   Parking and outhouse **⌷ 🚐**

The main parking area for day-exploring Myra Canyon.

135.9   Washout

The trail skirts around the washout.

136.2   Cut in rock

In the initial stages of construction, this was to be a tunnel. However, upon encountering loose rock near the centre of the tunnel, a decision was made to excavate a deep cut instead. Dynamite, which had replaced black powder, was just starting to be used when the KVR was being built. Its use presented a major problem in that the dynamite readily froze under the winter conditions. Due to carelessness and lack of experience many fatalities resulted from workers attempting to quickly heat dynamite in frying pans.

Hand-fitted loose rock retaining walls precede the abutments of most of the trestles in Myra Canyon, km 137.22.

136.76   Frame trestle #18 t55x10

The Myra Canyon Trestle Society numbered the 18 trestles in Myra Canyon from west to east.

137.16   Frame trestle #17)(27x8

137.22   Frame trestle #16)(27x12

137.27   Frame trestle #15)(46x12

137.48   Frame trestle #14)(73x12

137.73   Frame trestle #13)(87x15

137.81   Frame trestle #12)(24x10

137.96   Tunnel **⬛**114

138.22   Frame trestle #11)(132x24

This is the summit of the Carmi Subdivision at 1274 metres.

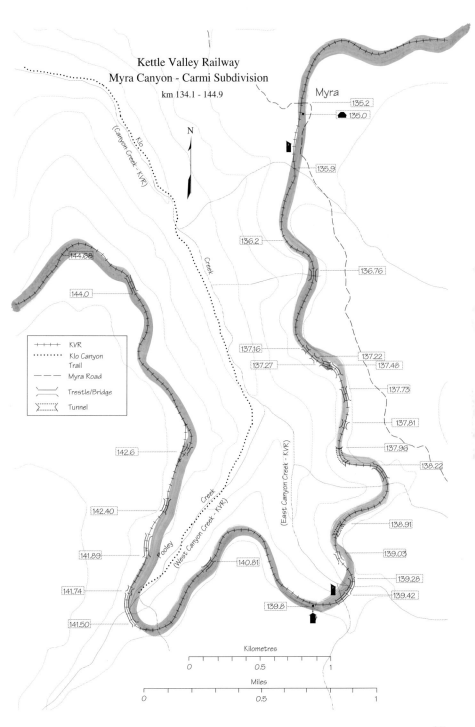

Kettle Valley Railway
Myra Canyon - Carmi Subdivision
km 134.1 - 144.9

N

Myra

135.2
135.0
135.9
136.2
136.76
144.68
144.0
137.16
137.22
137.27
137.48
137.73
137.81
137.96
138.22
142.6
138.91
142.40
139.03
141.89
139.28
140.81
139.42
141.74
139.8
141.50

(Canyon Creek - KVR)
Klo
Creek
(East Canyon Creek - KVR)
Pooley
Creek
(West Canyon Creek - KVR)

Legend:
- ┼┼┼┼ KVR
- ········· Klo Canyon Trail
- ― ― ― Myra Road
- Trestle/Bridge
- Tunnel

Kilometres
0   0.5   1

Miles
0   0.5   1

67

West Fork Canyon Creek Bridge, km 141.50.

Chute Lake Resort, km 171.5, is a welcome sight for weary cyclists.

138.91 Tunnel ■*84*

139.03 Frame trestle #10)(*59x9*

139.28 Klo Creek—East Fork Canyon Creek Bridge #9)(*111x48*
This was originally a frame trestle, changed when CPR upgraded the line. The present bridge consists of five steel through-plate girder spans on steel towers.

139.41 Outhouse ▌

139.42 Frame trestle #8)(*73x21*

139.68 Bench overlooking the second tunnel and trestle #10.

139.80 **Water tower** ▐
The concrete foundation blocks are still here.

140.81 S-Curve frame trestle #7)(*90x25*

141.50 Pooley Creek—West Fork Canyon Creek Bridge #6)(*220x55*
This is the longest and highest bridge in Myra Canyon. Originally a frame trestle, it was replaced in 1931-32 with steel. The bridge consists of twelve steel through-plate girder spans on steel towers.
This is the site where the last spike was driven for the Carmi Subdivision on October 2, 1914. On October 6, the first train ran from Penticton to Midway. Regular service started May 15, 1915 with the completion of the line to Merritt. Fifty-eight years later in June 1973, the final train operated over the tracks in Myra Canyon when the Canadian Broadcasting Corporation filmed segments of "The National Dream."

141.74 Frame trestle #5)(*23x3*

141.89 Frame trestle #4)(*150x37*

142.40 Frame trestle #3)(*82x9*

142.6 The KVR was relocated, diverting a 142 metre-long trestle. Sections of the original trestle are still standing and the original grade is passable and worth exploring.

144.0 Frame trestle #2)(*110x15*

144.68 Rock oven
A small rock oven used to bake bread for the crews building the railway can be found just down and off to the south (left) of the rail bed.

145.5 Frame trestle #1)(*78x15*

145.6 End of Myra Canyon

A rock barricade prevents motor vehicles from entering the canyon. Parking is limited and turning around can be difficult for larger vehicles.

145.8   Parking 🚐

One of the larger limited parking areas on this side of Myra Canyon.

146.1   Myra Canyon Bailout Trail - Parking ▮ 🚐 🚵

Myra Canyon Bailout trail heads down the hill becoming an old forestry road which connects to Little White Forest Service Road approximately 1.5 km from the end of pavement on June Springs Road.

146.5   Ruth Station i1247 ⬛ ⌇ ▮ 🚵0.2

Originally named Kelowna, but because of confusion with the community of Kelowna, it was renamed Ruth after Andrew McCulloch's younger daughter. The station house is still standing but not for much longer, as it is showing the ravages of time and vandalism. Far below in the valley, Kelowna can be seen through the trees. There are many picturesque viewpoints along this stretch and photo opportunities you will not want to miss.

148.8   Little White Forest Service Road ⌖ 🚐

Becomes June Springs Road toward Kelowna. There is another parking lot here for day tripping in Myra Canyon.

151.8   Crawford Hiking Trail access 👫

151.9   Crawford Hiking Trail 👫 ⋔

A staircase comes up from Kelowna. Just down the stairs is a small wilderness campsite with benches and a pond. The trail continues down to Crawford Estates in Kelowna. A second trail branches off to Little White Forest Service Road. The Crawford Hiking Trail follows on the KVR to km 154.8.

155.2   Bellevue Creek)(238 ⌖ 👫 ⛺ ▮ ⌐

The Crawford Hiking Trail diverts south and continues to the summit of Little White Mountain. A short distance up the trail is a wilderness campsite. The Bellevue Creek trestle was also upgraded in the 1930s from a frame trestle to steel plate girder spans on steel towers. Hand rails and planking were installed the summer of 2000.

155.7   Water tower ▮

Square concrete blocks placed in an octagonal shape mark the place where the water tower stood.

157.5   Lorna Station i1230 ⬛ ⌇ ▮ 🚵0.3

Lorna was named after the youngest daughter of J. J. Warren, president of the KVR. Hidden in the alders is the foundation of the station house. Very little evidence is visible from the rail bed and it is very easy to miss Lorna Station.

159.1 Gillard Creek

The trestle over Gillard Creek has been bypassed using a large fill. The original trestle, minus the top deck, still stands next to the fill.

159.4 Bypass reconnects to old grade

159.9 Chute Lake Road—Gillard Creek Forest Service Road ⍏

This road leads down into the valley to intersect with Lakeshore Road in Okanagan Mission. Beware, a few cyclists have mistaken Gillard Creek FSR as the rail grade. The rail grade is very flat at this point.

165.5 Pine Beetle Control Area—Lebanon Lake †

A large area was deforested due to an infestation of the mountain pine beetle. The area was reforested with new seedlings in 1992.

170.3 Chute Lake wye. ⍦

171.4 Chute Lake Station ⁍1191 ▰ ⬤ ⧵ Ⅹ ⛪ ⋔ ⊪ ⬤ ⬤ ⬮2.0

Chute Lake Station was named after the lake of the same name. The name Chute Lake came from the creek that resembled a chute or waterfall in its rapid descent to Okanagan Lake. On July 15, 1915, two months after the official opening of the Midway to Merritt line, a steam locomotive with a load of 530 Penticton residents climbed up to Chute Lake for a day picnic. It has been said that the Penticton residents very much enjoyed this new railway.

One can see how the rugged beauty of Chute Lake made this a choice spot for visiting back in 1915 and with very little changed, many still find their way up for a visit. Located at Chute Lake today is Chute Lake Resort, owned and operated by Gary and Doreen Reed. The octagonal-shaped foundation of the water tower can be found in the picnic area. Some of the original red KVR buildings are still in use on the property.

The facility offers picnicking, a playground, fishing (the lake is stocked with rainbow trout), boating and canoeing (rentals available), camping, a bathhouse, laundry, six rustic log cabins (each equipped with a fridge, wood-burning stove and kitchen supplies), and a lodge with eight sleeping rooms and a large dining area complete with pool table, an old jukebox and antique decor with many KVR artifacts and pictures.

171.6 Chute Creek)(18

171.7 Elinor Lake Forest Service Road ⍏ Ⅹ ⬤B

A primitive campground is found on the southeast corner of Chute Lake. After leaving Chute Lake, the KVR crosses many small wooden bridges and trestles spanning small creeks. The rail bed from Chute Lake to Penticton is downhill allowing you to cruise at a pleasant 13 to 14 km/hour. Unfortunately, the KVR is also being used by logging trucks and can be a little bumpy in spots with loose gravel and washboard.

TIP: Deflating tires to around 20 psi gives you a better ride and more control as you cruise over the rough Texas pea gravel and loose sand that is encountered on this downhill stretch.

Behind Chute Lake Lodge, km 171.4.

Rock ovens, km 187.1. Ovens such as this one enabled the KVR construction crews to enjoy fresh baked goods.

171.9 Chute Creek)(9

172.0 Chute Creek)(14

172.1 Chute Creek)(14

172.2 Chute Creek—Rock Oven #12)(14 |▀

Since about 1990 the KVR Woodwackers have been the unofficial stewards of the KVR from Chute Lake to Penticton. This volunteer group of mostly retirees has been responsible for most of the upgrades on this section. Ray Ward (of the KVR Woodwackers) has found and rebuilt many of the Rock Ovens. Rock Oven #12 found on the right just after the bridge is the first of these rock ovens encountered along the trail

172.3 Chute Creek)(14

174.1 Access road to Chute Lake Road ⌇

177.1 Cattle guard

180.4 Rock Oven #11 |▀

180.8 Elinor Lake Forest Service Road- North Fork Smethurst Road —Rock Oven #10 |▀ ⌇

Just before this intersection you cross over a cattle guard. To the east is Elinor Lake Forest Service Road, which follows Robinson Creek to Naramata Lake (3.6 km), Elinor Lake (4.7 km) and Chute Lake (8 km). To the west is North Fork Smethurst Road, which switchbacks down 100 metres in 1.5 kilometres to again intersect with the KVR at the middle segment of the giant loops at km 186.5.

181.4 Rock Oven #9 |▀

181.9 Adra Station ┆981 ▬ ▐ ┊ ┆ ⤳2.1

Adra Station was located just before the switchbacks that McCulloch used to avoid a grade of 4.5% that would have been required for the descent from Chute Lake to Penticton, an elevation drop of 850 metres over 24 kilometres. Instead, a grade of 2.2% was used with two giant loops. The line doubled back on itself through a spiral tunnel just past Adra, and doubled back again in a second giant loop just past Glenfir Station. The beautiful view from this location, overlooking Okanagan Lake and Summerland, was reminiscent of the Spanish seaport of Adra and Adra Station was appropriately named after it. The water tower and section house foundations, complete with sidewalk, remain at this site.

182.9 Rock Oven #8 |▀

183.1 Adra Tunnel Bypass Trail ┆➔⋮

This 150 metre-long single track bypasses the collapsed Adra Tunnel and rejoins the rail bed at km 184.4.

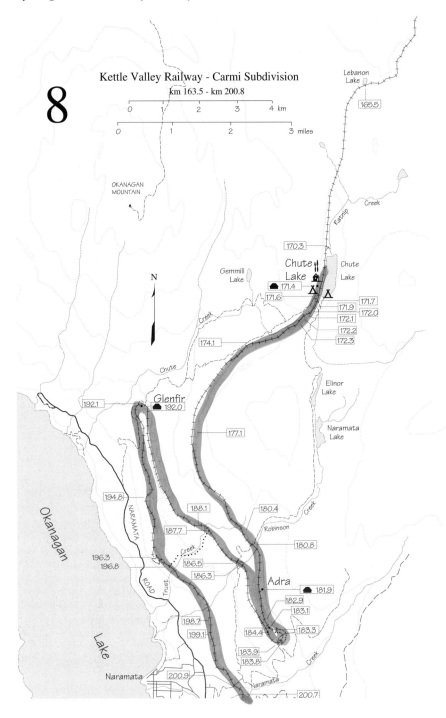

8

Kettle Valley Railway - Carmi Subdivision
km 163.5 - km 200.8

183.3 Adra Tunnel (The Big Tunnel) ■*489*

This spiral tunnel is the longest tunnel on the KVR. Safe travel through the tunnel can not be guaranteed as the ceiling and walls have given way on the outside of the curve near the lower entrance and there can be over a foot of water at the lower end. In 1992 the entrances of the tunnel were partially blocked with walls of cement blocks. A short trail, 140 metres before the tunnel entrance, bypasses the tunnel and reconnects with the rail bed just past the exit of the tunnel.

During the building of the KVR many hazards were encountered. One hazard in particular was rattlesnakes. During the rock blasting above Naramata, rattlesnakes were jarred out of their rock hiding places resulting in more than one worker suffering the bite of an angry rattler.

183.8 Tunnel exit

Owing to the heavy grades when descending from Chute Lake to Penticton, brakemen were to stand ready at the brakes. Brake wheels of the freight cars could only be turned from atop the cars, thus requiring brakemen to ride standing atop the freight cars. Such a task was exceedingly risky and more than one brakeman lost his life when the train unexpectedly lurched or stopped.

183.9 South Fork Smethurst Road ⌁

Following this road southward, you cross the KVR at km 200.9 to intersect with Naramata Road. Locals prefer to take the heart pumping scramble up this 4x4 road from km 200.9, rather then endure dragging out the ascent on loose sand and gravel switchbacking up the KVR. Going up, this road leads over the top of the tunnel. Many cyclists have gotten lost mistaking this road for the trail to the other end of the tunnel.

184.4 Adra Tunnel Bypass Trail ↤⋮

The trail joins the rail bed 550 metres from the exit of Adra Tunnel. This trail is signed if coming from Penticton. Take note of where it is before continuing up to look at the tunnel so you can be sure to get on the right trail to bypass the tunnel.

186.3 Rock Ovens #1, 2 & 3 ⌐

The two smaller rock ovens are up the trail to the east (right). The first one is on the right about 10 metres from the rail bed. The second is at 20 metres. Rock oven #3 is on the opposite side of the railway.

Steam locomotive emerges from the "Little Tunnel" at km 196.3 of the Carmi Subdivision. (Penticton Museum)

Cycling this part of the Kettle Valley Railway is becoming increasingly popular and why not with such incredible scenery? Looking back at the 48 metre-long "Little Tunnel."

186.5 Elinor Lake Forest Service Road—North Fork Smethurst Road ⚐ ▌

This road first crossed the rail bed farther up the hill, just prior to Adra Station at km 180.8. 4.6 kilometres south along this road connects you to the South Fork Smethurst Road. This road does cross a couple of private properties and use of it may be restricted. Please heed any notices. Turning south on Smethurst Road and travelling another 0.6 kilometres reconnects you with the KVR at km 200.9. Smethurst Road then continues another 0.8 kilometres to connect with Naramata Road.

187.1 Rock Ovens #4, 5 & 7—Tote Road Trail (Horse Shoe Trail) 🚴 👫 ⚑

The rock ovens were constructed by railway workers for baking bread and other goods for the men working on the KVR.

The signed trail to the rock ovens #4 & 5, is a faint 4x4 path on the east (right) side, that leads you up a steep climb to the rock ovens. Follow the path for a couple of hundred metres, keeping a watch on your left (close to Trust Creek) for the igloo (beehive) shaped rock ovens. From the trail, the ovens appear as rock piles covered with pine needles and moss, and are hidden back in a pine grove. They can be difficult to find with such good camouflage.

Rock Oven #7 can be found down the Tote Road Trail about 1400 metres. This trail is rather steep in places and should only be ridden by experienced cyclists. This trail reconnects to the KVR at km 196.8. It is easier to access this rock oven from km 196.8.

187.9 Trust Creek—Rock Oven #6 ⚑

A log bridge starts the trail to rock oven #6.

188.1 Power line—Power line Trail 🚴

Following this trail under the power lines will take you to North Fork Smethurst Road.

192.0 Glenfir Station ⅰ788 ◖ ⍭ ▐ 🚲2.2

This station was named after a large grove of fir trees that were growing beside the railway. A gravel fill marks the site of the Glenfir Station.

192.1 Chute Lake Road

The apex of the switchback meets the road to Chute Lake.

192.3 Outhouse ▌

194.8 Bench looking north toward Paradise Ranch

Paradise Ranch, a former orchard is now a large producer of grapes and produces it's own label ice wine. Canadian filmmaker Sandy Wilson grew up at the ranch and wrote and directed the feature film "American Cousin", about a summer at the ranch in her early teen years. The movie was shot on location at Paradise Ranch and Penticton.

Path overlooking Okanagan Lake. If you look closely, you may see the Ogopogo Monster, km. 195.0. Photo: Robbin McKinney.

196.3 Little Tunnel 📷48

The views along this section are unsurpassed as the KVR winds its way down the side of Okanagan Mountain and out of the Okanagan Highlands. Looking down into the valley you can see Okanagan Lake, Summerland, Naramata, Penticton and even as far as Skaha Lake.

Okanagan Lake, 340 metres below this point, is 128 kilometres long and 274 metres deep, and has been noted as a lake of much mystery and folklore. It is known as the home of the fearless lake monster "Ogopogo." This lake monster was originally identified by the Indians as N'ha-a-itk. His home was believed to be a cave at Squally Point at the big bend in the lake. New settlers were warned by the Indians not to go on the lake alone or near his cave, as the monster could rise out of the waves to claim a life. Animals were regularly sacrificed by being thrown overboard in an attempt to calm the beast. Today, people still look out onto Okanagan Lake and wonder if they will catch a glimpse of the sea serpent from the past.

196.8 Horseshoe Trail (Tote Road Trail)—Rock Oven #7

The rock oven is found about 300 metres up the trail. The trail continues another 1400 metres to connect to the KVR at km 187.7

198.7 Bench overlooking Okanagan Lake.

199.1 Outhouse 🚻

199.3 Bench over looking Okanagan Lake and Summerland.

200.2 Bench over looking Naramata.

200.9 Smethurst Road (Naramata Creek Road)—Naramata ⚑ ⌂ ⌂ ● ‖ ⊤ 🚐

Down Smethurst Road 1.6 kilometres connects you with North Naramata

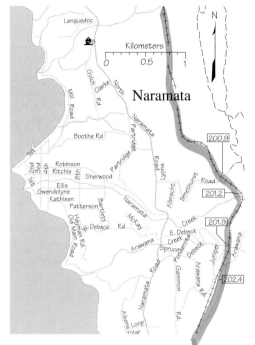

Road. 600 metres south on North Naramata Road brings you to the intersection with Robinson Ave. (Naramata Road). West on Robinson Ave. will bring you into the town centre of Naramata. 1.4 kilometres north on North Naramata Road from Smethurst Road is Vista Treks (Gulch Road and North Naramata Road). ⊤ Nichol Vineyard (250) 496-5962.

Up the road, the North and South Forks of Smethurst Road intersects the KVR at kms 186.5, 183.9 and 180.8.

201.2 Naramata Creek ⧓

The trestle is missing across Naramata Creek, but it is not difficult to cross the creek through the small gully. In the next 0.6 kilometres, trestles are also missing across Arawana Creek and another small creek. This requires you to climb in and out of one steep gulch and a second smaller one to cross each of these creeks. If conditions are wet these gullies are a mud bath.

201.9 Arawana Creek 🏕 ⧓

202.2 Arawana Station ╎566 🏠 🎒 ╎ 🚵1.8

This was originally named Naramata because of its proximity to the community of Naramata, but confusion between the two locations resulted in a name change. Arawana was named after a song popular at the time, "Aeeah Wannah." The water tower foundation, on which a picnic table and shelter have been built, marks the site of Arawana Station. Some of the red KVR buildings have been moved farther down the railway and are being used as a shed and an outhouse.

202.4 Arawana Road—Arawana Creek Forest Service Road ⚑ ⊤

⊤ **Lang Vineyards (2493 Gammon Road, 496-5987)**

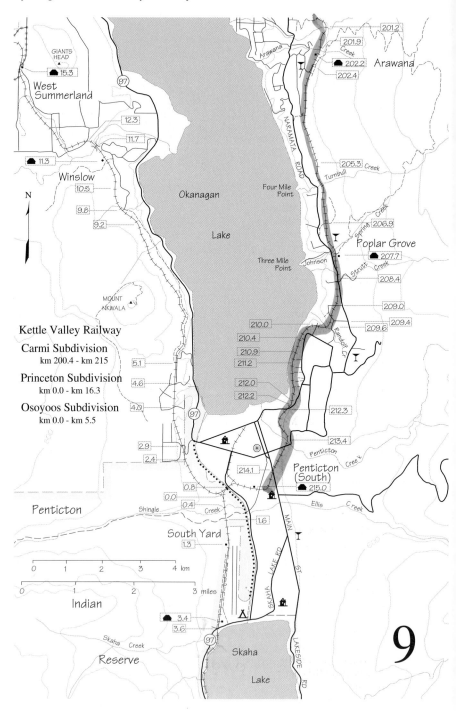

Kettle Valley Railway

Carmi Subdivision
   km 200.4 - km 215

Princeton Subdivision
   km 0.0 - km 16.3

Osoyoos Subdivision
   km 0.0 - km 5.5

9

205.3 Loose

The right-of-way becomes loose with section being quite rough and bouncy with large rocks, black sand and a disturbed trail from use by horses all the way to Naramata Road.

206.9 Sutherland Road ⊤

207.4 Hillside Estate Winery ⊤ ⅋

1350 Naramata Road, (250) 493-6274, right on the trail. Great place for lunch.

Arawana Station, km 202.2.

207.7 Poplar Grove Station - Riddle Road ᵢ461 ▬ ⊤ ⅋ ⬚1.6

The intersection of Riddle Road marks Poplar Grove Station.

208.4 Naramata Road ⊤ ⊤ ⊢→

The railway crosses to the other side of Naramata Road. This section has been upgraded by the City of Penticton and has been resurfaced in fine crush gravel. This section is also bordered by some of the orchards that have made the Okanagan Valley famous.

209.0 Davenport Road ⊤

209.4 Lochore Road ⊤

209.6 Randolf Creek - McCulloch Trestle)(

In the fall of 2001 the City of Penticton restored the railway grade through the orchards. Wine Country Walkways Society raised $300,000 with the help of many donations to build McCulloch Trestle across Randolf Draw.

210.0 Carder Road—Orchard ⊤

210.5 ▟▆▆▆▆▆ Lakeview Cemetery ▆▆▆▆▆▟

On December 13, 1945, Andrew McCulloch passed away. He was buried in Lakeview Cemetery overlooking the railway that was such an important part of his life. His grave site can be found in Section D, the first section directly to the right of the main entrance and below the fire hydrant. Access to the cemetery from the trail can usually be gained at this point.

212.0 Wreck of Little Joe Raymond ⊩

The benches surrounding Okanagan Lake are remnants of a beach consisting of glacial debris and can be quite unstable, giving way in slides. It was upon this bench on November 30, 1949, that train #12 was dumped down the side of the bench when it gave way. Irrigation of the orchards along these benches is also increasing the benches instability.

Lunch at Hillside Estate Winery, km 207.4. Photo: Goetz Schildt.

The recently rebuilt trail through the orchards and along Okanagan Lake, km 211.0.

212.2 Fork in trail - Vancouver Place ╞➔╎

Take the right fork and follow Vancouver Place 100 metres to Vancouver Avenue. Across Vancouver Ave. the railway becomes a paved path through the City of Penticton. (The left fork will take you down the back alley to Vancouver Avenue.)

212.3 Vancouver Avenue ↑ ┇▪ ╡←╎

The City of Penticton in conjunction with the Rotary Club have developed the KVR right-of-way as a multi-use walking/biking trail from Vancouver Avenue through to Main Street.

A memorial was erected in Penticton's Gyro Park in 1959 to honour Andrew McCulloch. Gyro Park can be found by following Vancouver Avenue west, over Penticton Creek to Lakeshore Drive. Gyro Park is located on the corner of Main Street and Lakeshore Drive.

212.4 Townley Street ↑

212.6 Westminster Avenue ↑

212.8 Nanaimo Avenue ↑

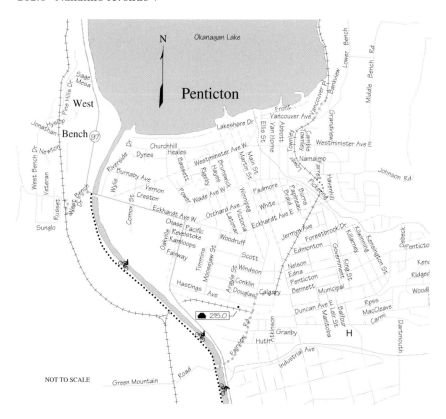

213.3 Pickering Street

Just before Pickering Street the pathway departs the original rail bed to detour around a large apartment complex built on the rail bed. The pathway reconnects with the original rail bed across Pickering St. at the old railway bridge.

213.4 Penticton Creek—Government Street)(15

This railway deck plate girder span has been converted to a pedestrian bridge over Penticton Creek.

213.5 Eckhardt Avenue East

213.7 Gahan Avenue—Penticton Secondary School sports grounds

After crossing Gahan Avenue the pathway zig-zags across the sports field, whereas the rail bed had cut diagonally across the field.

213.9 Jermyn Avenue

214.1 Edmonton Avenue—Main Street

The VV&E was more than just a paper railway before it fell into the hands of J. J. Hill. In 1898, with the dream of being the coast-to-Kootenay railway, a grade was constructed from the government wharf on Okanagan Lake, south toward Skaha Lake and down the Okanagan Valley toward Midway. In less than a year the dream would fizzle with no more than a partially completed rail bed between the two lakes. Today, the rail bed lies under Front Street and generally follows parallel and just west of Main Street toward Skaha Lake.

North on main is downtown Penticton where the majority of bike shops are found. Also two blocks north is the Penticton Museum. Penticton Museum (785 Main Street, 250-490-2451).

An interesting side trip is to the Kettle Valley Station Restaurant and Pub, which has many KVR artifacts in its decor. This restaurant can be found adjacent to the Ramada Courtyard Inn at 1050 Eckhardt Avenue West, which intersects Main Street just north of the museum.

Cartier Wines (2210 Main Street, 250-492-0621)

214.4 Calgary Avenue

Past Calgary Avenue the trail may be difficult to find. Turn west (right) on Calgary Ave. to Fairview Rd., then south on Fairview. Two blocks down Fairview is Hastings Ave. The Penticton Station can be seen east on Hastings. If continuing on to the Osoyoos or Princeton Subdivisions continue to follow Fairview Ave. across Highway #97 (Channel Parkway) and the Okanagan River Channel. Just after the channel bridge is the Jaycees bike path. North 800 metres, the path connects with the Princeton Subdivision. South, the path parallels the Osoyoos Subdivision. This detour is due to the Okanagan River Channel Bridge at km 0.7 being removed by CPR in 1996.

Arrival of the first passenger train from Merritt at Penticton Station, May 31, 1915. (Penticton Museum)

214.8 Fairview Road

215.0 Penticton Station 341

Penticton was the selected location for the KVR headquarters where a station, roundhouse and shop facilities were located. Many "helper" engines also resided here to assist trains up the 2.2% grade out of the Okanagan Valley. The original Penticton Station was located on Okanagan Lake, reached by a short spur from the main railway yard. This site was conveniently situated between the KVR trains and the CPR lake boats. The station site was changed in 1941 after passenger service on Okanagan Lake was discontinued, and a new station was then built at the railway yard.

The Penticton Station of 1941 can still be found on Hastings Avenue. It is now called the Kinsmen Station, housing the Kinsmen Club of Penticton, the Kanettes and the Jaycees.

OSOYOOS SUBDIVISION
Penticton to Osoyoos, 58.1 kilometres

The section of the Kettle Valley Railway from Penticton to Osoyoos became known as the Osoyoos Subdivision. This subdivision encompasses 58 kilometres through the best of the Okanagan, including orchards and vineyards, sandy beaches and warm lakes, the bird and wildlife sanctuary of Vaseux Lake, and south of Oliver, Canada's only true desert. Much of this area is fairly well inhabited, and the railbed at times can be difficult to follow. Successful efforts are being made to preserve the right-of-way through this area, but for now a fair bit of detouring off the railway is required. This unfortunately necessitates you to leave the relatively flat grade of the railbed to tackle the heavier grades of the highway. However, this detouring is not a totally disappointing feature as you do not find too many fruit stands on the KVR!

You start your journey by leaving the Penticton Station and immediately detour on the road to connect with the Jaycees Bike path. The KVR grade past the bike path to km 7.1 lies within the boundaries of the Penticton Indian Reserve. A detour is easily found by following the bike path to Skaha Lake, then taking the highway along the west side of the lake. The highway entails a wicked climb, especially in the Okanagan's summer heat, but you can then coast into Okanagan Falls for a dip in Skaha Lake, enjoy an ice cream at one of the many shops, or stay for a day or two in the town.

The railbed may be explored past Okanagan Falls, and along the west side of Vaseux Lake, but your exploration ends short because of a missing trestle. To continue your journey to Osoyoos, you return to Okanagan Falls and follow Oliver Ranch Road. This road takes you up into some beautiful orchards and vineyards. The Oliver Ranch Road then reconnects to the highway at the northeast end of Vaseux Lake. This lake, being a bird and wildlife sanctuary, offers great opportunity for sightings. You may also spot a herd of California bighorn sheep that are frequently seen in the cliffs to the east of this lake.

After following the highway for a short distance, you connect to a cycling trail. The International Bicycling and Hiking Society of Oliver have developed a 17.4 kilometre-long hiking and cycling trail from Highway #93 to Osoyoos Lake. Passing through Oliver, you find the original Oliver Railway Station, which has been converted into the tourist information centre. The full length of this trail is not actually atop the KVR grade, but along the Okanagan River. It ends abruptly at the north end of Osoyoos Lake where you then reaccess the highway and follow it into Osoyoos.

Except for the highway, the grade along this route is relatively flat. The biggest challenge is cycling in the heat of the desert sun. The heat alone can sap your energy just as any challenging uphill climb can. As you look around, you notice the unirrigated land is dry and parched, and don't be surprised if you see a turtle or rattlesnake cross your path! But then the advantage to this desert climate is seen where the irrigation starts. From

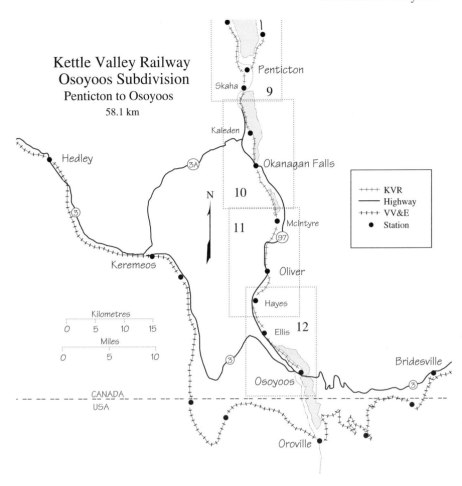

Kettle Valley Railway
Osoyoos Subdivision
Penticton to Osoyoos
58.1 km

Penticton

Skaha

9

Kaleden

Hedley

3A

Okanagan Falls

N

10

McIntyre

11

97

Keremeos

Oliver

Hayes

Ellis

12

Bridesville

Osoyoos

CANADA
USA

Oroville

KVR
Highway
VV&E
● Station

Kilometres
0   5   10   15

Miles
0   5   10

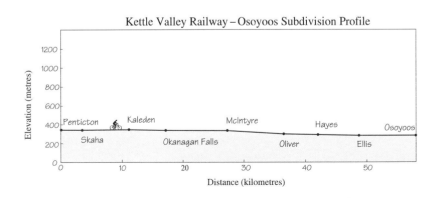

Kettle Valley Railway – Osoyoos Subdivision Profile

Elevation (metres)

1200
1000
800
600
400
200
0

Penticton   Kaleden   McIntyre   Hayes   Osoyoos
Skaha   Okanagan Falls   Oliver   Ellis

0   10   20   30   40   50

Distance (kilometres)

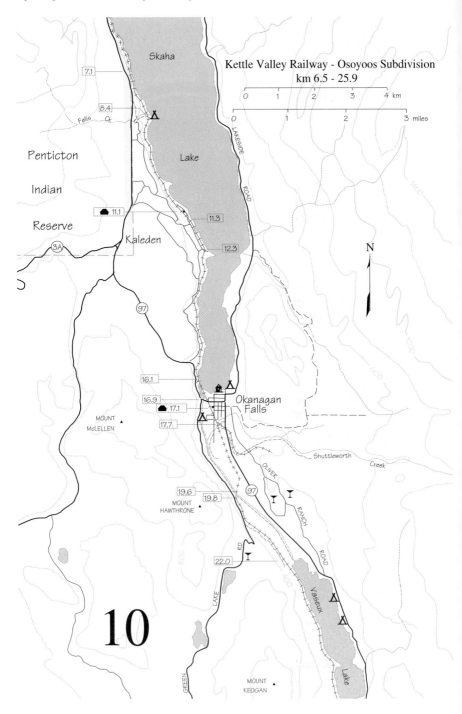

Kettle Valley Railway - Osoyoos Subdivision
km 6.5 - 25.9

the roadside, you can see an abundance of fruit growing in the orchards. An interesting detour is to visit one of the many vineyards for some wine tasting. The vineyards of this area are known to produce award-winning wines. You also won't want to pass up the chance to stop for some cherry cider at one of the numerous fruit stands that are found throughout this valley, or stop and pick some fruit at a U-pick orchard.

Even though the majority of travel along this route is not on the rail bed it still can be worth exploring. The 58 kilometres from Penticton to Osoyoos can be easily cycled in one day, though you may want to take your time to enjoy all this valley has to offer, as many camping and lodging accommodations can be found all along this route. The warm and welcoming people of this valley, not to mention the opportunity of travelling through the beautiful orchards and vineyards, stopping at a fruit stand or winery, experiencing the desert land of sand and scrub, then completing the venture at Osoyoos Lake, give reason enough to cruise the distance. In fact, you may never want to leave ▄▄

km	**Penticton Station**
0.0	

Penticton was a junction point for the Osoyoos Subdivision. The trains connected to either the Carmi or Princeton subdivisions, or to the Okanagan Lake boats. The construction of this subdivision began with a line from the Penticton Station to a station at Skaha Lake. The section from Penticton Station to Skaha Station was completed in 1920, with the line from Okanagan Falls to Hayes being completed in 1923. The KVR right-of-way is easily followed west from Penticton Station.

The Osoyoos Subdivision mileposts start at km 0.9 along the Princeton Subdivision where the Osoyoos Subdivision connects with it.

0.7   Channel Parkway)(/ Okanagan River Channel ⅋27

Two railway bridges, one right after the other, cross the Channel Parkway and the Okanagan River Channel. The Okanagan River Channel bridge was removed by CPR in June of 1996. A detour is required to get around the missing bridge. Take Fairview Road south across Channel Parkway and the Okanagan River Channel. After crossing the bridge turn south (right) on the Jaycees bike path.

0.8   "Jaycees" bicycle path

The bike path is the western boundary of the Penticton Indian Reserve. Permission is required to cross the reserve and may be gained by calling the band office. It extends south along the channel's length to Skaha Lake. You must detour from the railway to this bike path, as the railbed to the south becomes impassable with six foot-high barbed wire fences within the boundary of the Penticton Indian Reserve. During the building of the KVR the land between km 0.0 and km 7.1 was expropriated from the Penticton Indian Band. The use of this land was granted for as long as railway service was in operation. Now that the line has been abandoned, this land has been reclaimed by its original owners.

Vineyards and Orchards

The Okanagan Valley is blessed with ideal conditions for growing wine grapes, which has led to a wine making history that is decades old. The local wineries have developed a reputation for producing top quality wine, meeting world-class standards. Tours and tastings are offered daily at most wineries we have listed (phone ahead for confirmation).

South Okanagan Valley: Blossom and ripening times

Apricots: April 15 - 30 / June 18 - July 15

Cherries: April 18 - May 10 / July 8 - August 18

Peaches: April 20 - May 10 / July 25 - September 15

Pears: April 28 - May 10 / August 10 and on

Apples: May 1 - May 20 / July 31 and on

Grapes: June 15 - 25 / August 15 and on

0.9/0.0 Princeton-Osoyoos Subdivision junction

0.4   Shingle Creek ⋊₄₅

0.7   Green Mountain Road ⵏ

1.3   South Yard ⌡

The South Yard was a busy station in its prime. Trains loaded with fruit would travel up the Osoyoos line to Penticton. These reefers stopped at the ice house in the South Yard to be iced that afternoon. They then continued their journey by rail, or were loaded onto the Okanagan Lake barge. It was boasted that with this type of transportation fruit could be on market counters within 48 hours.

The South Yard site lies within the boundaries of the Penticton Indian Reserve, and is inaccessible without trespassing. Building foundations, railway platforms and scattered lumber remain at this site.

3.4   Skaha Station   ⌐340 ⬛ ⌡ ⬥

Between 1920 and 1931 trains were shuttled the 12 kilometres down Skaha Lake by barge from Skaha Station to Okanagan Falls. When the railway along the lake was completed in 1931, the tug and barge service ended. Today there is little evidence of the existence of the station.

3.6   Highway #97 ⵏ ⌐⇐¦

The railbed south of this point is still within the Penticton Indian Reserve. Access to the rail bed through the Penticton Indian Reserve has been off and on through the years. The lock gate across Highway #97 can be found open and the band has welcomed it use. Access has been gained in the past years a few hundred metres up Highway #97 where a trail runs down the hillside to the rail bed. Check with the band as to the policy at the time you wish to go. If you need to detour there are two options. One is to follow Highway #97 on the west side of Skaha Lake and attempt to reaccess the railbed at km 8.4 or km 12.3. Due private land issues check with the landowners as to accessibility and head postings. The second is to turn east on Highway #97 to connect to South Beach Drive, which then connects you with South Main Street. South Main Street becomes Lakeside Road and follows the east shore of Skaha Lake to Okanagan Falls, a detour of 15.2 kilometres. Both routes entail a steep climb and the hazard of motorized traffic. Highway #97 is particularly busy with car and truck traffic, but the shoulders are adequate for safe travel. Lakeside Road does not have wide shoulders, but it also does not have the traffic volume or speed found on Highway #97, which may provide for a more relaxed ride.

7.1   Penticton Indian Reserve boundary

The rail bed south of the reserve boundary has been fairly well travelled. South to Okanagan Falls the rail bed is the property of CPR with sections being sold off to private interests. Please respect and heed all notices. Access may be restricted at any time.

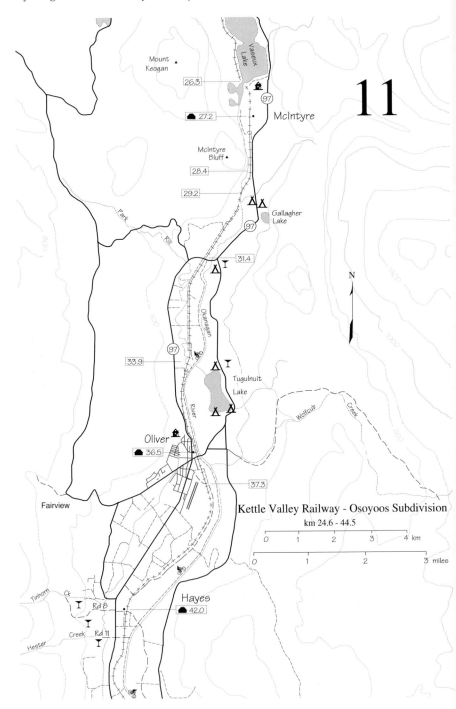

11

Mount Keogan ▲

26.3

McIntyre

27.2

McIntyre Bluff ▲

28.4

29.2

Gallagher Lake

31.4

Okanagan

33.9

Tugulnuit Lake

Wolfcub Creek

Oliver

36.5

37.3

Fairview

Kettle Valley Railway - Osoyoos Subdivision
km 24.6 - 44.5

0 1 2 3 4 km

0 1 2 3 miles

Tinhorn Ck

Rd 8

Hayes

42.0

Creek Rd 11

Hester

8.4   Banbury Green RV Park (tenting welcome)   ⵣ **⚠** ⮜

Access this park by taking Pineview Drive from Highway #97. The KVR grade runs through the middle of this privately run RV Park. Access to the rail bed may be restricted by the owners/operators of the park. The rail bed south to km 16.1 is easily cycled, except for a few sandy spots, allowing you to really cruise on this level grade. The scenery is also impressive as you skirt along the shore of Skaha Lake.

11.1   Kaleden Station   ⌐344 🚐 ⵣ 🏕 � 🍎 🚲

The distance between Penticton and Okanagan Falls was originally linked by barge service. This involved loading the train on and off the Skaha Lake barge, with delayed service in the winter if the lake froze over. In 1931, the CPR upgraded this subdivision with a connecting line along the west shore of Skaha Lake. This was the last work to be done on the Kettle Valley Railway by Andrew McCulloch, as he formally retired January 31, 1933, after 23 years of service.

Kaleden Station was named after the community of Kaleden, which adopted this name in 1909. It was formed from a combination of "Kalos," the Greek word meaning beautiful, and the biblical orchard Eden. The first fruit trees were planted in 1910 and some began bearing fruit in 1913 (apricots). By 1914 apples were being shipped to market.

11.3   First Street—Kaleden ⵣ ⵏ

Pieces of the railbed after this point have been sold to private hands and continuing down the rail bed may not be possible. Paralleling the rail bed is Ponderosa Avenue which can be followed to Ponderosa Resort where it may be possible to reaccess the rail bed.

12.3   Ponderosa Point Road ⵣ 🏢 ⮜

Ponderosa Resort.

16.1   Okanagan River)(169

This long pile trestle across the outfall of Skaha Lake has been decked and hand rails installed.

16.9   Highway #93 ⵣ

The railbed is marginally passable from here to the missing trestle at Shuttleworth Creek at km 17.7.

17.1   Okanagan Falls Station ⌐337 🚐 ⵣ ⚠ 🏢 🏕 ⵏ 🍎 (🚲

It is here at Okanagan Falls that the Okanagan Indians maintained a year-round village. The rapids and falls of the Okanagan River provided one of the best salmon fishing grounds. The Indians lined the banks to spear fish as they passed by en route to their spawning grounds.

The present dam has disrupted the original series of falls and rapids, which gave Okanagan Falls its name. However, the Okanagan River still offers good fishing, with trout and whitefish throughout the year and large and small mouth bass during the summer.

The section along Skaha Lake is particularly scenic.

The station in Oliver has been beautifully restored and is now an information centre.

Although sections of the railbed south of Okanagan Falls can be explored, you must backtrack to Okanagan Falls because of missing bridges. A detour is therefore required at this point. To detour, take Highway #97 through Okanagan Falls to Maple Street and turn south. This street then becomes Oliver Ranch Road. There is a bit of a climb involved, but the great scenery of orchards and vineyards will make up for the extra effort. The Oliver Ranch Road reconnects you to Highway #97 at the north end of Vaseux Lake.

If you wish to further explore the railbed on the west side of Vaseux Lake, head south on Green Lake Road on the west end of Okanagan Falls. Just past Okanagan Falls Provincial Park is a small road that gives access to another road running along the west side of the Okanagan River, intersecting with the KVR at km 19.8. Watch for the raspberries that grow wild along this stretch.

Ⲧ LeComte Estate Winery (Green Lake Road, 250-497-8267)
Ⲧ Wild Goose Vineyard (Sun Valley Way,
off Oliver Ranch Road, 250-497-8919)
Ⲧ Blue Mountain Vineyards and Cellars
(Oliver Ranch Road, 250-497-8244)

17.2   Northwood Mill spur Ⲭ

This 2.6 kilometre spur climbs the east hillside at a steep 4% grade to the Northwood lumber mill. The grade runs alongside the road to the mill and is passable though weedy.

17.7   Shuttleworth Creek Ⲭ18

19.6   Okanagan River Ⲭ55

19.8   Vaseux-Bighorn National Wildlife Area

Vaseux Lake was named using the French word "vaseux," meaning muddy or miry. Vaseux Lake Provincial Park encompasses the Vaseux-Bighorn National Wildlife Area, a sanctuary for birds and wildlife. Some birds that can be seen include trumpeter swans and Canada geese that nest there yearly. California bighorn sheep can also be seen on the cliffs across Highway #97 to the east of Vaseux Lake. Sheep crossing signs are posted on the highway to try to avoid mishap.

The intersection of the road along the Okanagan River Channel and the railbed is the northern border of the Vaseux-Bighorn National Wildlife Area. The railway from here is quite weedy around a small rock slide area making travel difficult. One option is to continue to follow the road along the top of the canal to the north end of the lake, then cut across a small flood control dam to the railway. This detour can be difficult. The weeds are about six feet tall at the dam, and there are breaks in the dam that are bridged by three inch-wide beams. It makes for quite a balancing act to get your bike and yourself across without getting wet. But don't worry, the fall is only about two feet. The other

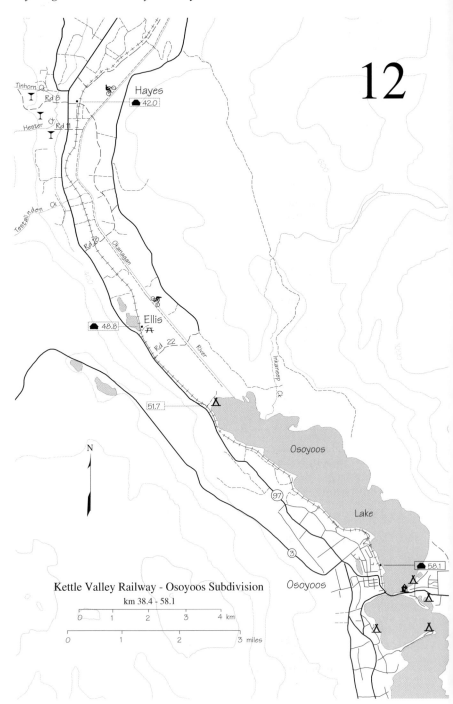

12

Hayes
▲ 42.0

Tinhorn Ck.
Rd 8
Hester Ck.
Rd 11

Testalinden Ck.

Rd 18
Okanagan
Ałc.

Ellis
▲ 48.8
Rd 22
River

51.7
Inkaneep Ck.

Osoyoos

N

97

Lake

3

Osoyoos

▲ 58.1

Kettle Valley Railway - Osoyoos Subdivision
km 38.4 - 58.1

0   1   2   3   4 km

0   1   2   3 miles

option is to reaccess Green Lake Road on your west, head south on Green Lake Road and turn on to the first major road on the left. The end of this road crosses the railbed just prior to some private property at the north end of Vaseux Lake.

22.0   Access road ⵏ

The railbed along the west shore of Vaseux Lake is a well-travelled one-lane road, although sandy in some spots. You can follow the railbed until the missing bridge at km 26.3. This area of the Okanagan is a land of cactus and rattlesnakes. The landscape is very dry and sandy, and scattered with clumps of cacti and patches of sun-bleached grass.

26.3   Vaseux Lake ⵜ*115*

A small road branches off to the right at the terminus of the railbed, but it quickly dwindles out after one kilometre.

27.2   McIntyre Station |*333* 🚂

McIntyre Station was named after Peter McIntyre, one of the "Overlanders" of 1862 who settled at the base of McIntyre Bluff in 1886. McIntyre Bluff is the location of the great ice dam that formed after the last glacier, causing Lake Penticton to back up all the way to Sicamous. Evidence of its great depth can still be seen in the horizontal benches of former beaches all along the Okanagan hillsides. As the ice dam slowly melted, the lake dropped in stages, creating level after level of remnant beach. This scenic bluff is steeped in Indian legends about buffalo and rival Indian bands being driven over its edge. Indian pictographs can be found inscribed on rocks at the base of the cliff.

The McIntyre Station site can be found by taking a short back road from Highway #97. However, no evidence of this station is found. The right-of-way is weedy, rough and barely passable to km 29.2.

ⵏ Brights Wines (North Highway #97, 250-498-4981)
ⵏ Inkameep Vineyards (Tuculnuit Road, 250-498-3552)

28.4   Irrigation canal ⵜ55

29.2   Okanagan River ⵜ*66*

31.4   Highway #97 ⵏ

You can access the bicycling/hiking trail or the KVR railbed just past the McAlpine Bridge on Highway #97, which crosses the Okanagan River. As part of an envisioned International Hike and Bike Corridor from Brewster, Washington to Vernon, B.C., the International Bicycling and Hiking Society has already developed 17.4 kilometres from McAlpine Bridge to the north shore of Osoyoos Lake.

The trail has not utilized the true KVR right-of-way, but is located slightly to the east of the railbed. Because the railbed had been mostly claimed by bordering landowners, the corridor of the Old River Road

The International Bicycling and Hiking Society has established an excellent trail that follows beside the Okanagan River Channel, km 48.8.

Osoyoos Station, km 58.1, has been restored and now houses the Osoyoos Lake Sailing Club.

was used. This narrow road has been turned into a multi-use trail that follows along the Okanagan River Channel.

33.9   Park Rill ⅄36

36.5   Oliver Station ℹ297 🚌 ⵏ ⵔ 🏛 ⅏ 🚻 🔌 🚮🛁 (🚴0.1

The original KVR Station at Oliver has been restored and designated an historic site. The building now houses the Oliver Tourist Infocentre and the International Bicycling and Hiking Society.

The true railbed around Oliver is at times difficult to follow. The KVR right-of-way at Oliver Station is actually to the west side of the station/infocentre in the middle of the parking lot. If you wish to explore the railbed, follow 93 Street across 348 Avenue from the parking lot. It then disguises itself as an alley. As you cross 346 Avenue the right-of-way follows along the west side of 91 Street. The remaining KVR to Osoyoos is barely passable at best. Where the railbed is used as an access road to fields, it can be in good riding condition. However, many sections have been fenced and have seen little traffic resulting in an overgrowth of tall weeds, bushes and trees. To continue your journey to Osoyoos, follow atop the bicycling and hiking trail.

Oliver Museum (#9728-356 Avenue, 250-498-4027)

41.1   Tinhorn Creek ⅄26

41.7   Wye ⅄

42.0   Hayes Station ℹ289 🚌 ⅏ 🚴0.1

The purpose of this branch line was for the transportation of fruit. No formal passenger service ever operated on the Osoyoos Subdivision, although passengers were permitted to ride in the freight train caboose. The stations instead served the freight from the fruit packing houses and a small number of sawmills along the route. At Hayes Station you can still find the remains of an old fruit packing plant. This can be reached from the bike path by heading west on No. 8 Road.

🍷 **Gehringer Brothers (No. 8 Road, detour 2.1 km, 498-3537)**
🍷 **Divino Estate Winery (No. 8 Road, detour 2.1 km, 498-2784)**
🍷 **Okanagan Vineyards (No. 11 Road, detour 1.8 km, 498-6663)**

43.3   Fruit warehouse spur ⅄

48.8   Ellis Station ℹ281 🚌 ⅏ ⵔ ⅏ 🚲

Ellis Station was situated at the south end of Deadman Lake. As with the other small stations in this subdivision, there is not much evidence of its existence. What can be found at this site is the Oliver Kiwanis

Desert Oasis Picnic Park. To reach this park, take No. 22 Road up to the highway, then turn north back to No. 21 Road.

Number 22 Road crosses the Okanagan River Channel and intersects the bike trail. At this intersection, there is a small parking area and a covered information pavilion. The bike trail continues past this point for only a short distance, then ends abruptly at the north end of Osoyoos Lake. You cannot access the highway or railbed from this point but must return to No. 22 Road. Following up No. 22 Road you can see the railbed just prior to Highway #97. You can follow the highway into Osoyoos. The railbed from No. 22 Road to Willow Beach Trailer Park was passable except for a couple of gates, though changes in owner ship may restrict access.

51.7 Willow Beach Trailer Park

Just past the trailer park the railbed is disrupted, overgrown and marginally passable. Although the majority of the right-of-way was in good shape, from here to Osoyoos Station it has been subdivided and parcels have been sold to home builders and adjacent landowners. It's disheartening to be cycling lazily along this beautiful orchard-lined path and run into a new house blocking further progress. As the KVR is divided up from the trailer park to Osoyoos, take the trailer park access road to Highway #97, then follow the highway into Osoyoos.

55.1 Fruit warehouse spur

57.3 Osoyoos wye

58.1 Osoyoos Station *i281*

There is little evidence of the KVR railway in Osoyoos, the terminal point of this line. The Osoyoos Station can still be found beside Lions Centennial Park. It has been restored and now houses the Osoyoos Lake Sailing Club.

With the exception of a few industrial spurs, the completion of the Osoyoos Subdivision from Hayes to Osoyoos in 1944 was the last piece of trackage built on the Kettle Valley Railway. When the line from Hayes farther south into orchard country was extended, an increase in the amount of fruit being transported on the KVR resulted.

Even today, fruit is part of the very existence of this valley. The city of Osoyoos boasts of having the earliest fruit season in the valley, with crops of cherries, plums, pears, apples and all kinds of vegetables. You can even find a banana farm!

Osoyoos Museum (Lions Centennial Park)

58.6 End of track.

Returning to Midway on Highway #3

The 69 kilometre return trip to Midway from Osoyoos requires a 955 metre climb up and over Anarchist Mountain. The majority of this climb is right out of Osoyoos as Highway #3 switchbacks up the hillside. Grades average 6% continuously for over 14 kilometres. If attempting this route start your trip very early in the morning to take advantage of the cooler temperatures and shade of the mountain, and take plenty of water with you. Allow up to 4 hours to make the summit Also note that the Highway is narrow in spots as it makes it's climb up the mountain with limited shoulders and sometimes heavy truck traffic. That said, the reward is the spectacular views up and down the Okanagan Valley and the view of the Cascades off to the west.

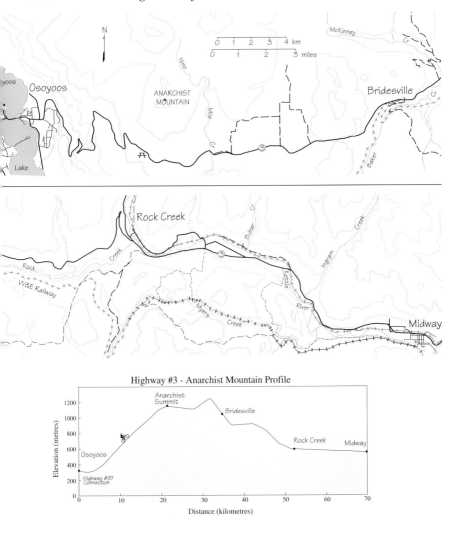

Burt Sharkey's Horse Motel, Spearing Station, km 168.5, Princeton Subdivision.

PRINCETON SUBDIVISION
Penticton to Brookmere, 174.9 kilometres

The section of the Kettle Valley Railway between Penticton and Brookmere was known as the Princeton Subdivision. This subdivision offers 174.9 kilometres of recreational riding into some unspoiled backcountry that has changed little since the turn of the century. The railbed is well travelled, enabling you to really push your endurance to go the distance. Along this route, as you cycle into the past, you experience the peaceful and scenic surroundings of this country. It is a truly a fascinating place to explore.

Leaving Penticton to begin your venture, you must pedal your fat tires up and out of the Okanagan Valley. The railbed is in great condition, and don't worry too much about the uphill grade. Remember, you are still on a railway. Views from this upper bench are impressive. You can stop to rest as you look down into the valley toward Okanagan Lake and the surrounding communities. Once back on your bike, you have to stop short of the Trout Creek bridge, 73 metres high and 76 metres long. It was constructed by McCulloch to cross this deep canyon to reach Summerland. Don't be surprised if your adrenalin surges as you glance down between the open ties to the gaping chasm below your feet. It is the highest bridge on the KVR.

Past the bridge, the railbed is in good condition—for a train. The tracks are still in place for the next 16 kilometres, where the Kettle Valley Steam Railway makes regular trips along Prairie Valley. There is no side path for cyclists, so you have to cycle the detour road or take the train. You can reaccess the gravel railbed at Faulder. From there, cruise the gentle but steady uphill grade along the steep-walled Trout Creek Valley.

The summit of the Princeton Subdivision is reached at Osprey Lake, a nice place to camp for the night or stay at one of the B&Bs. For the next 30 kilometres, you wind your way out of the Hayes Creek Valley. However, even with the downhill grade of the railbed, the valley bottom falls at a steeper grade leaving you high on the side of the bordering hills. This offers some impressive views of the lakes and ranchland below.

As you reach Jura, you share a short length of the trail with some local cows. For this reason, be sure to watch for any hazards that may have dropped on the trail—if you know what I mean. You descend by cruising along the loops of the KVR across the open rangeland on the hills above Princeton. Upon reaching the Princeton Station site, you will have put 113.4 kilometres between you and Penticton. The city of Princeton offers most services, and makes a nice break in the journey, be it for lunch or the night. You can also spend the day exploring the Copper Mountain Subdivision of the KVR. This branch line runs from Princeton to the Copper Mountain Mine.

Continuing on the Princeton Subdivision, the railbed is still well-travelled and easily cycled. As you pedal up the gentle grade, you find yourself in the steep-walled Tulameen River Valley. The trail follows along the winding corridor carved by the clear waters of the Tulameen River, an

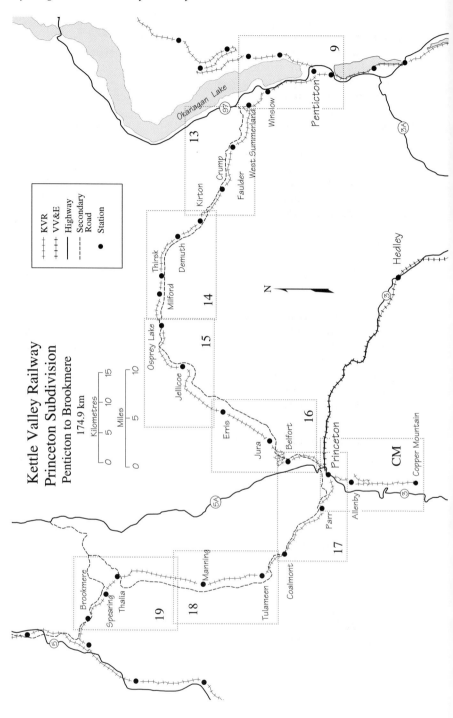

Kettle Valley Railway
Princeton Subdivision
Penticton to Brookmere
174.9 km

interesting river that at one point can be racing and roaring over huge boulders and then at the next be quietly lapping a sandy beach. Wildlife abound in this area, and it is not uncommon to see a group of deer or even a black bear picnicking in the berry patches.

Twenty kilometres up the trail from Princeton you come across the near ghost town of Coalmont and the site of Granite City. Don't be in too much of a hurry. You'll want to stop and explore the area and visit the historic Coalmont Hotel. This hotel was built in 1912, and has recently been restored. Coalmont can be an overnight stop or just a refuelling break in either the hotel dining room or pub.

Once back on the railbed, continue to pedal the easy grade along the river valley, winding your way through the green forests. Only six kilometres from Coalmont, You come to the town Tulameen, and the entrance to Otter Lake Provincial Park, which offers great camping facilities. Past Tulameen you follow Otter Creek to the town of Brookmere. This small town sits quietly in the pines, 35 kilometres down the railbed from Otter Lake. Coyle Creek Lodge is the only service in Brookmere, with just a few remaining local residents and some KVR artifacts, such as the water tower and a wooden caboose, reminding you that this town was once a bustling railway centre.

You can hardly deny the feeling you get when cycling this section. With its remote stretches of backcountry leading you deep into the wilderness, there are times where you, your bike and the trail seem to merge into one, and all that surrounds you is peace and solitude. Even when encountering more populated areas, the laid-back pace and local lifestyle of this region make you feel right at home on your three-to-four day cycle of the Princeton Subdivision of the Kettle Valley Railway ⬛

km	**Penticton Station** ⫶341 ⬛ 🏠 ⫙ 丫 🛆 🏛 ⼌ (🛅 🚲1.1
0.0	From Penticton Station to West Summerland Station the grade of the railway varies more than any other section. Although the average is a comfortable 1.1% uphill grade, it does vary from 0.0% to 2.2%.

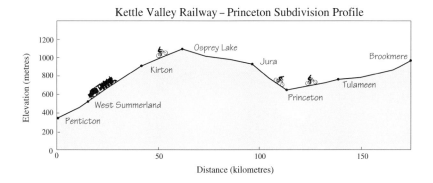

105

From the upper bench, km 6.0, some scenic views of the Okanagan Valley await you.

The Kettle Valley Steam Railway may soon be running across the tracks of the famous Trout Creek bridge to re-create an incredible piece of history, km 11.7.

0.7 Channel Parkway)(/ Okanagan River Channel ⨉27 ⊢→

Two railway bridges, one right after the other, cross the Channel Parkway and the Okanagan River Channel. The Okanagan River Channel bridge was removed by CPR in June of 1996. A detour is required to get around the missing bridge. Take Fairview Road south across Channel Parkway and the Okanagan River Channel. After crossing the bridge turn north (right) on the Jaycees bike path. Eight hundred metres down the path turn west (left) on to the KVR at km 0.8.

0.8 "Jaycees" bicycle path ⊢⇐⦙

The bike path is the western boundary of the Penticton Indian Reserve. Permission is required to cross the reserve and may be gained by calling the band office. To bypass the Reserve take the bicycle path to Highway #97, north on #97 to West Bench Drive. Follow West Bench Drive up the hill and just before the road crosses the KVR on a bridge (km 2.9), access to the rail grade can be gained.

0.9 Osoyoos Subdivision junction Y

The railway splits, the south line heading for Skaha Station on the Osoyoos Subdivision, and the northwest line heading for West Summerland Station on the Princeton Subdivision.

2.4 Entering West Bench—leaving Penticton Indian Reserve

Alternating between deep cuts and large fills over coulees, the KVR climbs steadily to mount the bench. As the bench is attained, the KVR bisects the community of West Bench, passing through orchards and behind private residences.

2.9 Right-of-way passes under West Bench Drive ⊢⇐⦙

If you bypassed the Penticton Indian Reserve you can gain access to the railbed just before the bridge.

4.0 Right-of-way passes under Newton Drive

4.6 Right-of-way passes under Hyslop Drive

5.1 Pine Hills Golf and Country Club Road ⥮

As you leave West Bench, the railway hugs the hillside as it climbs up along Sage Mesa. The views down the Okanagan Valley are spectacular, with views of Okanagan Lake and Penticton to the south and Naramata to the north. The views improve as the railway continues its uphill climb on an excellent hard-packed lane toward West Summerland.

9.2 The KVR hangs high on a rock face overlooking the Okanagan Valley

9.8 Small access road from West Bench and Research Centre ⥮

The Pacific Agri-Food Research Centre is fenced and locked with no access.

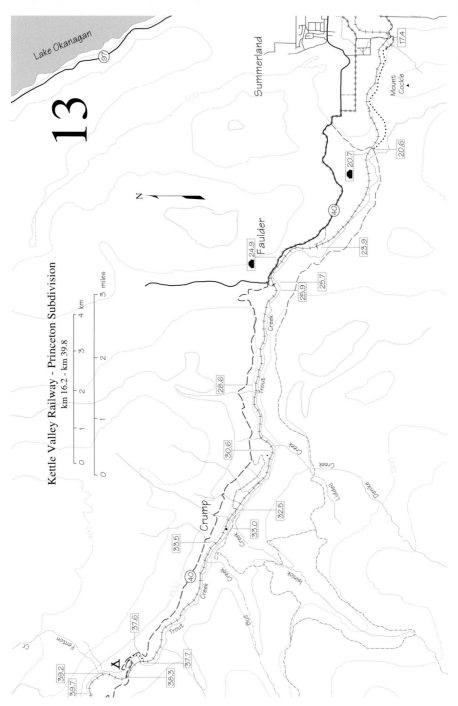

Kettle Valley Railway - Princeton Subdivision
km 16.2 - km 39.8

Lake Okanagan

Summerland

Faulder

Crump

Mount Cockle

10.5 Beginning of Winslow siding ⌐

Winslow siding is located on a wide upper bench. This is the planned terminus of the Kettle Valley Steam Railway. Plans include a railway station with access to the Agricultural Research Station.

11.1 End of Winslow siding

11.3 Winslow Station ⌐460 🚃 ┃ ⚷1.6

Winslow Station was named after R. M. Winslow of the provincial department of Agriculture who was primarily responsible for the development of the Dominion Experimental Farm. It was established in 1914 to assist the development of the agricultural industry in the unique environmental conditions of the Okanagan Valley. The name was later changed to the Summerland Agricultural Research Station and then to Pacific Agri-Food Research Centre, and borders the KVR at Winslow Station. The research centre has become an international tourist attraction providing tours of the botanical gardens. Although there is a gated road coming out of the research station here, there is no access to the botanical gardens or research centre. The only access to the centre is from Highway #97.

11.7 Trout Creek)(76x73

Trout Creek was a major obstacle for the KVR as the creek had cut a deep canyon in its plunge to Okanagan Lake. For this reason, bypassing Summerland was a cheaper and shorter route. However, at the insistence of the residents of Summerland who wanted to have the KVR run to their community, McCulloch engineered a 73 metre-high and 76 metre-long deck truss bridge to cross the canyon. The wooden approach trestles were replaced by steel structures and later by fills in 1928. It is the highest of its type in North America.

The tracks are in place from the south end of Trout Creek bridge to Faulder Station.

12.3 Canyon View Road - Canyon View Station 🚃 🚂 ⚐ ┃ ⇥

With the tracks still in place and an active steam railway operating on them, the best option is to detour from here and reaccess the railbed at Faulder, km 24.9. An even better idea is to take the train from Canyon View Station to Faulder before reaccessing the railway. The train makes regular runs between Canyon View Station and Prairie Station (km 20.7) and Faulder Station. Check with the Kettle Valley Steam Railway ((250) 494-8922 www.kettlevalleyrail.org) for scheduled service. Reservations are suggested to insure space for you and your bike.

To detour, take Canyon Road north (right) to Hillborn St. Turn west (left) on to Hillborn St., then north (right) on to Lewes Ave. and east (left) on to Victoria Road South. This route takes you for the most part alongside the KVR. Just before Victoria Road South intersects with Simpson Road is the former site of West Summerland Station. Continuing down Victoria Road South will take you to the town centre of Summerland.

All aboard—the Kettle Valley Steam Railway, West Summerland Station, km 15.3.

Switching ends of the train at Prairie Valley Station for the return trip to West Summerland, km 20.7.

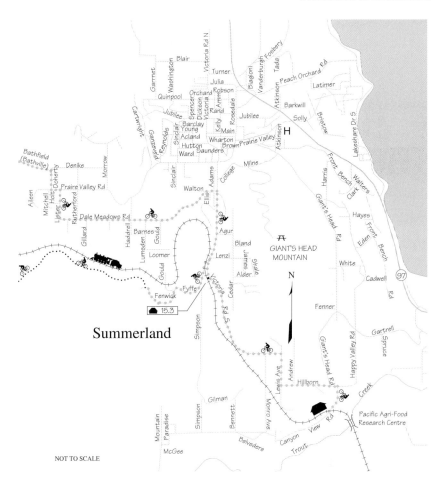

Summerland

NOT TO SCALE

Alternatively, if you are looking at accessing Summerland directly from Canyon View Road, just after you turn left on Hillborn Street turn right (north) on Giant's Head Road. Giant's Head Road will take you into downtown Summerland on a fairly level road.

Note: Canyon View Station is not one of the original stations of the KVR.

13.6   Monro Avenue †

15.3   West Summerland Station 523 ⛽ 🏛 🚂 🍴 ⛺ 🏠 ⛩ 🍴 🥤 🚴 1.5

Foundations of the original station and the octagonal water tower foundation can be found beside the tracks

From it's start in 1989, the Kettle Valley Heritage Society succeeded in keeping a small piece of KVR alive for generations to come. With a 1924 Shay logging locomotive restored by the B.C Forest Museum at

A large log like this one makes a good substitute for a bridge or trestle at Trout Creek, km 37.7.

Trout Creek Bridge, km 39.7.

Duncan, the society started passenger service from West Summerland to Faulder on September 17, 1995. With the help of many volunteers and organizations, the railway will continue to expand, eventually running from Winslow to Faulder.

Summerland Museum
9521 Wharton Street, 250-494-9395

As the railway leaves the station it starts a climb along the north side of Mount Conkle. Rows of fruit trees carpet the valley bottom as you skirt the southern perimeter of Prairie Valley. This section contains those postcard views that the Okanagan is famous for.

Two options exist in detouring around the active tourist railway;

By road, continue north up Victoria Road South. Turn west (left) on Dale Meadows Road and follow it for 2.9 kilometres. Turn north (right) on to Lister Avenue, east (left) on to Prairie Valley Road, north (right) on to Doherty Avenue and east (left) on to Bathfield (Bathville) Road. After turning east on Bathfield the road forks with the left fork heading to Prairie Valley Station and the right fork (Fish Creek Road/ Faulder Road / Princeton - Summerland Road/ Highway #40) going to Faulder. Of course, this detour requires that you climb more than the elevation difference between Faulder and West Summerland in less than three kilometres.

In 2001 a trail was constructed to bypass this active railway. To access this trail turn left (west) off Victoria Road South, just north of West Summerland Station, onto Simpson Road, right on Fyffe Road, and left on Fenwick. This will take you to the old flume line trail above the railway tracks and through the rodeo grounds to Prairie Valley Station. A trail is in the works following along the railline between Prairie Valley and Faulder and may be completed in short order. Check locally or on the web site for further updates on the status of these trails.

15.6   Lenzi Avenue ⊤

17.4   Gould Avenue)(

20.6   Bathville Road ⊤

20.7   Prairie Valley Station
This is the current home base of the Kettle Valley Steam Railway. The train can be taken to this point or picked up at this point.. From here to Faulder continue to take the train, trail (when finished) or take Bathville Road out to the Summerland-Faulder Road (Highway #40) and turn west (left) to Faulder. Distance from station to end of track at Faulder by road is 6.4 kilometres.

Note: Prairie Valley Station is not one of the original stations of the KVR.

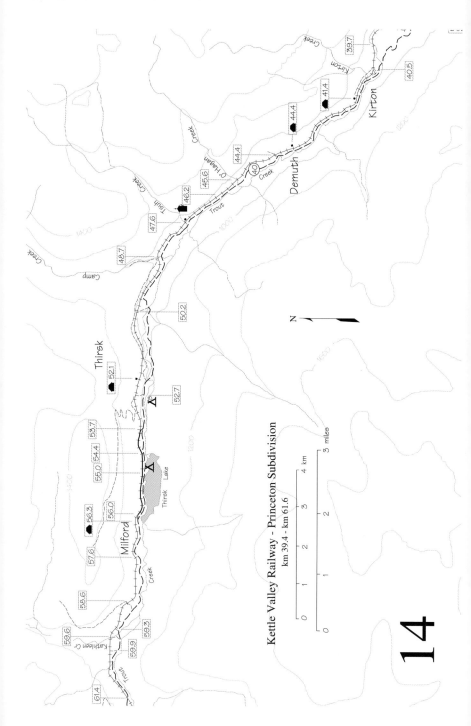

Kettle Valley Railway - Princeton Subdivision
km 39.4 - km 61.6

14

23.9   Local access road ⦆

24.9   Faulder Station ⫯670 🚂 🚃 ⫴ ⦆ 🚻 ⌀ 🚲1.5
This is the western terminus of the Kettle Valley Steam Railway.

25.7   Community of Faulder. ⦆
If approaching by roadthere is a junction of roads as you come into Faulder on Highway #40 (Princeton – Summerland Road). Take the left turn into the cluster of homes that is the community of Faulder. This short road will connect you with the KVR.

25.9   Both Faulder siding and the tracks end here ⫯⇐⫯
Reconnect with the KVR here.

28.6   Loose sandy railbed

30.6   Trout Creek Canyon narrows
The KVR squeezes between the roaring rapids of Trout Creek and the vertical canyon walls. Beware of rock slides and rocks on the trail.

32.5   Crump ⦆
Crump was a flag stop named after a KVR superintendent.

33.0   Twenty Mile Tank 🏴

33.5   Shallow creek to ford—won't get too wet

33.6   Power line

37.6   Gravel mounds and ditches- Trout Creek Bypass trail ⫯⇒⫯
Large mounds of gravel and deep ditches cut across the railbed to prevent vehicle traffic from falling into Trout Creek owing to a missing bridge. Just prior to the trail leading down to the creek is the Trout Creek Bypass trail. This 500 metre trail skirts the along the bank of the creek to connect with Highway #40. 600 metres after turning left on the highway, and after crossing the highway bridge over Trout Creek, the railway can be reaccessed as it crosses the highway. This trail starts out with a rather steep down hill that can be very difficult to negotiate when wet. It is a single lane track, that can be a little tough to push a fully loaded bike along, but may be the only alternative when the creek is running high.

37.7   Trout Creek ⫽58 ⚠B
This bridge was removed by CPR in 1995. All that remains are the two concrete towers that once held up the three deck plate girder spans. A steep trail on the north side of the railbed leads down to the creek. During low stream levels the creek can be forded. A large log across the creek makes a natural bridge for those with good balance. Located on the west side of the creek is a natural backcountry campsite. The trail is a little less obvious when coming from the other direction, but is just before the gravel mounds and ditches on the west side of the missing bridge.

Fixing a flat in the shade, km 38.9. Photo: Goetz Schildt.

Missing bridge across Kathleen Creek, km 59.6.

38.3   Highway #40 ⚊ ⚊ ⚊
The KVR enters Kirton Canyon, another narrow steep-walled canyon of Trout Creek. Trout Creek Crossing Forest Service Campground is just east down the Highway.

39.2   Cave

39.7   Trout Creek)(23
Kirton Canyon widens out.

40.4   Access road to Highway #40 ⚊

40.5   Kirton Station wye, overgrown with trees ⚊
A wye was built at Kirton, the end of the 2.2% grade from Penticton, for turning helper engines.

41.4   Kirton Station ¡910 ⚊ ⚊ 1.1
The name Kirton was derived from the first part of J. Kirkpatrick's name, the KVR's first agent at Penticton, and the last part of the name from Penticton.

44.4   Demuth ⚊
This station was formerly called Altamont, but there is very little left to mark the passing of this station.

44.9   Private access road to Highway #40 ⚊ ⚊
Demuth Forest Service Campsite is a small semi-open site just off Highway #40 on the shore of Trout Creek.

45.6   O'Hagan Creek

46.2   Viewpoint
The KVR is high on the north slope of Trout Creek Valley overlooking a pastoral green valley bottom.

47.5   Thirty Mile Tank ⚊

47.6   Tsuh Creek

48.7   Camp Creek
A very high fill carries the KVR over Camp Creek.

50.2   Access road to Highway #40 ⚊
An old siding to the north reconnects with the main line.

52.1   Thirsk Station ¡1008 ⚊ ⚊ 1.0
Named after the Thirsk community in Penticton. Thirsk is a district in England.

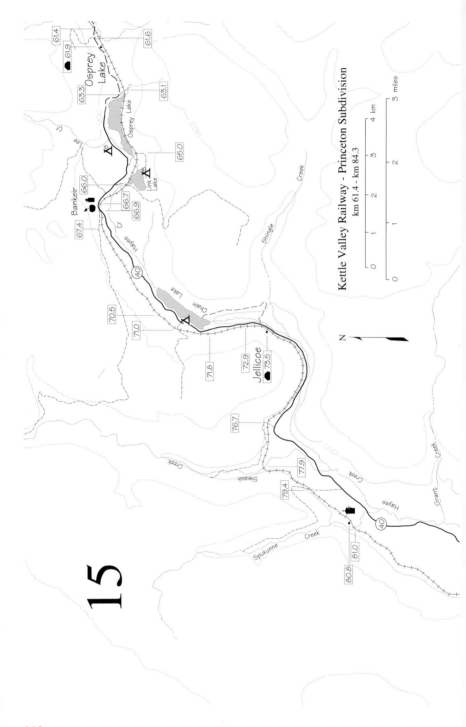

Kettle Valley Railway - Princeton Subdivision
km 61.4 - km 84.3

15

52.7 Access road to Highway #40 ⌄ ⚐

Demuth Forest Service Campsite is east on Highway #40 on the shore of Trout Creek.

53.7 Highway #40 →

Unfortunately, the highway jumps up onto the railgrade for the next 2.3 kilometres. The original road runs parallel to the road on the railway.

54.4 Thirsk Lake

The beginning of Thirsk Lake can be seen across the original Highway #40.

55.0 Thirsk Lake Recreation Area ⚐

A beautiful little spot on the north shore of Thirsk Lake.

56.0 Highway #40 departs KVR ←

The railway is found up on the right as the road makes a slow down hill turn to the left. This is easily missed so keep a good look out to the right.

56.3 Milford Station ⅼ1050 ▬ │ 🔄0.8

There is very little evidence of the station that once was here.

57.6 Fills and cuts in rock

58.6 Logging access road to Highway #40

59.3 Kathleen Creek Bridge detour │→

Take the trail to the south (left) 110 metres to the highway. Five hundred metres west on Highway #40 turn north (right) on a small road and travel two hundred metres to reconnect with the railbed. Do not take the small 4x4 road immediately after the highway bridge. This road does lead to the railway, but it is on a high, loose fill which is very difficult to climb.

59.6 Kathleen Creek ⋈50

The bridge over Kathleen Creek was removed by the CPR in 1995. Owing to the high, loose fills on both sides of the creek, it is best to detour using the highway bridge to cross the creek.

59.9 Kathleen Creek Bridge detour ends │←

A small road from Highway #40 crosses the KVR.

61.4 Highway #40 ⌄

61.6 Access road to Highway #40 ⌄

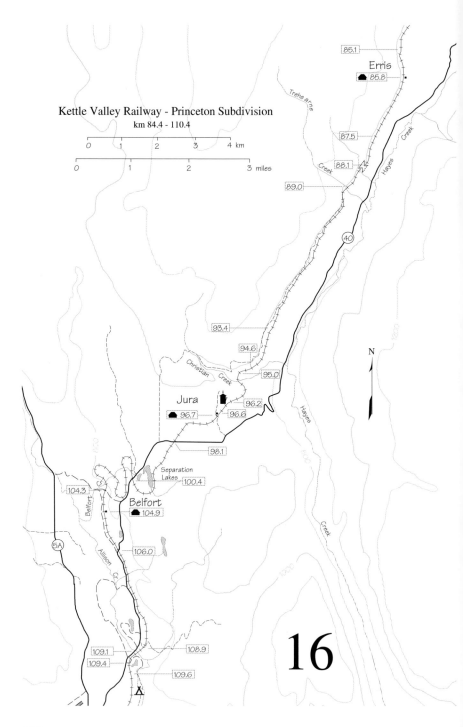

Kettle Valley Railway - Princeton Subdivision
km 84.4 - 110.4

61.9   Osprey Lake Station   i1095 ⬛ ⬛ ⸲ 🚲0.6

The concrete water tower foundation is found just prior to where the section house use to stand. Just past the station the ballast has been stripped for approximately one kilometre. To the south there is a small rough airstrip running parallel to the KVR.

63.1   Osprey Lake summit   i1098 —Wong Way ⛺ ⸵

Mr. Wong may have a campsite here in the near future.

63.3   Osprey Lake)(142

A pile trestle spans the east end of Osprey Lake, across from the numerous summer cottages that line the north shore.

Before the advent of mechanical refrigeration, large amounts of ice were cut by hand from Osprey Lake during the winter months. They were transported by the KVR and stored in blocks in sawdust-insulated icehouses in Penticton. The ice was used during the summer months to cool the reefer cars transporting fruit and to supply air conditioning for railway passenger cars. Ice was also taken from Otter Lake at km 139, by the Great Northern Railway to supply their icehouses in Washington state. In 1919, 3,000 cars of ice were loaded and shipped in 15 days. By the early 1920s mechanical ice had come of age, and a rapid decline in the need for natural ice resulted.

65.0   Link Lake Road ⸵ ⛺B

A small forest service campground can be found south on Link Lake Road and another one can be found taking Link Lake Road north to Highway #40, then east to the campground.

65.3   Country Lane ⸵ ⛺

Country Lane Campsite is found here.

66.0   Access road to Highway #40 ⸵

66.7   Bankeir ⬛ ⬛ ⬛ (

3 Lakes General Store is just a few metres north of the railbed. This is the only store, coffee and snack bar on the route from Penticton to Princeton. A small road runs between the store and the right-of-way.

66.9   Highway #40 ⸵

67.4   As the Hayes Creek Valley bottom falls, it leaves the KVR high on the north slope. Magnificent views of this narrow valley can be glimpsed through the trees. Ranches and swamps fill in any broadened areas of the valley.

70.5   Overlooking Chain Lake

Erris Tunnel, km 88.1.

71.0   Chain Link Campground—access road to Highway #40 ⛺ 🏠ᵇ ⵜ

Located at the intersection of this road with Highway #40 is Chain Lake Campground on the shore of Chain Lake. It is 300 metres down the hill to the campground.

Uphill this road will take you to Jellicoe B&B.

71.8   End of Chain Lake

72.9   Jellicoe B&B access trail 🚶 🏠ᵇ

Steep trail up to Jellicoe B&B

73.5   Jellicoe Station ⁞1017 🚃 ⸾ 🚲0.3

This was formerly named Usk Station but later named after the British admiral who distinguished himself at the Battle of Jutland in 1916.

The wide railbed results from the siding that once existed here.

76.7   Access road to Highway #40 ⵜ

77.9   Siwash Creek

A large curved timber trestle once took the KVR across Siwash Creek. This trestle was later filled. The half moon fill now wraps around Pine Valley Resort & Horse Centre. The trail for several kilometres in both directions has been chewed up badly by horses making it difficult to cycle.

79.4   Spukunne Creek Road ⵜ

80.8   Fifty Mile Tank 🛢

The water tower foundation is found slipping over the hillside.

81.0   Spukunne Creek—five through plate girder spans)(78

85.1   Logging area near the KVR, resulting in a chewed up railbed

85.8   Erris Station ⁞981 🚃 ⸾◌ 🚲0.5

Named after the mountain of the same name in Ireland. A widening in the grade marks the location of Erris Station.

87.5   Open area and gravel pit, small trail crosses railbed

88.1   Erris Tunnel ▮91

Much of this 91 metre-long tunnel was excavated through loose rock, requiring wooden timbers to be used as bracing. With the timbers still in place during the final operation of this line, it became the last tim-ber-lined tunnel to be used on the CPR system. A metal water trough at the west exit helps keep the railbed from being washed out.

89.0   Trehearne Creek

A major washout occurred here on April 9, 1934.

Crossing Spukunne Creek bridge, km 81.0.

Rainbow over the KVR, km 90.0.

🚂 *Coquihalla Agreement* 🚂

Before the echoes of clanging picks and shovels subsided from the Battle of Midway, another hot spot in the war between the KVR and the VV&E started to flare up in the race to Princeton. In 1905 both railways were boasting that each would be in Princeton before the other. J.J. Hill was first out of the blocks pushing the VV&E from Midway ever closer to Princeton, while the KVR was buying up property around Princeton, not only for its own right-of-way but also to block the VV&E from entering their community. By 1907 the VV&E had reached Keremeos, and in 1909, Princeton. Passenger service out of Princeton aboard the VV&E commenced with the KVR still six months away from even starting construction at Midway. In the shadow of its competitor's success the KVR in 1910 started construction at Midway, Merritt and Penticton. In November 1911, the VV&E had tracks into Coalmont and the rich coal seams of the Tulameen Valley. Coal began flowing south in long strings of coal hoppers along with the hopes of a "coast-to-Kootenay" connection. Construction by the VV&E slowed after reaching Coalmont, confirming the fears of many that the rush to Princeton was for the coal and not to complete the line to Hope. But by the middle of 1912, with the sound of KVR steam engines breathing over the VV&E's shoulder, the fight to claim the narrow Coquihalla Valley commenced. The difficulty was that, owing to the extreme ruggedness of the valley, it was not practical to construct two independent railways through this constricted gouge. The surveys by the two railways through the canyon placed each with the upper hand in different sections. It became clearly evident that the duplication of what would be the most expensive section of railway in North America was unjustified.

The two competitors came together in the spring of 1913 and agreed to work on a single line, thereby bridging the final piece of the coast-to-Kootenay dream. This became known as the Coquihalla Agreement. As per the terms of that agreement, the VV&E completed the trackage from Princeton to Brookmere and granted running rights to the KVR. In exchange, the KVR agreed to build and maintain the line from Brookmere to Hope and grant running rights to the VV&E for the annual fee of 2.5% of the total cost of construction. With this agreement the VV&E and the KVR both realized the dream of the coast-to-Kootenay rail link.

93.4   Scenic views down Hayes Creek Valley to Similkameen Valley

94.6   Gate

95.0   Mileage post 59, just prior to crossing Christian Creek

96.2   **Sixty Mile Tank** 🚰

The open range land at Jura, km 96.0.

An example of the easy opening gates installed along the KVR. This one near Jura, km 98.1.

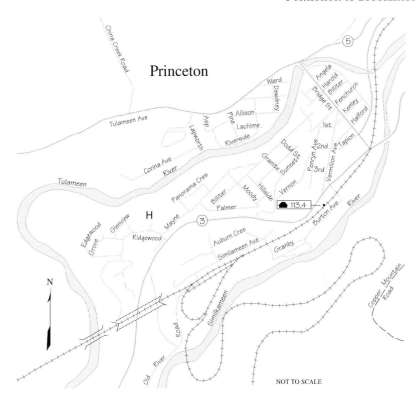

Princeton

NOT TO SCALE

The octagonal foundation of the water tower remains and the right-of-way widens for the Jura siding just after the water tower. In 2000 a gazebo was built on the base of this water tower.

96.6   Mileage post 60

96.7   Jura Station ⏸930 🚂 ⛏ 🏠 Ŷ 🍴 🚲1.9

A siding and a wye were built at Jura where the heavy 2.2% grade eased to 1%. The wye was used for turning the helper engines. The KVR departs the Hayes Creek Valley at Jura and the railbed then crosses an open, grassy plateau speckled with small lakes and stands of pine. In spring and summer the open hills above Princeton are carpeted with wild flowers.

In 1912, a decision was made to route the KVR into Princeton. The railway, high in the Hayes Creek Valley at elevation 930 metres, had to descend 282 metres into Princeton, less than 12 kilometres away. McCulloch chose to maintain a 2.2% grade over this abrupt descent by laying out three extraordinary loops on the open rangeland northeast of Princeton.

98.1   Highway #40 Ŷ

The gated fence of the Jura Stock Ranch greets you on the other side of Highway #40. Thirteen kilometres of the railbed winds its way through

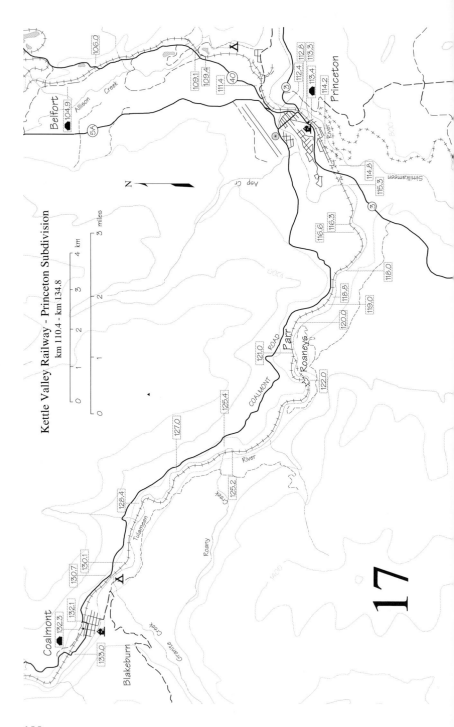

Kettle Valley Railway - Princeton Subdivision
km 110.4 - km 134.8

the ranch. Watch for cattle and city-slickers on horseback looking for cattle rustlers. Don't get caught with fresh steaks in your panniers. Past the gate, the KVR begins the first of the Jura Loops as it rounds Separation Lakes and passes the Maverick Hitch 'n' Post.

100.4 Highway #40 ⍏

Gated fences prior to and after Highway #40. The entrance to Maverick Cattle Drives is just to the west.

104.3 Access road from Highway #40 to Highway #5A ⍏

104.9 Belfort Station i*776* 🚂 ⍭ ❙ 🚲*1.5*

This station was named after the famous French garrison in the "Jura" mountains that resisted the German invasion of 1870. The only visible evidence of Belfort Station is a noticeable widening of the right-of-way due to the past existence of a siding.

106.0 Highway #40 ⍏

The KVR is earth bermed on both sides of the highway to restrict motorized vehicle traffic.

108.9 Private drive ⍏

109.1 Allison Creek

Loose sharp rocks make up the railbed.

109.4 Rainbow Lake Road ⍏ 🏛 ⛺ ❙ ⍭ 🚶

Following the road to the east brings you to Princeton Castle Resort and the old stone ruins of the Portland Cement Plant finished in 1908. It took four years to build the plant and yet was in operation for only nine months due to a lack of coal and limestone. This building was a grand architectural and engineering achievement of the times. The VV&E constructed a spur from the line across the Similkameen River up Allison Creek to the plant in 1908. This line continued 700 metres past the plant, weaving its way up the creek, and crossing it five times to reach the tramway that came down from the mine.

The Portland Cement Plant is now the site of the Princeton Castle Resort. This resort covers 110 acres and has many services, such as a lodging, campsite, restaurant, hiking trails and tours of the historic ruins.

109.6 Access trail to Princeton Castle Resort. 🚶 ·🚲·.

111.4 Old Hedley Road and Sawmill spur ⍒ ⍏

KVR is high on the hillside overlooking the Princeton Sawmill. The spur line follows down the hill to the sawmill.

112.4 Tulameen River �*67*

The highway bridge running parallel to the west can be used to cross the river.

Tulameen River Bridge, km 115.3.

Trail pavilion in Tulameen Canyon, just before Parr Tunnel, km 121.9.

112.8   Highway #3 ⍓

Just before you cross Highway #3 you find that a car dealership is using the right-of-way as a parking lot.

113.3   Vermilion Avenue - Princeton Gateway ⍓ ⍓ 🚐

One of the official access points starting to spring up along the trail. Parking and trail information.

113.4   **Princeton Station** |648 ⬛ ⍓ ⍓ Υ Λ ⍓ ⍓ ⍓ ⍓ ⍓ ⍓ ⍓ ⍓ 0.4

Prior to 1860 Princeton was known as Vermilion Forks, "Vermilion" meaning the mercuric sulphide compound that produces a brilliant red pigment, and "Forks" because the Similkameen and Tulameen rivers converge here. In 1860, Vermilion Forks was renamed Princeton, after the Prince of Wales.

The mercuric sulphide compound is found in the red earth up the Tulameen River. Tulameen is a Salish Indian word meaning red earth. The Indians commonly used this pigment for face painting. This feature was so prized by the Indians that many tribes would come to trade for it.

🚂 Princeton Museum 🚂
117 Vermilion Avenue, 250-295-7588

The Princeton Station is still standing, white vinyl sided and home to a real estate office and a Subway restaurant. Just past the station site is the junction of the Copper Mountain Subdivision. West of Princeton, the KVR trains operated on the VV&E tracks as far as Brookmere. At Brookmere the VV&E then joined onto the KVR line. The KVR's use of the track was permitted under the "Tulameen Agreement" of 1914. Only a few VV&E trains even ran as far west as Coalmont, and ultimately the trackage was sold to CPR in 1945.

114.0   Auburn Crescent ⍓

114.2   Copper Mountain Subdivision ⍓ (see page 141)

114.8   Tunnel 🔲324

This 324 metre-long tunnel was constructed in 1910 by the VV&E and carries the railway under Highway #3.

115.3   Tulameen River)(96

In 1885 the Tulameen River and its tributaries were the site of a gold rush. Placer gold and platinum were mined from Princeton up to Champion Creek. Present-day prospectors still search for their fortunes along the watershed of the Tulameen.

115.5   Tulameen Coal Mines spur ⍓

A short spur ran downstream along the side of the river.

116.3 Pleasant Valley Mining spur
Another short spur crossed the river to a tipple.

116.6 The Tulameen River shows the reason for its name with bright red banks framing a blue river.

118.0 Hoodoos

118.8 Gate

119.0 Coalmont Road is suspended high on the slope above the KVR. The walls of the canyon are unstable resulting in a constant flow of rubble cascading down on the KVR. Over the next few kilometres watch for rocks on the rail bed.

120.0 Gate

121.0 Parr
The name Parr came from the name of the engineer in charge of the tunnel construction. Parr was the name of the short spur at this location. Originally two bridges took 1.5 kilometres of the railway along the south bank of the Tulameen River. On January 25, 1935, an ice jam washed out one of the bridges on which the railway crossed. Repairs were not completed until February 11, 1935. Continuing difficulties in maintaining the two bridges resulted in the construction of the tunnel. The tunnel was built in 1948-49, allowing 1.3 kilometres of the railway to relocate to the north bank of the river, bypassing the two bridges. The railbed, with rotting ties still in place, can be seen across the river and the remains of the abutments of the two bridges against the banks of the river.

Roaneys, a former flagstop, was located on the bypassed section at km 121.5.

121.9 Trail pavilion

122.0 Parr Tunnel ◼147
Owing to the curvature of this 147 metre-long tunnel, both ends of the tunnel cannot be seen when in the middle.

125.2 Tulameen River)(71
Through truss bridge.

125.4 Roany Creek

127.0 Beautiful rust-coloured slope falling down to the river. Coalmont Road hangs precariously high above on the wall of the canyon.

128.4 Tulameen River)(105
Rust-coloured cliffs provide a contrasting backdrop to the green pines, golden sand beach, and blue waters of the Tulameen River.

130.1 Spur ⤾

130.7 Granite Creek

Across the Tulameen River was the site of Granite City, named after Granite Creek, which enters the Tulameen River at this point. Granite City became a bustling town of about 2,000 after the discovery of these gold-laden waters in 1885. In 1886 Granite City was considered the largest city in the interior of British Columbia. However, when the gold boom ended less than four years later, the town became deserted. The mounds of tailings and a few dilapidated log buildings lost amongst the trees are all that remain.

One of the frustrations of panning the placer gold on Granite Creek was a white metal of similar weight inter-

Coalmont Hotel, km 132.1.

mixed with the gold. Hence, it was difficult to separate the two. Years later it was discovered that the white metal was platinum, with a value well exceeding that of the gold. There was a renewed interest in Granite Creek as prospectors reworked old claims and searched for the discarded piles of platinum.

The site of Granite City is now a campground which can be accessed through Coalmont.

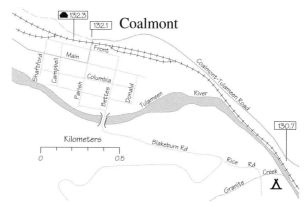

132.1 Coalmont-Tulameen Road / Parish Avenue ⚕ ⛺ 🏨 🛏 🍴 🍺

The Coalmont Hotel still operates among the false-fronted wooden buildings on Main Street. It was recently restored with original antique decor including the sleeping units, a public dining area and pub. Also found in Coalmont is the Coalmont General Store just north of the hotel. To reach Granite Creek Forestry Campground, 1.6

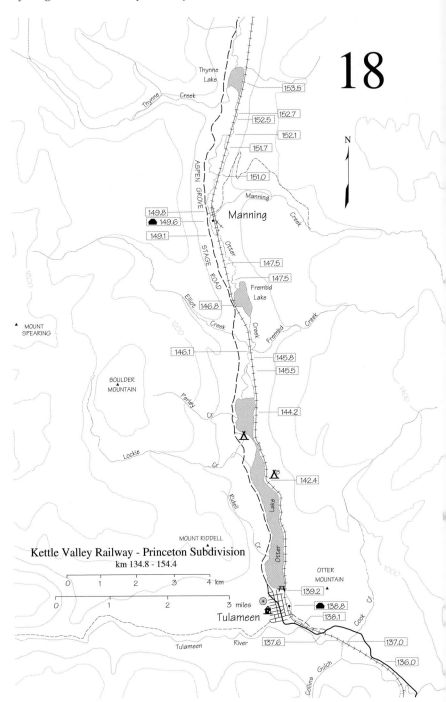

18

N

Thynne Lake

Thynne Creek

153.5

152.7
152.5

152.1

151.7

151.0

Manning

ASPEN GROVE

Manning

149.8
149.6
149.1

STAGE ROAD

Otter Creek

147.5
147.5

Frembd Lake

Elliot Creek

146.8

MOUNT SPEARING

Frembd Creek

146.1

145.8
145.5

BOULDER MOUNTAIN

Perley Cr

144.2

Lockie Cr

142.4

Riddell Cr

Otter Lake

MOUNT RIDDELL

OTTER MOUNTAIN

Kettle Valley Railway - Princeton Subdivision
km 134.8 - 154.4

0   1   2   3   4 km

0   1   2   3 miles

139.2

138.8
138.1

Tulameen

Tulameen River

137.6

137.0

Cook Cr

Collins Gulch

136.0

kilometres from the hotel, follow Bettes Avenue through Coalmont and across the Tulameen River, turn left on Blakeburn Road, then left on Rice Road. This leads you to the campground and the site of Granite City. The remains of Blakeburn can be found about five kilometres up Blakeburn Road.

132.3 Coalmont Station ¡727 🚆 ♪ ⊬ ☕ ◊ 🚲0.6

Named for the seemingly endless "mountain of coal" in the area. Now almost a ghost town, Coalmont flourished in the early 1900s when J. J. Hill's VV&E reached Coalmont and immediately started transporting coal from the Columbia Coal and Coke Company to the iron horses of the Great Northern Railway. The surface coal was quickly spent and it soon proved uneconomical to mine the deeper coal seams. As mines in the area disappeared, so did the residents of Coalmont.

133.0   Coalmont—Tulameen Road ⊤

136.0   Gate

137.0   Gate

137.6   Coalmont—Tulameen Road ⊤

138.1   Otter Creek)(13

138.6   2nd Street—Tulameen Gateway 🏛 🛉 🍴 ☕ �𝍖 🚐
Offical trail access point with parking and trail information.

138.8 Tulameen Station ¡763 🚆 🛉 ♪ ⊬ 🚲0.2

This area was called Campement des Femmes, "Camp of the Women." When the men went into the countryside to hunt, Salish Indian women and children were left here on this fertile flat, which served as a base camp. During the Gold Rush, the area was known as Otter Flats and later renamed Tulameen.

Had there not been the threat of the KVR beating J. J. Hill's VV&E to the coast, Hill would have preferred to construct a grade west from here up the Tulameen River Valley. Approximately at the intersection of Railway Creek and the Tulameen River, an eight mile-long tunnel was to be constructed through the Hope Mountains to emerge at

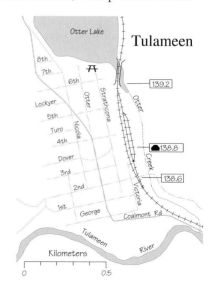

Tulameen Trading Post

Tulameen Gateway at km 138.6

Dewdney Creek in the Coquihalla River Valley. Such a tunnel would have taken years to construct. The restraint of time played a part in the final route chosen, as the KVR and VV&E raced to the Coquihalla River Valley since it was wide enough for only one rail line.

A spur ran from here to the shore of Otter Lake Provincial Park beach where the VV&E cut ice from the lake to feed its ice houses in Washington state. Each year thousands of boxcars of ice made their way south. The Tulameen Station built in 1914 was moved within the townsite and now serves as a private residence. An old red freight shed has been moved a short distance from the railbed and can be seen in use as a storage shed.

139.2 Otter Lake - Otter Creek)(102 ㅠ

Just before you cross the outlet of Otter Lake you come to Otter Lake Provincial Park. A second section of the park is found 4.6 kilometres north on the west side of the lake. The southern parcel of the park has picnicking and swimming, and the northern parcel has camping and swimming. The KVR follows the east side of Otter Lake constrained between the shore and the steep mountainsides.

142.4 A beautiful little campsite on the lakeshore in a small rock cut beside the railway 𝕏

144.2 Gate

145.5 Gate

145.8 Washed out area

Frembd Creek appears to have cut a new channel that flows down the railbed for few metres at this point during spring run off.

146.1 Otter Creek)(37

Just downstream of the confluence of Otter Creek and Frembd Creek, the KVR crosses Otter Creek to travel the west side of the valley.

146.8 Frembd Lake

The KVR squeezes along the narrow valley between the steep forested mountain slopes and Frembd Lake.

Cycling along Frembd Lake, km 146.8.

147.0 Gate

147.5 Otter Creek)(14
A pile trestle crosses an old channel of Otter Creek.

148.0 Pile Trestle)(

149.1 Otter Creek)(41

149.4 Pasture
The railway grade has been removed by a local rancher for the next 400 metres but the trail runs through the field.

149.6 Manning Station i785 ◼ ⸗ ♣0.5
With the exception of a widening of the right-of-way and some scattered concrete pieces, there is not much evidence of Manning Station. Past Manning the KVR continues to cross and re-cross the serpentine Otter Creek.

149.8 Manning Creek)(9 ⸆
Double pile trestles, one for the main line and one for the siding, cross the creek. The railbed resumes and crosses a small road.

151.0 Otter Creek)(27

151.7 Otter Creek.)(27

152.1 Otter Creek.)(41

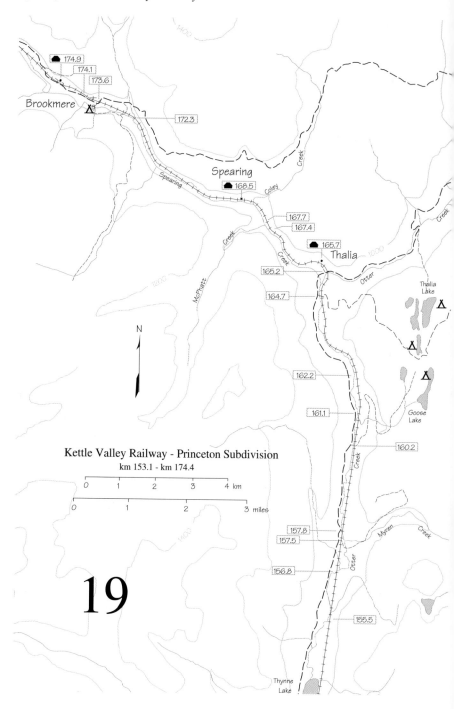

Brookmere

174.9
174.1
173.6
172.3

Spearing

168.5
167.7
167.4
165.7
Thalia
165.2
164.7

Thalia Lake

162.2
161.1
160.2

Goose Lake

N

Kettle Valley Railway - Princeton Subdivision
km 153.1 - km 174.4

0   1   2   3   4 km
0   1   2   3 miles

157.8
157.5
156.8
155.5

Thynne Lake

19

152.5 Otter Creek)(27

152.6 Washed-out gully through railbed

152.7 Otter Creek)(32

153.5 Thynne Lake - Gate
With the lake pressed against the valley's east wall, the KVR skirts the west shore of Thynne Lake.

155.5 Gate

156.8 Otter Creek)(27

157.6 Private drive ↑

157.8 Otter Creek)(37

160.2 Private drive ↑

161.1 Gate

162.2 Rockfall

164.6 Gate

164.7 Youngsberg Road ↑ |⇒|
The railbed is gated on both sides of this road. The trestle over Otter Creek and Aspen Grove Stage Road was burned down. If you wish to avoid negotiating the trails along the steep gravel abutments, detour west (left) on Youngsberg Road (130 metres). Turn north (right) on Aspen Grove Stage Road and cross the bridge and cattle guard (820 metres), then turn west (left) on to the small road just in front (south) of the gravel abutment of the missing trestle. Follow the road though the gate up to the railbed (340 metres).
Following Youngsberg Road east there are primitive forestry service campsites at the fishing lakes of Thalia, Goose and Lodwick.

165.2 Aspen Grove Stage Road and Otter Creek ⋈61
This frame and pile trestle was set ablaze in 1996. A trail now runs down the sides of the high gravel abutments on both sides of the missing bridge and a small foot bridge spans Otter Creek. The trails are relatively narrow and steep with some loose gravel. If you are heavily loaded you may wish to use the detour mentioned at km 164.7
Just north of the east abutment is a cave used by the famous CPR train robber, Bill Miner. The KVR did not exist when Bill Miner was robbing trains.

165.6 Detour road joins railbed ▮ |⇐|

165.7 Thalia Station |866 ⛺ ⫿ ⫯1.9

This station was formerly named Canyon.

167.4   Fixed washout

The local residents have built a 110 metre-long bypass road alongside the washed-out railbed.

167.7   Canyon narrows

The railbed and creek fit shoulder to shoulder through this tight canyon.

168.5 Spearing Station |917 ⛺ ⫿ ⛺0.9

This was formerly named Koyl Station, but the name was changed when confusion was noted between it and Coyle Station on the Merritt Subdivision. Spearing was named after Gus Spearing, a civil war veteran who spent his final days trapping in the Otter Valley.

Today you will find Burt Sharkey's Horse Motel, a privately owned campground for horse back rideres and cyclists.

172.3   Spearing Creek)(27

173.6   Brookmere Road ⫠ ⛺8

A rough campsite used mainly in the winter by snowmobilers.

174.1   Gate

174.5   Brookmere community grounds.

174.8   Private drive ⫠

174.9 Brookmere Station |962 ⛺ ⬤ ⫿ ⫽ ⌂ ⛺ ◊

This area was originally known as Otter Summit, and later named Brookmere with the coming of the railway. Brookmere was the divisional point of the KVR from the VV&E tracks. The presence of the two railways accounted for an unusual nature to the Brookmere railway yard. The KVR and GNR shared the station house and locomotive watering facilities. This created the unique feature of having Brookmere Station squarely in the middle of the yard so that it would equally serve both railways. Similarly, the water tank at the west end of the yard was equipped with a spout on each side to permit use by either railway. North of the tracks, the KVR built a bunkhouse, coal tower, turntable and a three-stall roundhouse.

You will find that many of the KVR buildings have been preserved at Brookmere. The water tower was relocated for preservation, and a wooden caboose was also given as a gift from the town of Merritt to the citizens of Brookmere. Brookmere is one of the few towns on this route that has been able to preserve some of its railroad heritage.

Coley Creek Lodge access can be found on the far west end of Brookmere as Brookmere Road leaves Brookmere. Turn right (east) on Brookmere Station Road and follow to the campground and lodge. ⬛

COPPER MOUNTAIN SUBDIVISION
Princeton to Copper Mountain, 21.4 kilometres

In the early 1900s, Canada Copper owned a mine on Copper Mountain, just south of Princeton. With an increased demand for copper during the First World War, Canada Copper approached the KVR in April of 1917 requesting that a rail line be constructed from Princeton to Copper Mountain. The KVR would haul raw ore from Copper Mountain Mine to a concentrator plant that was to be built between the mine and Princeton, then to the smelter at Trail, B.C. By November 1917, McCulloch had completed the survey work and by the spring of the next year, construction began.

With the work involved and wartime shortages, this branch line was not completed until October 1920. The Copper Mountain Subdivision ran for 21.4 kilometres, and included 24 trestles and four tunnels. One section even required 360,000 cubic yards of solid rock to be blasted from the mountainside to create a ledge for the track. A secondary spur ran to the top of the concentrator mill, a site called Allenby. Both Copper Mountain and Allenby had turntables in order to turn locomotives around for the return trip.

After only a few months of operation, depressed postwar copper prices closed the mine in December 1920. Canada Copper then sold the mine to Granby Consolidated Mining and Smelting Company. Granby reopened the mine in August 1925, for an extremely productive period of five years. During this time, the KVR had a 15-car ore train making three round trips per day between the mine and mill. In an average year, the KVR handled 13,696 cars of ore and 861 cars of concentrates along this line.

Late in 1930, the mine closed only to again reopen in 1937. Copper prices had increased due to the Spanish Civil War, along with an increased demand for copper when Canada entered the Second World War. The Copper Mountain Mine and rail line operated continuously for the next 20 years, but in April of 1957 the mine again closed, this time permanently. Shortly afterwards, the Copper Mountain Subdivision was abandoned and the line dismantled.

Today, sections of the original railbed from Princeton to km 16.5 can still be ridden. Unfortunately, the route is discontinuous because of the missing bridge across the Similkameen River and the construction of houses on the right-of-way. Pieces of this subdivision are slowly being sold off. On the loops overlooking Princeton, a residential development already has the right-of-way running into someone's outdoor swimming pool at km 3.4. Farther along, at km 5.8 the front door of Tanglewood Hollow abruptly stops further progress. If there was a way to get around the private property, you would find the railbed to Allenby is unreasonable condition. Of course, it may be possible to cycle from Allenby to the back of the property.

For the determined mountain biker who needs to do it all, it maybe possible to access most of the discontinuous sections between those privately held. The flat and dusty 6.1 kilometre-long section reclaimed

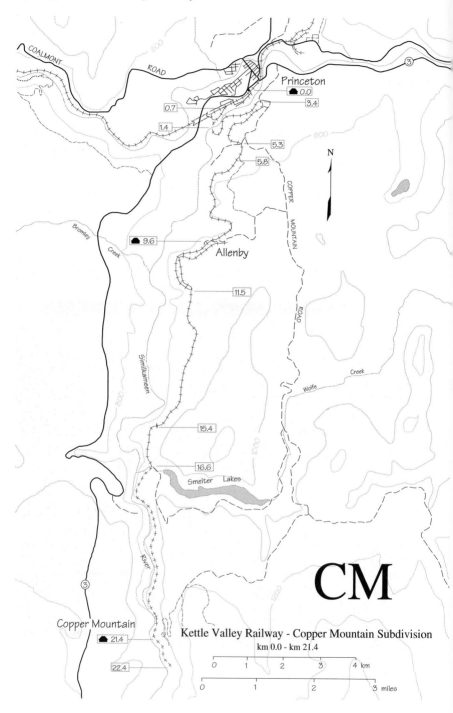

COALMONT

ROAD

800

Princeton

0.0

0.7

3.4

1.4

5.3

5.8

COPPER MOUNTAIN ROAD

800

N

Bromley

Creek

9.6

Allenby

11.5

Similkameen

Creek

Wolfe

800

15.4

1000

16.6

Smelter Lakes

River

CM

3

1000

Copper Mountain

21.4

Kettle Valley Railway - Copper Mountain Subdivision
km 0.0 - km 21.4

22.4

0   1   2   3   4 km

0   1   2   3 miles

by Allenby Road, from Allenby to the locked gate into Copper Mountain just short of Smelter Lakes, can be tackled. Past Smelter Lakes, the forest and time have reclaimed this most fascinating section of the KVR with all its trestles and tunnels, making it totally impassable. The remains of the trestles and the abandoned tunnels still clinging to the side of the Similkameen Canyon on this impassable section can be viewed from the Newmont Mines just across the canyon ➟

Using 24 trestles and four tunnels, this 21.4 kilometre-long branch line ascended nearly 300 metres from Princeton to the mine on Copper Mountain. (Princeton Museum)

km   **Princeton Station** ¡648 🚍 🛈 ⸗ ⸗ ⸗→⸗
0.0

A detour is necessary because of the missing bridge over the Similkameen River and the rough shape discontinuous nature of the KVR from Princeton to Allenby. From the boarded up Princeton Station head east on Highway #3 and hang a right (north) on to Copper Mountain Road. After a muscle tiring climb of 5.3 kilometres, turn east (right) on to Allenby Road. 2.9 kilometres down Allenby Road is the remains of the Allenby concentrator mill. At this site, Allenby Road turns on to the original KVR grade.

0.7   Copper Mountain Subdivision departs from Princeton Subdivision. ⸌

1.4   Similkameen River ⋇122

3.4   Private residence
The right-of-way runs into the outdoor pool of the private residence.

3.5   Access road to Copper Mountain Road ⸗⇐⸗

5.3   East Similkameen Road ⸗⇒⸗ ⸗⇐⸗

5.8   Tanglewood Hollow
The KVR runs right into the front door of this private residence. It is difficult to bypass without trespassing.

9.6   **Allenby** 🚍 🛈 ⸗ ⋏ ⸗ ⸗⇐⸗
The decaying remains of the old concentrator mill are found in every direction. The majority of it is hiding in the vegetation surrounding the main site. Up the hill, behind where the plant stood, is the High Line spur, which the KVR used to deliver the raw ore to the concentrator. From Allenby to Smelter Lakes, Allenby Road runs on top of the original railbed with a few jogs to bypass missing trestles.

11.5   High Line spur ⸌
This 2.6 kilometre-long spur heads back to the top of the old concentrator plant at Allenby. This spur line is marginally passable, being rather rough and overgrown.

15.4   Locked gate into Copper Mountain

16.6   Smelter Lakes ⋇233
Smelter Lakes no longer exist in reality. Years of dumping tailings into the lakes have completely filled the narrow valley. At this point the road leaves the railway grade and climbs the valley wall along Smelter Lakes. The KVR is not passable beyond this point, even on foot, as the forest has reclaimed the grade and the tunnel portals are blocked by slides. In this last 5.8 kilometres the railway had 17 trestles and four tunnels. Many of the trestles still cling to the side of the Similkameen Valley.

21.4   **Copper Mountain.** 🚍 ⸗

22.4   Turntable and end of line. ⊨

Myra Canyon, Trestle #4, Carmi Subdivision, km 141.89.

Kettle River Bridge, Columbia & Western, km 139.0.

Myra Canyon, Trestle #11, Carmi Subdivision, km 138.22.

Second tunnel and trestle #10, Myra Canyon, Carmi Subdivision km 139.0.

Caboose built by Paul Lautard of the cyclists reststop, Carmi Sibdivision, km 39.9.

1924 Shay Locomotive building steam in preparation for hauling the Kettle Valley Steam Railway train up Prairie Valley, km 15.3, Princeton Subdivision.

Tunnel #7, Coquihalla Subdivision, km 44.4.

Osprey Lake, Princeton Subdivision, km 63.3.

Tunnel on the Columbia & Western, km 23.6.

The only remaining water tower on the KVR. This tower is unique in that it had two spouts to service both the KVR and VV&E at Brookmere Station, km 174.9 Princeton Subdivision.

A small tuscan red shed built into the hillside at Coykendahl Station, Columbia & Western Railway, km 28.7.

Farr Creek Bridge, Columbia & Western, km 24.8.

MERRITT SUBDIVISION
Brookmere to Merritt, 47.3 kilometres

The section of the Kettle Valley Railway between Brookmere and Merritt is known as the Merritt Subdivision. This subdivision was not part of the KVR coast-to-Kootenay main line, but was simply a branch line to connect the KVR main line with the CPR main line. However, this branch line was frequently used during the winter season when the Coquihalla Subdivision was closed because of heavy snow, forcing trains to be diverted north. After the permanent closure of the Coquihalla Subdivision in 1959, the Merritt Subdivision became part of the KVR main line.

The pleasant cycle through this short section is very scenic as you follow the Coldwater River Valley on a gentle downhill grade and well-travelled railbed. This route passes through the Coldwater River Canyon with high rock walls to either side as both the railbed and the river squeeze through the canyon along the valley bottom. The valley then opens up to rolling hills covered with grass and speckled with pine trees as it leads you into the city of Merritt nestled in the Nicola Valley. Continuity problems in this ride begin at 25.9 kilometres from Brookmere. A major washout can slow and sometimes stop progress and then at 32.6 kilometres is the Coldwater Indian Reserve which has in the past not allowed passage on the railbed through their property. Lack of access to the railbed and washouts at the bridges across the Coldwater River at kilometre 40.4 and 43.1, after the reserve and before Merritt keeps cyclists on the Coldwater Road into Merritt, which is a nice ride in it's self.

The only designated campsites or lodging facilities along the Merritt Subdivision are in Brookmere and Merritt. Back country camping opportunities exist around Brodie. Your legs will be pleased that the accessible trail is a good one and the grade falls gently downhill from Brookmere. Once you've made it to Merritt, you can easily reward yourself as all amenities are available to you in this friendly town in the Nicola Valley ◄

km	**Brookmere Station** ╎*962* ● ♟ ⌇ ◊ 🚲*0.6*
0.0	Brookmere was a busy railway town in its day, being the junction point for the three subdivisions of the Kettle Valley Railway, Princeton, Coquihalla and Merritt. It was also the junction point of the VV&E line. Brookmere is presently a quiet little community with a few KVR buildings and a wooden caboose and water tower preserved in memory of Brookmere's KVR history.
0.4	Brookmere Road ⸸ ⌂ 𝍄
	Access to Coley Creek Lodge can be found on Brookmere Station Road, 100 metres down Brookmere Road.
1.1	Brook Creek)(*6x3*

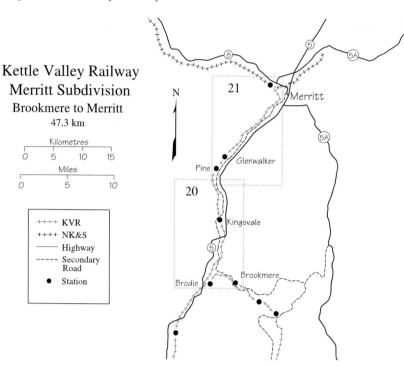

Kettle Valley Railway
Merritt Subdivision
Brookmere to Merritt
47.3 km

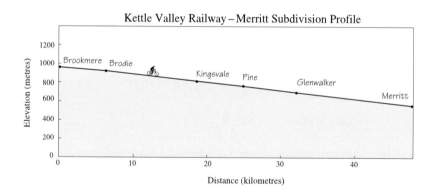

Kettle Valley Railway – Merritt Subdivision Profile

1.3   Brook Creek)(6x3

2.8   Brook Creek)(5x3
        Railbed is composed of large, loose gravel and is a little better packed
        where the tire tracks are.

5.4   Major washout
        Thirty metres of railbed has been swept off the face of the mountain. A
        trail cuts up and around the missing railbed.

5.9   Sand slide
        Fifty metres of the railbed is covered by a sand slide that is easily walked
        or ridden over.

6.4   Brodie i923 🚂 ♪ ⼁ 𝕏 | 🚴0.9.
        This spot on the KVR was known as "the Loop." Brodie Station was at
        the apex of this large loop, where the main line turned back on itself to
        continue north along the branch line to Merritt. At this apex, the main
        line continued south on the Coquihalla Subdivision to Hope.
            Brodie can be accessed from Coquihalla Highway by the Larson Hill
        Exit (Exit 250) and taking Brodie Siding Road following down along
        the highway.
            All around Brodie is some of the most beautiful backcountry camp-
        ing spots on the KVR. The only drawback is the highway noise from the
        Coquihailla.

An original CPR wooden caboose and KVR water tower are found at Brookmere, km 0.0.

155

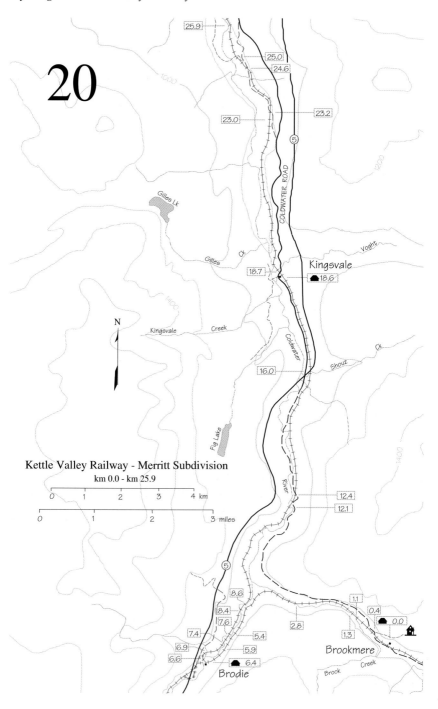

20

Kingsvale

Kettle Valley Railway - Merritt Subdivision
km 0.0 - km 25.9

Brookmere

Brodie

6.6   Coldwater River—through-plate girder)(31x6

This is one of the more beautiful sections of the KVR with the railway and the Coldwater River continually trading sides as each tries to gain the advantage through the narrow Coldwater River Canyon. Because of the tight quarters with the walls of the canyon, there are frequent rockfalls requiring a lot of rock dodging along this section. The trestles in the canyon have all been planked and handrailed in 2001.

6.9   Salt Creek—Washout)(3

A seasonal creek has washed across the rail bed. In the 2001 the Nicola Valley Explorers Society E-Team built a pedestrian/horse bridge across this creek.

7.4   Coldwater River—pony truss)(33x6

7.6   Coldwater River—deck truss)(33x6

8.4   Coldwater River—deck truss)(33x6

8.6   Coldwater River—deck truss)(33x6

12.1   Coldwater River—through truss)(34x6

12.4   Gate—Coldwater Road ⍏

16.0   Coquihalla Highway Overpass/access to KVR ⍏

Coldwater Road, KVR and the Coldwater River pass under the Coquihalla Highway. Access to both Coldwater Road and Coquihalla Highway can be gained here. Exit 256 from the Coquihalla Highway will bring you to this place.

16.9   Minor washout.

18.6   Kingsvale Station ℹ817 🛏 🛖 ⸗ ⸗ 🚴0.8

The section house in this picturesque little community was being used as a private residence until late 2000 when it burned to the ground. Between the station house and the now missing bridge over Voght Creek / Coldwater Road was the concrete foundation of the water tower. Which was removed when the Coldwater Road was realigned.

18.7   Coldwater Road / Voght Creek ⤬20

This bridge was taken out in 2001 when Coldwater Road was realigned. The Nicola Valley Explorers are working on approaches to the trail from the road. Watch for signage. Past Kingsvale the KVR enters farmland and with it comes the problem of gates and fences.

23.0   Gate

23.2   Peterson Road ⍏

*Katharine Shewchuk riding across the newly built bridge spanning the washout at km 25.9.
Photo Murphy Shewchuk.*

24.6   Peterson Road ⸸

24.8   Olsons spur ⱶ

25.0   Road ⸸
A small road leads down to the river or up to Peterson Road.

25.9   Major washout
One hundred and eighty metres of railbed was washed away when the Coldwater River changed its course in 1994. A single track trail and a 10 metre long bridge has been built into and along the slope of the hillside by the Nicola Valley Explorers Society, that gets over this washout.

26.6   Sand slide

27.5   Sand slide

28.1   Private drive ⸸

28.3   Patchet Road ⸸ ⱶ→
This is the last exit before Coldwater Indian Reserve. Detour here up Patchet Road to Coldwater Road which will take you the rest of the way to Merritt. The Nicola Valley Explorers Society is working on a trail from this point to Merritt and when ready, signage will direct you on to this new trail. Check the Society's website for updates.
Past this point, the right-of-way is still explorable to the boundary of the Coldwater Indian Reserve. Across Patchet Road the rail bed passes though a farmyard that has gated fences at both ends.

28.4   Pine i*764* ⱶ 🚴*0.9*
A 24.1 kilometre-long logging spur was constructed here in the 1920s by the Nicola Pine Mill of Merritt. Operated by the mill, the line was extended along Midday Creek as logging operations proceeded up the valley. Operation of the spur line ended in the Depression years of the 1930s.

32.2   Glenwalker Station i*697* ▰ ❙ 🚴*0.7*
This section is again in the midst of farm land. When passing through this stretch, you may find irrigation sprinklers on, watering not only the crops, but also the railbed and you. This can actually be quite nice, especially if you are cycling in the heat of the day. There is a private road from the station to Coldwater Road.

32.6   Coldwater Indian Reserve Boundary
A gravel barricade and ditch erected to inhibit traffic through the reserve marks the Coldwater Indian Reserve boundary. When the right-of-way of the Kettle Valley Railway was acquired by the government of British Columbia, the rail bed that was contained within the bounda-

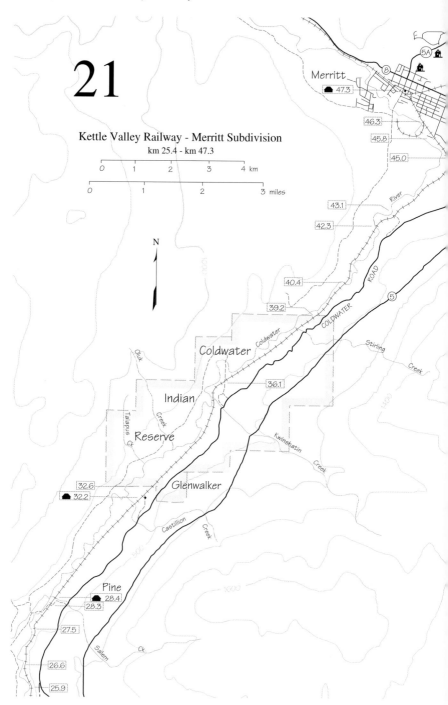

21

Kettle Valley Railway - Merritt Subdivision
km 25.4 - km 47.3

Merritt 47.3

N

Coldwater

Indian

Reserve

Glenwalker

Pine 28.4

ries of the Indian reserves turned over to the respective reserves. The Coldwater Indian Reserve has denied any request to cycle the rail grade through their property. Return to Patchet Road (km28.3) to detour around the Reserve.

36.1 Private access road to Coldwater Road ⊤

This access road crosses the rail bed, then continues across the Coldwater River. There is a small residential community that is part of the reserve to the west. This is not a public road.

39.2 Coldwater Indian Reserve Boundary

A gravel barricade across the right-of-way blocks traffic from entering the Reserve to the south.. If heading south return to Merritt and reaccess the railgrade at Patchet Road (km 28.3).

40.4 Coldwater River—through truss)(34

The Coldwater River has cut a new channel that has removed the railbed south of the bridge. The bridge now sits on its naked south abutment in the middle of the river. The river can be forded only at low water levels.

42.3 Coldwater River—through truss)(34

The northern approach has been washed out and the north abutment has been undermined, twisting the through-truss bridge. The river can be forded only at low water levels.

42.9 Private access road—Merritt Mountain Music Festival grounds ⊤

The Merritt Mountain Music Festival is a weekend-long music festival held in July. From here to Pooley Avenue the KVR is used as a road from the festival grounds to Merritt called Mountain Music Way.

45.0 Mountain Music Way ⊤ ⊦⇒⦚

Past this point the KVR is under constant change and may not be passable.

45.8 Douglas Street ⊤ ⊦→⦚

Weyerhauser Sawmill yard has swallowed up the railbed of the KVR.

46.3 Merritt Mine spur ⊬

This 1.4 kilometre-long spur was built in 1907 to reach the Middlesboro Collieries across the Coldwater River.

47.3 Merritt Station |567 ▰ ⓘ⌽ ⊬Υ Λ ▟ ⍦ ⓘⒸⓘ

Merritt was originally a flag stop along the Nicola Branch Line of the CPR. This CPR branch line was formally opened in April 1907 as the Nicola, Kamloops & Similkameen Railway, later changed to the CPR's Nicola Branch Line. It ran between Spences Bridge and Nicola giving CPR access to the wealth of coal in the Nicola Valley for their locomotives.

Nicola Valley Museum Archives
(2202 Jackson, 250-378-4145)

It was here at Merritt that the Kettle Valley Railway connected to the CPR's Nicola Branch Line. The KVR opened the Merritt Subdivision May 1915. It was October 1915, that the Nicola Branch Line was turned over to the Kettle Valley Railway, enabling the KVR trains to run directly through to Spences Bridge, the junction point of the CPR main line.

The tracks along the Merritt Subdivision were some of the last to be removed from the Kettle Valley Railway. The abandoned Merritt Station has been moved and can still be found along the NK&S east of Merritt. Merritt became a growing centre with the coming of the railway. Cattle and mining are still an important part of Merritt's economy. With the Coquihalla Highway passing through Merritt, just as the KVR did so many years earlier, this city is again a hub of activity.

COQUIHALLA SUBDIVISION
Brookmere to Hope, 91.1 kilometres

The final section of the Kettle Valley Railway, the Coquihalla Subdivision, was constructed in July 1916, completing the coast-to-Kootenay connection. The country through the Coquihalla Valley is magnificent and rugged, with high mountains and sheer rock cliffs reaching into the canyon below. It is ironic that Andrew McCulloch named the Coquihalla stations after characters from the plays of Shakespeare, in seemingly vast contrast to the rugged countryside around him. The rail line along this route is nothing more than a narrow ledge tucked up on the side of a steep canyon, with huge bridges and impressive timber trestles. It is no wonder that many stories were generated by the fact that the passenger train happened to travel this section at night thus preventing the passengers from seeing the rocky cliff edges and the canyon far below.

The path carved through the Coquihalla by the Kettle Valley Railway fell silent the winter of 1959, and was shortly thereafter abandoned. However, the Coquihalla again saw activity in 1985 with the construction of the Coquihalla Highway. Following basically the same path as the KVR, the highway consequently faced many similar obstacles such as dealing with both the unforgiving terrain and weather of the Cascade Mountains and with the overly high construction and maintenance costs. A toll booth is operational on the Coquihalla Highway to help cover some of these costs.

Cycling the 91.1 kilometres of the Coquihalla Subdivision from Brookmere to Hope lets you experience the sheer magnificence and harshness of this backcountry. The ride is not entirely easy going, because you are often off the less challenging grade of the railbed. Only half of the total distance cycled is actually upon the railbed itself. The reason for this is that many of the trestles are no longer safe for travel or even standing, some tunnels are collapsed, and at some spots the grade itself has been wiped off the side of the cliff. The main detour routes follow very closely or atop the original KVR grade.

You begin peddling this section from the town of Brookmere along the easy downhill grade toward Brodie. Past Brodie, you begin your ascent to the summit at Coquihalla Station. Impressive views await you all along this none-too-scenic route. Past Coquihalla Summit, the rail bed enters the steep walled Coquhallia canyon. Unfortunately until the permission can be gained to use the route though the canyon, at Coquihailla you will have to detour on the Highway to bypass this section to reconnect at Aurum. After a nice down hill run to Jessica, for now, you have to get back on the Highway to continue your journey to Othello, but things are changing fast, and in short order a trail may be built to avoid the highway.

You leave the highway to rejoin the railbed at Othello and the Quintette Tunnels. This is a truly spectacular spot where the thundering Coquihalla River carves its way through a sheer rock canyon. The railway hangs on the cliff wall, passing through tunnels and crossing over bridges in order

163

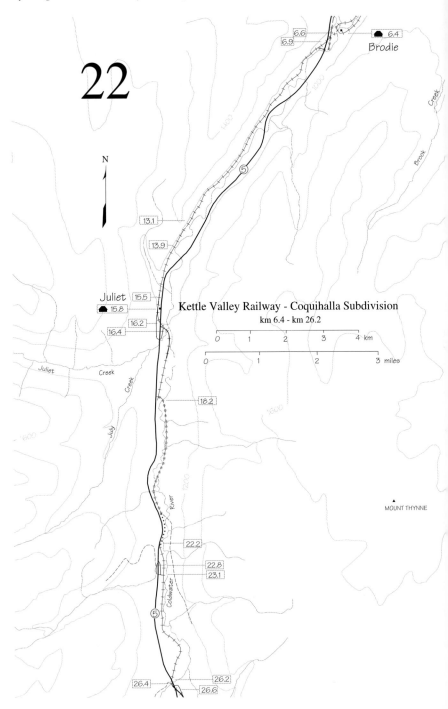

22

N

6.6
6.9
6.4
Brodie

5

13.1

13.9

Juliet 15.5
15.8

Kettle Valley Railway - Coquihalla Subdivision
km 6.4 - km 26.2

16.2
16.4

0   1   2   3   4 km

0   1   2   3 miles

Juliet   Creek

18.2

1600

1200

MOUNT THYNNE

22.2

22.8
23.1

5

26.4   26.2
26.6

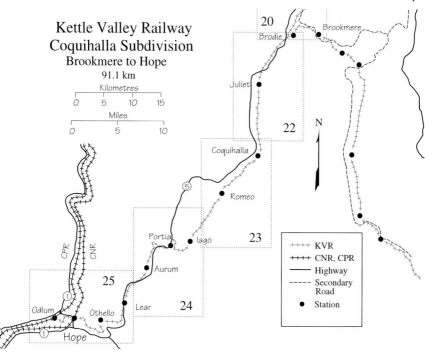

Kettle Valley Railway
Coquihalla Subdivision
Brookmere to Hope
91.1 km

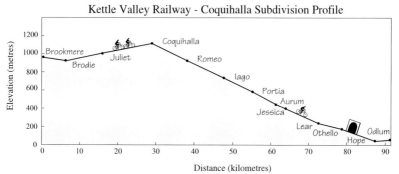

Kettle Valley Railway - Coquihalla Subdivision Profile

IMPORTANT NOTICE

A portion of the railbed in the Coquihalla Subdivision is owned by Trans Mountain Pipeline Company. Presently this portion of the railway is not open to public access (spring 2002). Trails BC is in the process of trying to come to an agreement with Trans Mountain Pipeline Company for the use of the rail bed and portions of the Trans Mountain Pipeline Road as part of the trail. Until such an agreement is reached, anyone who enters on to this section of the rail bed without Trans Mountain Pipline's expressed permission is trespassing. Check the website www.planet.eon.net/~dan/ or www.trailsbc.ca/southwest_region/coquihalla.asp for updates on this situation.

Nicola Valley Explorers E-Team working on the washouts by Juliet, km 13.1.
Photo Murphy Shewchuk.

Bypass trails around second washout, km 13.9.

to share this narrow canyon with the raging Coquihalla River below. Once through the last tunnel, a great cruiser ride awaits you. The railbed is packed gravel lined with a lush growth of coastal vegetation, encouraged by the high rainfall of this area. The railbed leads you to to Hope.

The time needed to cycle this section is one to two days, depending on your ability and endurance level. We strongly recommend taking time to cycle the Coquihalla, a place where two things take your breath away—the excellent scenery and the challenging ride ➤

km	
0.0	**Brookmere Station** ¡1962 ⬛ 👤 🚶 ♂ 🚲0.6

Brookmere Station was the divisional point between the KVR line and the VV&E line. The Coquihalla Agreement of 1913 allowed GNR to use the KVR tracks from Brookmere to Hope for a payment of $150,000 per year. It was felt by some that this healthy payment was all that kept the CPR from abandoning the line in the 1930s. In 1944, GNR had to pay $4.5 million to cancel the agreement after only one GNR train had used the line in September of 1916. This was no doubt the most expensive train ride in the history of railroads. The railbed is easily cycled for the next 18 kilometres, from Brookmere to Juliet except for two washouts at kms 13.1 and 13.9. Check the Merritt Subdivision for a description of the railbed from Brookmere to Brodie.

6.4 Brodie Station ¡1923 ⬛ 🚶 ♂ 🚲0.9

Apex of "the loop," where the railway tracks branch, the Merritt Subdivision going north and the Coquihalla Subdivision going south. The bridge over the Coldwater River heading to Coquihallia is out, continue to follow the loop around and cross the river on the Merritt leg and after crossing the River, back track back on the Bodie Siding Road to reconnect to the Coquihallia section.

6.6 Coldwater River—deck truss ✖33

the west abutment of this bridge had been undermined years ago by the Coldwater River causing the to twist. The bridge was uncrossable and was removed in 2001. The proximity of the Merritt Sub bridge made repairing or replacing this bridge unnecessary. Take the Merritt Sub to cross the river.

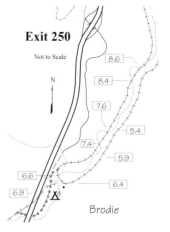

Exit 250

Not to Scale

N

8.6
8.4
7.6
5.4
7.4
5.9
6.6
6.4
6.9

Brodie

6.9 Coquihallia Highway—Bodie Siding Road. ↑

The railbed is lost due to the construction of the highway over it but by detouring on Brodie Siding Road to the south and crossing under the bridge of

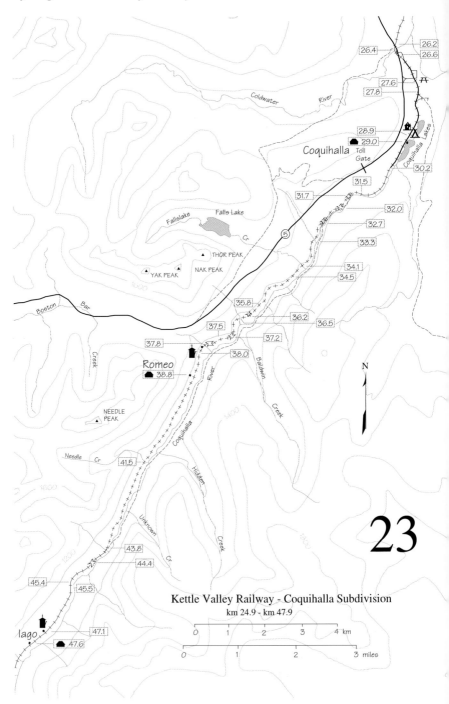

Coldwater River

26.4 | 26.2
26.6
27.6
27.8

28.9
29.0

Coquihalla Toll Gate

30.2

Coquihalla Lakes

31.5
31.7
32.0
32.7
33.3

Fallslake

Falls Lake

Cr

THOR PEAK

YAK PEAK   NAK PEAK

34.1
34.5

35.8

Boston Bar

36.2
36.5

37.5
37.8
37.2
38.0

Romeo
38.8

Creek

Baldwin Creek

N

NEEDLE PEAK

Coquihalla River

Hidden Creek

Needle Cr

41.5

Unknown Cr

43.8
44.4

45.4
45.5

23

Iago

47.1
47.6

Kettle Valley Railway - Coquihalla Subdivision
km 24.9 - km 47.9

0   1   2   3   4 km

0   1   2   3 miles

the highway, the KVR can again be picked up. On the west side of the highway the railbed is great shape all the way to Juliet except for the two washouts at km 13.1 and 13.9. The Coquihalla Highway can be accessed from Brodie by following the Siding Road north alongside the highway to the Larson Hill Exit (Exit 250).

13.1   Major washout →∴

The Coldwater River has washed away 120 metres of the rail bed. A trail has been constructed by the Nicola Valley Explorers Society that climbs the hillside to get around this washout. This trail is steep and can be difficult to climb and descend with a bike in tow. If loaded, two trips may be necessary to get you, your bike and your gear across.

Climbing down the rail bed to the river bed and squeezing between the cliff and the river may be done with some difficulty during low stream levels.

13.9   Major washout part two

Sequel to km 13.1. A excellent trail has been built into the hillside that is approximately level with the original rail grade and can almost be ridden.

15.5   Locked gate

An eight foot-high gate and fence impedes travel on the rail bed. There is a one-way animal gate 400 metres south along the fence that can be used to get out onto the road.

15.8   Juliet Station ⱼ1005 🚉 🏕 ▯ 🚲 0.8

There is very little evidence of Juliet Station, the site being destroyed by the construction of the highway. The original railgrade runs across the highway at this point. There is no way to get through the highway fences in order to follow the railbed.

16.2   Coquihalla Highway (Exit 240) ⚔ ⚑

The KVR crosses the Coquihalla Highway, which cannot be followed, but a small detour through an underpass reconnects back on to the right-of-way on the other side of the highway. The Coldwater River Provincial Park Road, from the Coquihalla Highway, turns on to the original KVR right-of-way to the Coldwater River Provincial Park (deactivated). Following the road south you will find an information sign that describes Andrew McCulloch's work on the Kettle Valley Railway.

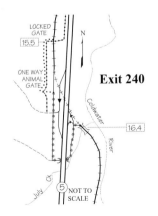

16.4   July Creek ⊼)(

This bridge is now part of the Coldwater River Provincial Park Road.

Tunnel #1 at km 31.7.

Snowshed #15, high above the Coquihalla River, is one of the few sheds still intact, km 45.4.

18.2 KVR rail bed disappears under highway

At this point the road atop the original grade of the KVR has deviated off the grade. Evidence of the grade has been obliviated during highway construction. Here there is a one-way animal gate through the fence that gives access to the highway. The one-way-animal gate is hidden by trees from the 4x4 road. It is before the bend in the river that brings the river against the highway.

The best option is to follow the pipeline and the trail along the highway for 4.1 km to reconnect with the rail bed at km 22.2. This route is to become the official route but does require fording the Coldwater River twice. Stream levels may not allow for this option year round until bridges over the river are built. To access the pipeline right of way follow the 4x4 road a few metres to the where the pipeline crosses the Coldwater River on the left. Ford the Coldwater and follow the trail 2.2 km to the second crossing. 500 metres after fording the river the second time the trail leaves the pipeline trail to follow along side the highway fence for 0.9 km to reconnect to the original KVR rail grade.

22.2 Rail bed emerges from under the highway.

There is no break in the fence to gain access from the highway. The trail along the highway fence connects to the rail grade

22.8 Mine Creek Bridge

Creek bed is easily crossed during dry periods.

23.1 Mine Creek Road (Exit 231)

If coming from the Coquihalla Highway, turn off on to Mine Creek Road and take the underpass under the highway. Note: there is no exit off the highway from the south nor is there an on ramp heading south at Mine Creek Road.

26.2 Short detour

The KVR runs into the high fence along the highway as the rail grade has been over run by the highway. Less then 100 metres down the trail to the south are the twin highway bridges and the KVR bridge that span the Coldwater River. The highway bridges can be walked under to regain the railway at the north end of the KVR bridge over the Coldwater River.

26.4 Coldwater River

The KVR loops briefly on the west side of the Coquihalla Highway. The old railway bridge still exists as a road bridge on Exit 228 on the west side of the highway.

Exit 231

N

22.2

22.8

23.1

NOT TO SCALE

26.6   Coquihalla Lakes Exit (Exit 228)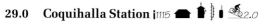

The KVR heads back across to the other side of the highway. Take the overpass across to the other side to reconnect to the rail bed. The road to the Coquihalla Summit Provincial Recreation Area turns onto the KVR and passes Briton Creek Rest Area.

27.6   Britton Creek Rest Area

Rest area with indoor shelter, washrooms and a seasonal concession stand.

27.8   Coquihalla wye

28.9   Coquihalla Lakes Lodge

29.0   Coquihalla Station 1115

Both the station and water tower foundations can be found along the east side of the railbed, beside Coquihalla Lakes.

30.2   Gate

This is the beginning of the Trans Mountain Pipeline Road through the Coquihallia Canyon. This road travels along the same route as the railway; the road bed is atop the KVR at some points and branches away at others. The road reconnects with the Coquihalla Highway at km 54.5.

At the time of writing (Spring 2002) the KVR in the Coquihalla Canyon is owned by Trans Mountain Pipeline and is not open to the public. Use of this road without Transmountain Pipeline's express permission is trespassing. Negotiations are underway between Transmountain Pipeline and Trails BC and an agreement on use of this corridor is expected in the Summer of 2002. Inclusion of this section in this book is not intended to promote the use of Trans Mountain Pipeline's property but is only preparatory to an agreement on the use of this corridor for cyclists. Until such time take the Coquihailla Highway to Carolyn Mines Road (km 51.7)

31.7   Tunnel #1 66

The pipeline road branches from the railbed just prior to a 66 metre-long tunnel. The railbed is impassable past this point to km 43.8.

32.0   Tunnel #2 85

32.7   Tunnel #3 55

33.1   Frame trestle 46

33.3   Frame trestle 123

On September 28, 1969, as part of a demolition exercise by the Canadian Armed Forces, this trestle was blown up.

Exit 228 ⑤

NOT TO SCALE

26.2

26.4

Coldwater

River

N

Britton Creek Rest Area

27.6

34.1   Falls Lake Creek ✝123
        The white lace of Bridalveil Falls and the rugged rock walls use to pro-
        vide a dramatic backdrop for the deck lattice girder bridge and frame
        trestle approaches of Falls Creek Trestle. In 1996 the northern frame
        trestle approach collapsed with the remaining bridge and approaches
        following soon after.

34.5   Tack Creek ✝96
        Frame trestle replaced by steel in 1954—the steel trestle towers remain.

35.8   Filled 89 metre-long frame trestle.

36.2   Tunnel #4—collapsed ◼76
        The line was diverted around this tunnel in 1959 after a slide blocked
        the entrance.

36.5   Frame trestle ✝192

37.2   Tunnel #5—collapsed ◼93

37.3   Frame trestle. ✝41

37.5   Frame trestle. ✝59

37.8   Tunnel #6—collapsed ◼67

37.9   Romeo water tower ♜

38.0   Frame trestle ✝101

38.8   Romeo Station ┇924 ◼ ┊ 🚴2.1

41.5   Needle Creek ✝98
        The bridge construction used to cross this creek was a through arch
        span on concrete towers with 15 and 18 metre deck lattice girder ap-
        proaches. This was the longest clear span on the KVR, at a length of 98
        metres. In 1981, the bridge was dismantled for its steel.

43.8   Pipeline road rejoins KVR grade ┤←┊

44.4   Tunnel #7 ◼50
        The road passes through this steel-lined tunnel.

45.4   Snowshed #15
        The road passes around this 98 metre-long concrete snowshed. Origi-
        nally, 15 snowsheds existed between km 38.3 and km 45.4, but with
        improved snow removal equipment, only five of the snowsheds re-
        mained during the final operation of this line.

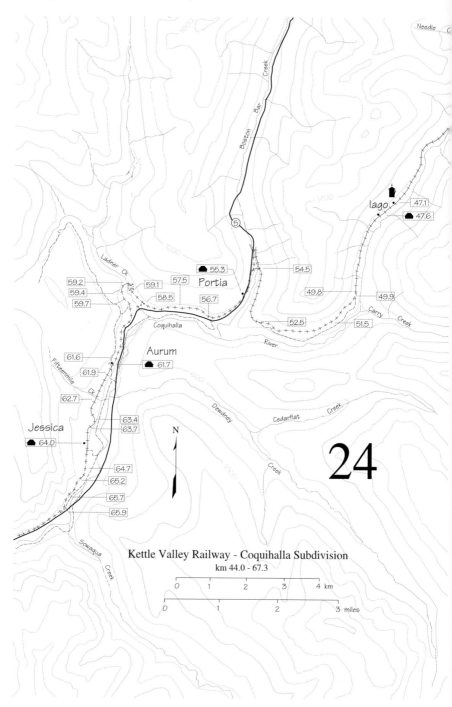

Kettle Valley Railway - Coquihalla Subdivision
km 44.0 - 67.3

24

45.5   A rock retaining wall can be found here. Like many others along the KVR, these walls were constructed by stone masons, who fitted the stones without the use of mortar. This mortar-free construction enabled water to drain between the stones, rather than build up a pressure that could possibly overturn the wall.

47.1   Iago water tower

47.6   Iago Station ¡739

49.8   Pipeline road leaves KVR grade

Just as the road leaves the relatively flat rail bed and heads down a steep hill an indistinct trail on the right continues on a level path. This narrow single track trail is just over 100 metres long and widens out on to the original railbed. The trail on the rail bed is a single track that winds it's way around rocks, fallen trees and saplings growing on the rail bed.

49.9   Frame trestle 37

A trail bypasses this missing trestle

51.5   Deck plate girder bridge 49

The abutments and towers remain for this bridge as a single track trail now runs along the edge of the hillside to bypass this missing bridge.

52.5   Pipeline road rejoins KVR grade.

High above the Coquihalla River on the trail, km 52.0.

54.5   Boston Bar Creek Bridge ⊬ *106* Y

A 24 metre deck plate girder with 46 and 36 metre-long frame trestle approaches. Foundations are all that's left to find.

The pipeline road branches from the railbed at this point and follows one of the arms of the Portia Station wye as it heads up the side of Boston Bar Creek. The road then connects with the Coquihalla Highway at the Portia Exit (Exit 202). The highway must then be followed south, as the KVR can not be reaccessed until Carolyn Mines Road at km 61.6.

55.3   Portia Station ¡*584* ◼ ⅃ Ⱶ ⅃ ❘ 🚵 *2.2*

An oval sign, with the picture of a steam engine and the station name "Portia," can be found on the Coquihalla Highway acknowledging the historic Kettle Valley Railway and the close proximity of the Portia Station site to the Coquihalla Highway. The KVR crosses the highway at this point and it is difficult, if not impossible, to follow because highway construction has obliterated most of the right-of-way. As the highway heads downhill toward Hope the remains of a ledge that was the KVR can be seen on the hillside.

The wye at this station was primarily used for turning snowplows that operated on this slide prone section between here and Coquihalla Station. The heavy snow conditions of the Coquihalla made this section the most difficult to manage in the winter. The KVR utilized rotary plows, wing plows, 15 snowsheds and numerous men with shovels. The rotary plows were often ineffective, as the snowslides usually contained rock and trees that could destroy the cutting blades. With the advent of bulldozers for snow removal, the CPR was able to eliminate all but five of the original snowsheds.

56.7   Frame trestle ⊬ *34*
Filled in 1954

57.5   Frame trestle ⊬ *108*

58.5   Trail from Highway #3 Bridge over Ladner Creek Bridge ⚶

Just northeast of the highway bridge over Ladner Creek is a trail that leads up the hillside to the rail bed. 600 metres down the rail bed is the east portal of Ladner Creek Tunnel (Tunnel #8). Although the rail bed is in ridable condition to the tunnel there is no where else to go but to retrace your tracks back to the trail.

59.1   Tunnel #8—collapsed ◼*56*

Todd Barker and a dedicated crew of individuals have built a trail over the collapsed tunnel. This trail is very steep and hangs on the edges of the cliffs.

59.2   Ladner Creek Bridge)(*170*

The last spike ceremony was held near the east end of Ladner Creek Bridge. The Coquihalla Subdivision was officially opened on July 31,

1916. The ties on the bridge deck have not fared well in recent years and rot has made them increasingly unsafe to cross.

The railway bridge can be seen from Highway #5 looking up the valley from the highway bridge across Ladner Creek.

59.4   Frame trestle. ✝41

This trestle and the next pile trestle have rotted in place. Any sections of these two trestles still standing are extremely soft with rot and unsafe.

59.5   Pile trestle. ✝14

59.7   Twenty Mile Creek—deck plate girder. ✝40

This missing bridge effectively stops further exploration south on the rail bed.

61.6   Tangent Creek ✝89

Filled in 1956 and washed out November 24th, 1959. The washout of this filled-in trestle was never repaired and contributed to the Coquihalla Subdivision's demise.

61.7   Aurum Station—Carolyn Mines Road i444 🚂 ✝ ⬧ 🚴1.9 ⬅

An oval sign on the highway marks the close proximity of the Aurum Station site to the Coquihalla Highway. The grade can be found by taking the Caroline Mines Exit and following it up a steep climb to where the two cross. South, the rail bed heads towards Jessica and was rebuilt for logging access. North the railbed is overgrown and not passible.

61.9   Frame trestle. ✝13

This trestle is bypassed by the logging road.

62.7   Fifteen Mile Creek—frame trestle ✝68

The bridge was replaced when the rail bed was rebuilt as a logging road. The bridge deck is made of two CN flat cars laid side by side.

63.4   Pile trestle. ✝55

Bypassed by the logging road.

63.7   Snowshoe Creek—frame trestle. ✝110

Bypassed by the logging road.

64.0   Jessica Station i398 🚂 🚩 ⬧ 🚴1.8 ➡

An oval sign on the highway marks the close proximity of the Jessica Station site to the Coquihalla Highway. The station foundation can be found alongside of the railbed. Past Jessica the rail bed again becomes overgrown. A gravel road leaves the rail bed just past Jessica and heads down hill to connect with the Jessica access road running north - south. North the road connects to Carolyn Mines Road, south on the road connects to the Coquihallia Highway just after the highway crosses the Coquihallia River.

Work by local trail groups is underway to clear and fix the rail bed south of this point.

64.7   Frame trestle. ⋊ 32

64.8   Frame trestle. ⋊ 110

65.2   Frame trestle. ⋊ 73

65.7   Frame trestle. ⋊ 14

65.9   Coquihalla Highway

The railbed lies mostly to the right (west) of the highway from this point until Lear. Highway construction has disrupted most of the rail grade from here to Lear but if you keep a close watch to the right you will see pieces of the grade still clinging on the hill sides. Plans are to take the trail to the east side of the highway but bridges over the Coquihallia River will have to be built in order to have a continuous route. Until that time the only option is to ride the shoulder of the highway to Othello Road (Exit 183, km74.6)

68.4   Eleven Mile Creek—frame trestle ⋊ 89

69.2   Pile trestle ⋊ 14

The beginning of the end occurred here on November 23, 1959. It had been raining hard the last two days so when the call came in that a washout had occurred north of Lear, it was not an unusual occurrence. After all, this was the Coquihalla and washouts were the norm. Repair crews were dispatched and a work train headed south from Brookmere. On arriving, it was discovered that not just one washout had occurred, but four separate major washouts had happened. While the immensity of the damage swamped the small army of workers, work started immediately on repairing the washouts. The next day another major washout happened at Tangent Creek. Up and down the line dozens of washouts took out the railbed that week. All told, the damage to the line exceeded $250,000. Work to repair and improve the line continued till winter forced a halt until spring. But spring did not see a renewed continuance in the work. The Coquihalla Canyon fell quiet. On January 9th, 1961, the CPR announced that because of the cost of repairs, the decision had been made to abandon the line, so the fate of the Coquihalla Subdivision was sealed. The rails and ties were removed. Nature took care of the rest.

69.3   Ten Mile Creek—filled frame trestle. ⋊ 37

72.7   Lear Station i238 ⬛ ⫙ ⫙ 🚲1.0

An oval sign on the highway marks the close proximity of the Lear Station site to the Coquihalla Highway. Lear Station was situated on the south side of the aerial tramway, but highway construction has removed any trace of the site.

74.6   Coquihalla Highway—Othello Road ⊩ Δ ⊩←

The KVR can be reaccessed by turning off the Coquihalla Highway (Exit 183) on to Othello Road toward the Coquihalla Canyon Provincial Recreation Area (Quintette Tunnels). Othello Road runs atop the original grade to the Provincial Recreation Area. Following the recreation area road keeps you on top of the KVR. An information plaque is found just after exiting the highway. It describes the engineering achievement of Andrew McCulloch in the construction of the Quintette Tunnels. Othello Tunnels Campground is also found along this road, just a short distance from the tunnels.

78.7   **Othello Station** ℹ176 🚌 ⫚ ⟟ ⊩ ▮ 🚐 ▮ ⚲1.5

Less than 10 kilometres from Hope, McCulloch faced a near impossible challenge. The Coquihalla River had cut a horseshoe path through a 91 metre-deep, straight-walled, narrow canyon. There was barely enough room for the river, and certainly no extra room for a railway. Confronted with this challenge, McCulloch and several fellow engineers surveyed the canyon from small woven baskets suspended down into the canyon by ropes from the cliff tops above. After several weeks, McCulloch engineered a perfect tangent alignment of tunnels, later known as the Quintette Tunnels.

In the fall of 1981, the area from Hope to Othello became the site for the filming of the movie *Rambo-First Blood*. The Coquihalla Canyon around the Quintette Tunnels (known as Chapman Gorge in the movie) is where Rambo (Sylvester Stallone) clung for his life on the rock walls above the rushing waters of the Coquihalla River.

Although called the "Quintette" tunnels, there are actually only four as the third tunnel was partially "day-lighted," giving the illusion of five. This section of the KVR through the narrow Coquihalla Canyon has been designated as the Coquihalla Canyon Provincial Recreation Area.

79.6   Tunnel #10 ▮200

Although Tunnel #9 was originally planned, it was never constructed.

79.7   Tunnel #11 ▮30

79.8   Coquihalla River)(23

It's hard to believe, but each autumn salmon struggle against the torrent meltwaters that funnel through this narrow gorge to find their way to spawning grounds.

79.9   Tunnel #12 ▮123

This tunnel is partially open—"day-lighted"—on its north side, creating the illusion of actually being two tunnels.

80.0   Coquihalla River.)(53

80.1   Tunnel #13 ▮101

Past the last tunnel, this next section is incredibly refreshing, not just for the excellent railbed and the welcome downhill grade, but as you cycle, the sights and smells of heavy coastal vegetation envelop you.

The Quintette Tunnels at Othello, km 78.7, were cut in tangent alignment despite the twisting nature of the narrow Coquihalla Canyon.

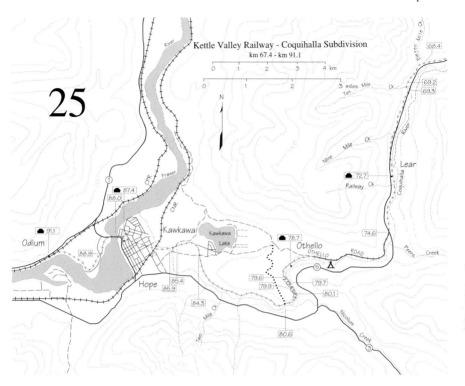

Kettle Valley Railway - Coquihalla Subdivision
km 67.4 - km 91.1

25

80.6   Nicola Valley Trail. 🚶

84.3   Kawkawa Lake Road ⅄

Kawkawa was a former flagstop on the Kettle Valley Railway. The
Kawkawa Lake Road intersecting the KVR can be followed west into
Hope. Following the road east will lead you back to Othello.
    The trail continues to follow a top the original rail grade across the
road.

85.1   Sucker Creek Fish Enhancement Area ⊢→⁞

The trail leaves the rail bed and runs parallel to the original grade. The
railgrade for the next couple of hundred metres makes a cut which has
been utilized as a gravel stream canal for spanning salmon. The trail
gets back onto the railgrade just before it comes to Union Bar Road.

85.4   Union Bar Road ⅄ ⊢→⁞

The bridge over the Coquihallia River has been removed. Take Union
Bar Road south (left) to Kawkawa Lake Road and turn west (right) across
the road bridge across the Coquihalla River.

85.9   Coquihalla River ✟115 ⛺

As you follow Kawkawa Lake Road into Hope, you first cross the Coquihalla River. Immediately after crossing the river a picnic site is on the

north, and Coquihalla Campsite, a large campsite with many services, is on the south. The trail is signed through Hope to downtown Hope starting at the picnic site on the west side of the bridge as the railgrade is not easily followed through Hope.

87.4   Hope Station i44 ▄ ▮ ⌿ Υ Λ 🏛 ⌂ ▮ (▮ 🐊 0.3

Just as at Penticton, many locomotives were based at Hope to be used primarily in "helper" service on the heavy grade up through the Coquihalla Pass. This was basically the terminus of the Coquihalla Subdivision, with the remaining line constructed in order to connect to the CPR main line.

Little evidence remains of the once active station at Hope. The railway is not easily found or followed. What you will still find is the original VV&E railway station that was built in 1916 by the Great Northern Railway. Over the years it served as a station for the Canadian National Railway. In 1985, the abandoned building was moved from its site at the corner of Hudson Bay Street and Fifth Avenue to the junction of Highways #1 and #3, now called the Rainbow Junction. The station retains its original look, but now houses a restaurant, a retail outlet and Hope's art centre. This is the last train station of its design in existence.

Past Hope there is not much left of the original KVR. The only section that can be cycled is a short 700 metre-long section from Lanstrom Road back to the Fraser River Bridge.

🚂🚃 Hope Museum 🚃🚂
(919 Water Avenue, 869-7322)

88.0   Fraser River Bridge Ӿ 290

This bridge consists of four 72.5 metre-long, double-deck through truss spans, making the total length 290 metres. The upper deck is still being used by motorized vehicles crossing the Fraser River. The lower deck was used by the Kettle Valley Railway to cross the Fraser River and connect to the CPR main line at Odlum. The cross ties of the lower deck have been removed and the bridge barricaded with a fence.

88.9   Lanstrom Road ⌃

Thick coastal plant life envelops the KVR from Lanstrom Road back to the Fraser River Bridge, turning the right-of-way into a beautiful tree-covered lane. West from Lanstrom Road, plant life has reclaimed the KVR where land developers have yet to remove the grade for housing projects.

91.1   Odlum Station ▮ i55

Odlum was originally named Petain after a World War I French army hero, but in 1940 was renamed Odlum after the head of Canada's overseas forces. It was decided to change the name after Petain sided with the pro-Nazis. Odlum was the terminal point of the KVR track, connecting the KVR main line with the CPR main line. The Canadian Pacific Railway main line continues to Vancouver. 🚃

Columbia & Western Railway (C&W)
(Boundary Pathway)
Castlegar to Midway, 162.3 kilometres

The C&W was originally chartered in 1896 by Fritz Heinze, with the objective to ensure a reliable connection between his smelter in Trail and the markets, without having his hands tied by either Daniel Corbin with the Spokane Falls & Northern Railway or the Columbia & Kootenay Steam & Navigation Company. His planned route was to Penticton, but if dissatisfied with the connection there to the CPR, he planned to take his railway to the coast. In spite of his grand plans, Heinze sold the C&W to CPR in 1898. CPR started construction from Castlegar in 1898, reaching Grand Forks in September of 1899. By 1900 the line reached Midway, with a spur line from Eholt to Phoenix, and a spur from Eholt to the Emma mine. A branch line was built to Deadwood, running behind the smelter at Anaconda. In 1992 the line was abandoned and the tracks removed.

Cycling the C&W is a spectacular experience. The right-of-way hangs on mountainsides and boundless vistas spread out below your wheels. Long tunnels and huge rock retaining walls help to keep the railbed glued to the cliffs. Views of Lower Arrow Lake and Christina Lake seem to go on forever. This is a trip that takes you far off the beaten path and into the wilderness. Between the three major centres, Castlegar, Grand Forks and Midway, the railbed does not follow the same valleys as the roads, thus leading the cyclist into backcountry not normally ventured into. This has to be taken into account before riding this railway, as there are very few access points along most of the C&W.

Starting at the C&W Station in downtown Castlegar, you find that the tracks remain and are still in use from the Castlegar Station to km 8.8. From km 8.8, the railway climbs at a grade greater than 2% to the summit at Farron. En route to Farron, the railway passes through the 916 metre-long Bull Dog Tunnel, connecting Pup Creek and Dog Creek valleys.

From Farron, the C&W follows the narrow McRae Creek Canyon down to Christina Lake. The creek falls faster than the railway, and leaves the railbed high on the canyon wall. In a downhill rush the railway finally bottoms out at Cascade, where it begins a slow climb to Grand Forks. The railbed is in great shape until Cascade, where it turns up the Kettle River Valley. Here to Grand Forks the rail bed was removed to install a gas pipeline and the original rail bed was replaced with a urban style gravel path.

Past Grand Forks, the C&W climbs to Eholt before descending into Midway. Although the railbed to Eholt is in excellent shape, the section from Eholt to Midway can have some weed growth on it in spots, but rarely does it inhibit cycling on it. Most of the problem areas are adjacent to pasture land and access has been restricted to motorized traffic ━

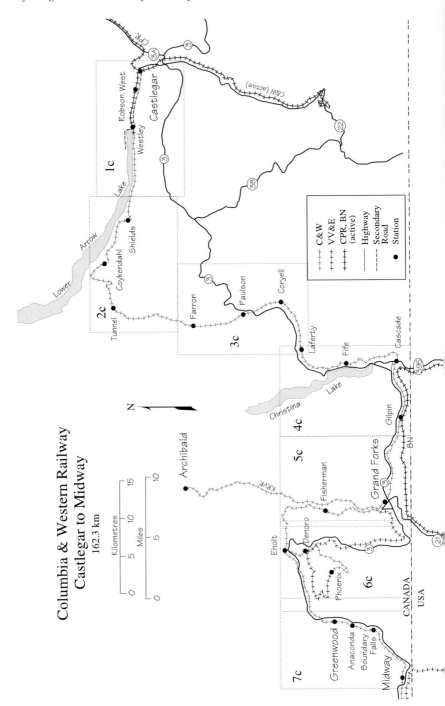

Columbia & Western Railway
Castlegar to Midway
162.3 km

Castlegar Station has been restored and serves as Castlegar's museum, km 0.0.

km   **Castlegar Station** i439 ⬛ 🏠 ⏸ 🍴 Ⅴ 🎯 ⛺ 🏛 🚻 🛈 🛤 ⊙ 🛈 🚲 0.9 →⌐

0.0   In 1902, the CPR completed a railway bridge across the Columbia River enabling the rail-lines to be linked between the Columbia and Kootenay, the Columbia and Western, and the Kettle Valley railways. Thus began the history of Castlegar.

     Although the original station burned to the ground in 1906, it was immediately replaced and remains one of the best preserved in the province. The station at Castlegar was moved from the middle of the wye intersection 100 metres east, to the corner of 13th Avenue and 3rd Street. Restored, it now serves as the Castlegar Museum. A detour down Arrow Lakes Drive to km 8.8 is required to bypass the still active section of the railway.

IMPORTANT NOTICE

At the time of writing (spring 2002), the railbed from Castlegar to Christina Lake is the property of the Trans Canada Trail Foundation (TCT). Local rails-to-trails organizations and the Provincial Government are in the process of trying to come to an agreement with TCT for the transfer of this right-of-way to public lands. Until such a transfer, anyone who enters on to this railgrade without TCT's express permission is trespassing. The inclusion of this section in this book is not intended to promote the use of TCT's property but is only preparatory to the transfer of these lands to public hands. Before venturing on to this right-of-way check with the TCT or the Boundary Rails-to-Trails Society as to the ownership status of the railbed.

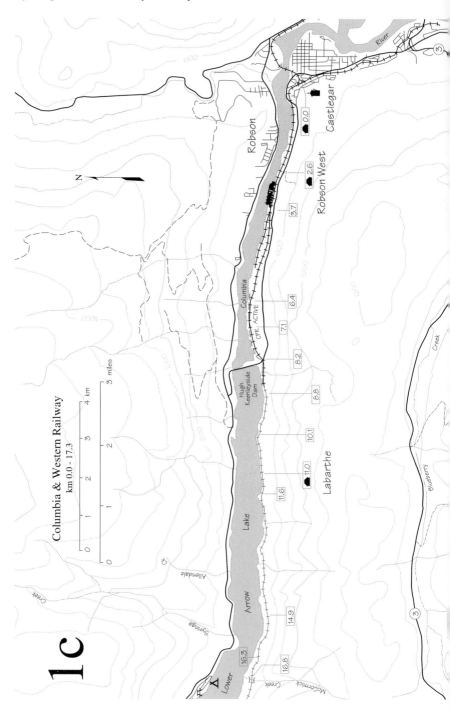

Columbia & Western Railway
km 0.0 - 17.3

Castlegar Museum
13th Ave. & 3rd St., 365-6440

2.6   Robson West Station ┆430 🚂 🚃 ┆ ┃ 🚵1.0

Robson West was the terminus of Heinze's C&W from Trail. Barges would ferry the train up Lower Arrow Lake to connect to the CPR.

3.8   Kraft Station 🚂 🚃 ┃ ⸝

This station came into existence when the Celgar Pulp Mill was built.

7.1   Westley Station ┃ 🚂

In 1964, a revision in the railway at this point was required owing to the construction of the Hugh Keenleyside Dam. The revision moved 5.6 kilometres of the line higher onto the hillside, bypassing the former station of Labarthe and the Labarthe Tunnel.

8.2   Arrow Lakes Drive ⸝

A small side road leads along the tracks to their end.

8.8   Locked gate across right-of-way—end of side road ┆←⸝

Access the railbed here. From here to km 10.1 the rails are still in place, but are now filled in with ballast.

10.1   End of ballast-filled rails

Some loose ballast from the end of the rails to km 16.3 can make cycling a little more difficult. As you climb the rail grade your views of Lower Arrow Lake will be of numerous log booms and a few tug boats awaiting their turn for the Celgar Pulp Mill.

11.6   Labarthe Tunnel ◼57

The current line bypasses the tunnel, which is submerged under Lower Arrow Lake during spring run off. Labarthe Station, at km 11.0 on the bypassed line, utilized a turntable for turning around helper engines that were required for the steep grade to Farron.

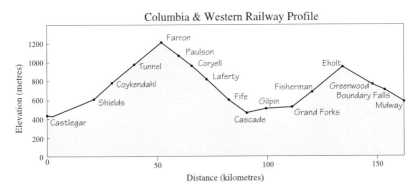

Columbia & Western Railway Profile

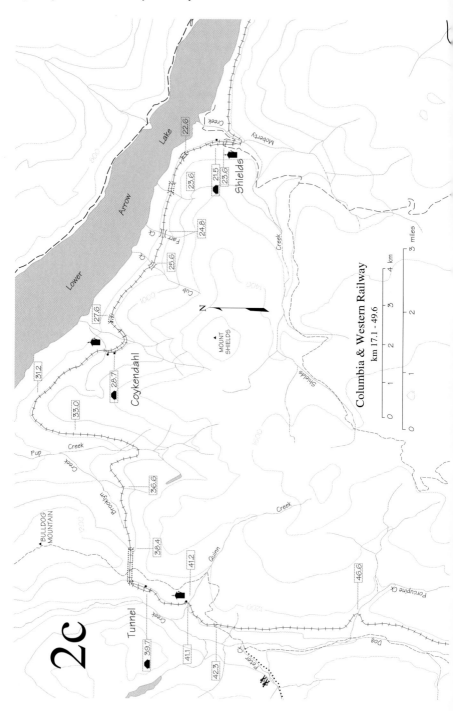

Columbia & Western Railway
km 17.1 - 49.6

14.9   Washout

A single track path up to the south skirts around this 50 metre-long washout. As you follow the rail bed you can't help but notice how for most of the way from Castlegar to Tunnel you hang upon the cliff as the valley seems to get farther and farther below. Helping to hold the railway on to the cliff are extensive rock retaining walls. Many of these massive walls are constructed of granite, finely crafted by Italian stone masons.

16.3   Loose ballast ends.

16.8   McCormack Creek Bridge   )(125x58

Five deck plate girders carried the railway over McCormack Creek.

21.2   Shields Creek Forest Service Road ⊤

Thirteen kilometres south on this road connects to Highway #3 400 metres east of the junction of Highways #3 and #3A.

21.5   Shields Station ¡609 🚂 ♠ ⸙ ⸗ ⚙⚡2.1

A large open area is all that is left of Shields Station.

22.6   Tunnel 🔲50

23.6   Tunnel 🔲118

24.8   Farr Creek)(102

A 65 metre-long through truss with deck plate approaches crosses Farr Creek.

25.6   Cub Creek—deck plate girders.)(125

27.6   Coykendahl Tunnel 🔲89

Enter this tunnel a little cautiously as the curvature makes for total blackness in the centre, and the railbed gets a little rough in places.

28.1   Coykendahl siding ⸙

28.7   Coykendahl Station ¡778 🚂 ◊ ⚙⚡1.3

A tuscan red shed built into the side of the hill remains at this station.

29.0   Coykendahl water tower. ♠

31.2   Rockfall

A path leads through this 40 metre-long rockfall.

33.0   Small rockfall

36.6   Major washout

Single track on top of what's left of a large fill that spans a tributary of Brooklyn Creek.

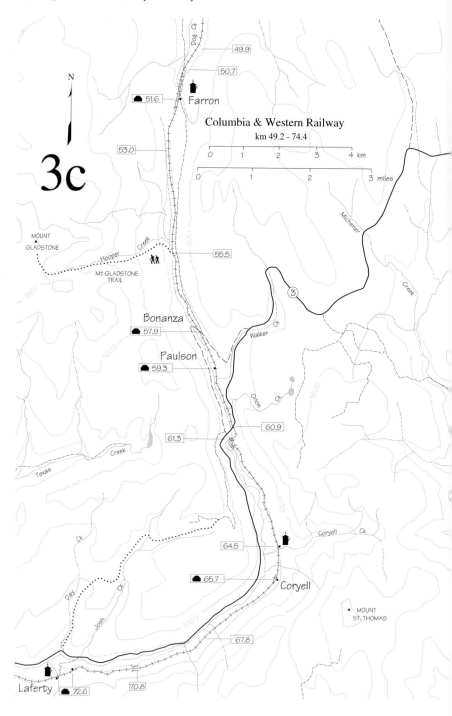

N

3c

Columbia & Western Railway
km 49.2 - 74.4

38.2 A small 4x4 road follows Brooklyn Creek down to the town site of Brooklyn.

Brooklyn

In the spring of 1898, William Parker's mining claim opposite Deer Park on the shores of Lower Arrow Lake became the construction headquarters of the C&W. In the three months of June, July and August, the town of Brooklyn came to life. By September, Brooklyn boasted 16 hotels, a hospital and stores supplying goods from boots to wholesale liquor. But before the year had ended the residents and businesses were leaving Brooklyn in droves for greener pastures farther down the line. By the next summer Brooklyn was little more than a ghost town.

38.4 Bulldog Tunnel 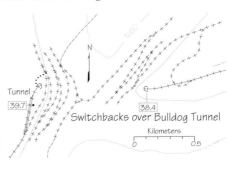 912

During the construction of this tunnel, a series of switchbacks carried the line over the top of the tunnel. Over a distance of 8.2 kilometres, a 4% grade up six legs of switchbacks took the trains up 155 metres to the summit, then a 4% grade down six legs of switchbacks brought the trains back down 123 metres to reconnect with the line. The switchbacks can be found by following the old telegraph line up, north of the west portal of the tunnel. The tunnel itself cuts a straight line from east to west with a slight hook at the west end. Travelling from west to east is preferable because once around the corner you just walk toward the light at the other end, but coming from the east you walk in total darkness for almost the total length of the tunnel. The east end of the tunnel almost always has water cascading down the side of the entrance.

39.7 Tunnel Station ¡980 ⬛ ⁞ 🚲 1.9

The station foundation can still be found, as well as an apple tree overlooking Dog Creek Valley. This spot would make a reasonable campsite except for the absence of a reliable water source.

41.1 Water tank 🏭

41.2 Quinn Creek

A large fill crosses the creek.

42.3 Dog Creek Trail—Peter Lake Trail 🥾 ⛺.

Dog Creek Trail follows along the shore of Dog Creek and reconnects with the railbed at km 49.9. Peter Lake Trail leaves Dog Creek Trail at the confluence of Peter Creek and Dog Creek and follows Peter Creek for eight kilometres to a beautiful lake surrounded by steep mountainsides.

Farron, km 51.6.

Poulson Bridge (Highway #3) crosses high above the railgrade, km 60.9.

46.6   Porcupine Creek

The large curved trestle that originally spanned this canyon was later replaced by fill when upgraded by the CPR.

49.9   Water flows have carved channels in the railbed.

50.9   Dog Creek Trail 🚶

51.6   **Farron Station** ⌐1212 🚗 🛏 🍴 Y 🚲1.8

Named after one of the railway construction engineers, Farron was the summit station of the Monashee Mountains and a turning point for helper locomotives. Along with the station house, the foundations of three other residences can be discovered here. The most prominent remaining item is the concrete diesel cistern alongside the rail bed.

53.0   Bomb monument

At this spot in 1924 a bomb planted on a passenger train exploded, killing nine people including Peter Verigin, leader of the Doukhobors. A small monument remains west of and adjacent to the rail bed.

55.5   Mount Gladstone Trail 🚶

57.3   Bonanza siding—Paulson Detour Road ⌐

Paulson Detour Road accesses Highway #3.

59.3   **Paulson Station** ⌐1074 🚗 🍴 🛏B X^B 🚲1.4

As work on the railway moved to Grand Forks, the Paulson Brothers established a hotel, store and stables here. Once the railway was completed, the hotel sitting alongside the railway became known as Paulson Station. Later a siding was added at km 57.3 to service ore shipments from the Bonanza mine and the station was sometimes referred to as Bonanza Siding. A stone foundation and the remains of other buildings along the banks of McRae Creek can be found.

The flat valley bottom alongside the railbed, with McRae Creek meandering through it, makes the area around Paulson a beautiful spot to set up a backcountry campsite.

60.9   Highway #3 Overpass

There is no access to the highway at this point, as the highway bridge passes high above the rail grade.

61.1   Snowshed site

This was the site of the longest snowshed on the C&W. The abutments in the hill side and timbers in the canyon are all that remains.

61.3   Paulson Tunnel ⬛111

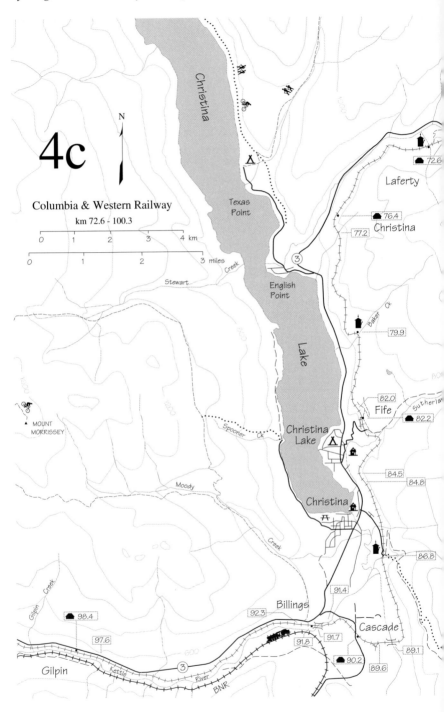

4c

N

Columbia & Western Railway
km 72.6 - 100.3

0   1   2   3   4 km

0   1   2   3 miles

Christina

Texas
Point

English
Point

Lake

Stewart

Creek

MOUNT
MORRISSEY

Spooner   Ck

Christina
Lake

Moody

Creek

Gilpin

Gilpin   Creek

Kettle

River

BNR

Laferty

Christina

72.6

76.4

77.2

Baker   Ck

79.9

82.0

Fife

Sutherla

82.2

84.5

84.8

Christina

86.8

91.4

Billings

92.3

Cascade

91.8   91.7

90.2   89.1

89.6

98.4

97.6

63.1   Rock retaining wall—another of the numerous retaining walls along this stretch of the Columbia & Western Railway.

64.5   Water tower 🏠

65.7   Coryell Station i*968* 🏠 🏠 2.2

The town of Coryell was founded in 1898 under the name of Gladstone. Gladstone sprung up from the news that the construction on the railway had begun at Castlegar and that Gladstone would be one of the stations on route. The railway was not the only reason for the town. Burnt Basin, about two kilometres from the town site, had been staked by miners as early as 1896. News of the possible mining riches in the area contributed to the influx of miners to the area at the same time the railway was being constructed.

At its height the town boasted four hotels, three general stores, a restaurant and bakery, livery stables and a dance hall. In the summer of 1899 the town's population jumped as track layers came through town, but by the beginning of 1900 the town had shrunk to one hotel and the railway station. On January 8, 1900, the station was renamed Coryell after John A. Coryell, the engineer who made the first surveys for a coast-to-Kootenay line.

Today little remains of the town except the station foundations and a red railway shed sitting off to the side of the rail bed.

70.8   Snowslide bridge)(*41*

72.6   Lafferty Station i*820* 🏠 2.2

Lafferty Station was named for a Rossland bank manager.

73.0   Lafferty Road ⵏ

Lafferty Road (a 4x4 road) makes a steep descent down to Highway #3.

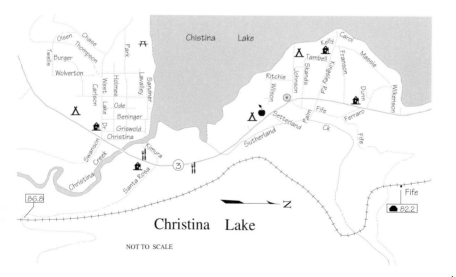

Christina Lake

NOT TO SCALE

195

Looking out to Christina Lake, km 76.0.

A wooden ore bin for a large lime quarry at Fife, km 82.0.

73.1   Lafferty water tower. ☗

76.5   Christina

Christina was a former flagstop named for Christina Lake. Large concrete rock retaining wall overlooks English Cove on Christina Lake.

79.7   Water tower ☗

Concrete foundation blocks remain.

82.0   Wooden ore bin for a large lime quarry here at Fife. ✕

82.2   Fife Station ⏀599 ⬤ ☗ ╱ ⫟ 𝕏 ⬕ ⬙ ⫟ ⬗ ⊛ ⬙ ⏀1.9

A small tuscan red section shed serves to mark the location of Fife. Two six foot-high fences line Fife Road with pedestrian walk throughs. Unfortunately, a bike will not fit through the openings. Bikes have to be tossed over the fences. Past Fife, the railbed becomes increasingly weedy, although the high traffic volume of cyclists from Christina Lake usually keeps twin tracks clear through the weeds.

1.9 steep, downhill kilometres on Fife Road will take you to Highway #3 and Christina Lake where most amenities can be found. Across the intersection of Fife Road and Highway #3 is Wildways Adventure Sports and Tours, which is the local bicycle repair shop. If you don't feel like tackling the steepness of Fife Road on the return journey, take Santa Rosa Road, 1.6 kilometres south on Highway #3, from Fife Road, which is not quite as steep.

84.5   Rock Retaining Wall

Spectacular views of Christina Lake and the town of Christina

84.8   Rock Retaining Wall

86.5   Water tank ☗ ⫞

A four-car siding was situated here.

86.8   Santa Rosa Road—Dewdney Trail ⫟ ⬕ 𝕏⬙ ⫟ 🏃 🚵.

The overpass that was here was removed in 1992 and replaced with a fill. A slight detour around the west side of the fill is required to reconnect to the railbed. Santa Rosa Road connects with Highway #3 and the town site of Christina, 1.3 kilometres down the hill.

The historic Dewdney Trail also crosses the railbed at this point, although mostly overgrown sections of it east of the railbed can be hiked and in some places ridden. Refer to Mike Wisnicki's *Over the Hill* for more information.

88.5   Texas gate

89.1   Kettle River.)(154

This six deck plate girder span bridge once had frame trestle approaches that have since been filled in.

The rock retaining wall holds the C&W high on the mountainside above Christina Lake, km 85.0.

Passing bikes over the fence at Fife, km 82.2.

In 2000, B.C Gas tore up the railgrade from here to Grand Forks to install a pipeline. The historic railgrade was replaced with an urban style crushed gravel trail. Some will find this section very tiring, particularly if loaded down, due to the constant grade changes. Bypassing this section using, Highway #3, by non supported cyclists is a common sight. Since the stable bed of the railway was removed the longevity of this section of the trail remains to be seen.

89.6   Cascade wye.

90.2   **Cascade Station** i463 ⛺ ⚊ ⛺ ♿ 0.5

Highway #395 crosses the C&W at the site of the former Cascade Station.

Cascade was known as "The Gateway City" and considered unique because it owed its existence to water power. The booming mines of the Boundary district needed electricity, and it was the availability of a hydroelectric power supply that sustained the dreams of this community for so many years. However, its birth must still be credited to the Columbia & Western Railway.

As with many of the turn-of-the-century boom towns, Cascade also met its demise, and today only a couple of homes remain with most of the 17-hotel town site converted into a golf course. The power house was demolished after heavy snows in 1998, collapsed the roof.

91.4   Power Station Bulkhead Trail ⚊

A short trail across the bulkhead of the power plant to views of the canyon.
Two 2.1 metre diameter wooden pipes 500 metres long connected to the bulkhead, took the water to a penstock that carried the water under the highway to the powerhouse

91.7   Kettle River—deck truss with deck plate girder approaches.)(52 🚐

A large wood and rock fill dam for the power plant in Cascade spanned the Kettle River a couple of hundred metres up stream of the bridge. Water to the power plant was diverted though a 125 metre tunnel that went under the railway east of the bridge, then flowed down the 150 metre rock cut, along side the railway to the bulkhead back at km 91.4 On the west end of the bridge is a trail head parking lot off Highway #3.

91.8   **Billings**

Billings was a flag stop on the railway and the site of the Yale Columbia Sawmill.

92.3   Gate

97.6   Gate

98.4   **Gilpin Station** i507 ⛺ ⚊ ⚊ ♿ 0.1

Named after the first customs agent in the area.

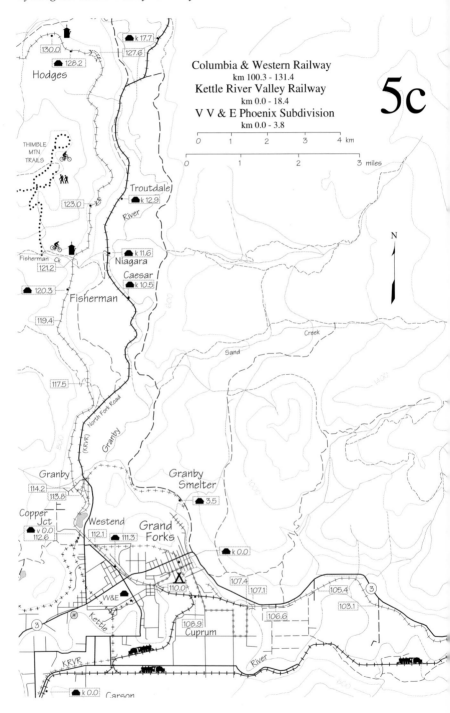

Columbia & Western Railway
km 100.3 - 131.4
Kettle River Valley Railway
km 0.0 - 18.4
V V & E Phoenix Subdivision
km 0.0 - 3.8

5c

103.1 Collins Road. ↑

105.4 White Hall Road. ↑

106.6 Nursery Road. ↑

107.1 Kettle River—through truss and half deck plate girder spans.)(70

107.4 Darcy Road ↑ |→¦
Darcy Road creates a deep cut in the fill. On the other side of the road the rails are still in and are actively being used by the Burlington Northern Railroad. Detour south on Darcy, west on Cameron, north on Kenmore, east on Sagamore Avenue, north on International, which immediately turns into 2 Street and crosses the C&W and then the Kettle River. Just across the bridge pick up the trail on the northeast side of the bridge that follows the shore of the river to the Municipal Park and Campground. From the Park take 7th St. out and turn east on 72nd Avenue, south on 8th Street and then west on Kettle River Drive. Pick up the railway again just as Kettle River Drive turns south.
   A new trail is being planned that will follow along top of the dike from Darcy Road to the 2nd Street Bridge along the Kettle River. Look for signs when this trail is completed.

108.7 2nd Street Grand Forks ↑

108.9 Cuprum—Kettle River Valley Railway junction.

110.0 Kettle River)(83
The active railway and the rails end at the east end of the bridge.

110.1 Kettle River Drive ↑ |←¦
Reaccess the railgrade here as it crosses the Kettle River Drive.

110.4 Boundary Drive ↑

110.9 Highway #3 ↑
There is quite a little hill on both sides of the highway to get off on the grade
   Grand Forks and area is blessed with a myriad of trails for the mountain biker. For more information get hold of the book *Over the Hill* by Mike Wisnicki.

111.2 76th Avenue ↑

111.3 Grand Forks Station i523 ⬛🏠❙ ❚ ∀ ∧ 🏛 ᴨ ❙ ‖ ● (⊙ ❙ 🏊1.6 |←
Grand Forks was an early settlement in 1865, the same year that Edgar Dewdney was cutting his famous trail from Hope to Fort Steele. In 1897, the settlement was incorporated as the city of Grand Forks. Other town sites rapidly grew with the discovery of copper at Phoenix and Mother Lode near Greenwood. The Granby Smelter was located at Grand Forks,

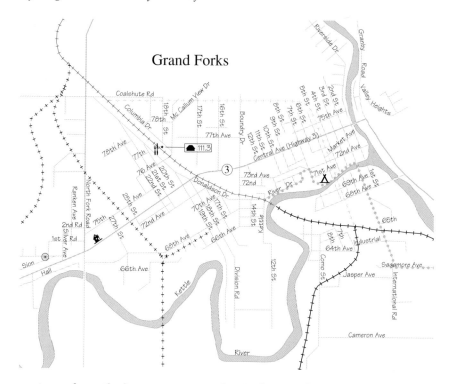

and was the largest copper smelter in the British Empire. With 20 years of prosperity, farming also developed with many orchards planted. The year 1919 saw a decline in copper and subsequent closure of the smelter. This was a blow to the area, resulting in little growth until seed growing, logging and sawmill operations again brought prosperity back to the community.

Many buildings and landmarks can still be found from the town's affluence during the turn of the century. A walking tour guide through historic Grand Forks can be obtained at the Boundary Museum.

As the Columbia & Western Railway could not obtain suitable right-of-way into the city of Grand Forks, its station was actually built in the city of Columbia, now know as West Grand Forks. The station has been beautifully restored and now houses the Grand Forks Station Neighbourhood Pub and Columbia Grill. It is the oldest CPR station in B.C., still in its original location and it is protected under a Heritage Designation Bylaw. Many historical artifacts of the railway can be found adorning the pub's walls, 442-5855. Boundary Museum, 7370 5th St., 442-3737

112.1 Westend—Kettle River Valley Railway Junction (KRVR).

Chartered in 1901 the Kettle River Valley Railway built north in an attempt to bulid a railway through Vernon to Nicola where it could connect to the Nicola , Kamloops & Similkameen Railway (NK&S) and onward to the mainline of the CPR. By 1907 the line reached Lynch Creek and by 1919 the line was ended at Archibald 32 kilometres north of Grand Forks. In 1935 the line was abandoned and now lies mainly under the highway from Grand Forks to Archibald.

In 1911 the name was simplified to the Kettle Valley Railway (KVR) and was leased to the CPR in 1913 which the CPR later used to built the Kettle Valley Railway from Midway to Hope.

112.4 North Fork Road

For the next 6 km the rail bed is soft and sandy due to the large amount of horse traffic this section is receiving.

112.6 VV&E Phoenix junction

This run up to Pheonix is being cleared and will make a nice circle route between Eholt and Grand Forks. Check the VV&E Phoenix Branch.

113.8 Granby—Granby Smelter spur.

114.2 Eagle Ridge Road

117.5 Goat Mountain Road

This 4x4 road connects to North Fork Road down the hill; up the hill it connects with Son Ranch Road, which connects to Highway #3 on the other side of the mountain range.

119.4 Ness Creek Trail

This very steep and technical trail leads down the mountain side to North Fork Road. The trail heads up the hill, further up the railway, and connects to Fisherman Creek Road further up the mountain.

120.3 Fisherman Station *679* 2.1

121.2 Fisherman Creek Road

Down the hill the road leads to Niagara and a connection with North Fork Road. Uphill the road leads to Thimble Mountain Trails and Highway #3. Just prior to the road is Fisherman Creek which is one of the few places water is found on this section.

Niagara

Niagara was another railway boom town that popped up because of the C&W. Construction in the town started in the fall of 1898 and peaked by the start of 1899. Before the summer of 1899, the town had already shrunk to half its peak and was declining fast. At its peak it boasted 12 hotels, nine general stores, three butcher shops, a couple of blacksmiths and a host of other businesses. By the end of year there were only a handful of diehard residents left in Niagara. When construction on the KVR commenced in 1906, Niagara saw a brief resurgence.

121.9 Cattle guard.

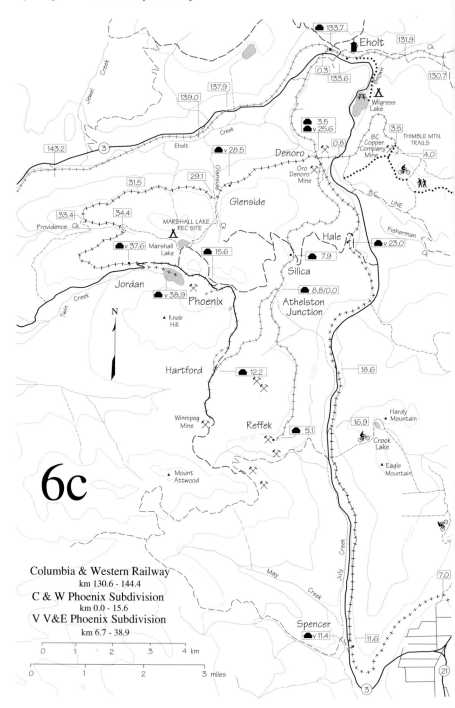

Eholt

133.7

131.9

0.3

133.6

133.6

137.9

139.0

Brown

Ck

130.7

Wlgress Lake

3.5
v 25.6

0.8

3.5

BC Copper Company Mine

THIMBLE MTN. TRAILS

143.2

3

Eholt

v 28.5

Denoro

4.0

29.1

31.5

Oro Denoro Mine

B.C.

LINE

Glenside

Glenside

33.4

34.4

MARSHALL LAKE REC SITE

Hale

Fisherman

v 23.0

Ck

Providence Ck

v 37.6

Marshall Lake

15.6

7.9

Silica

Jordan

Twin Creek

v 38.9

Phoenix

8.8/0.0

Athelston Junction

N

Knob Hill

Hartford

12.2

18.6

Winnipeg Mine

Reffek

5.1

16.9

Hardy Mountain

Crook Lake

6c

Mount Attwood

Eagle Mountain

Columbia & Western Railway
km 130.6 - 144.4
C & W Phoenix Subdivision
km 0.0 - 15.6
V V&E Phoenix Subdivision
km 6.7 - 38.9

May Creek

July Creek

Spencer

v 11.4

11.6

7.0

3

21

| 0 | 1 | 2 | 3 | 4 km |

| 0 | 1 | 2 | 3 miles |

122.9   Fisherman Creek Sectionman Shed ▐

This Tuscan red railway shed use to house an avalanche inspector for the railway. In the fall of 2001 the shed was refurbished and converted to a shelter for wary cyclists and cross country skiers. Shutters on the windows were installed and benches for throwing a sleeping bag on were built.

123.0   Tunnel ▐125

127.6   Tunnel ▐156

128.2   Hodges Station 🚂 ₫

130.0   Water tower ▐

Concrete foundation still remains.

130.7   Brown Creek Forest Service Road (F.S.R.) ↑

The railbed is used by logging trucks from this point to Eholt Road, thus turning it into a washboard.

131.9   Brown Creek F.S.R. ↑

133.1   Cattle guard

133.3   Eholt water tower- Willgress Campground Trail ▐Δ 🚶 🚴

In the fall of 2001 a campsite on Wilgress Lake, beside the Highway #3 rest stop, was built for cyclists. The trail to the site is approximately one kilometre long, and not necessarily rideable. Trail condition will improve over time.

133.6   Eholt Road ↑

133.7   Eholt Station & Phoenix junction ▮1951🚂 ▐ ₫ ⸾ Υ ↑ 🚲1.4

It was back in 1898 that the CPR designated Eholt as a railroad divisional point along the C&W, thus assuring its future as a town site. By 1899, over a hundred lots were sold only two weeks after they went on the market, and some 30 buildings were already in the course of construction. Later that same year Eholt had five hotels, a true symbol of prosperity in this time period. During its prime, Eholt boasted a population of about 300. However, with the collapse of the world copper market following World War I, the demise of Eholt began.

Today, not a single building from the town or the CPR operations remain, only a couple of foundations and some lilac bushes. Three farms now occupy the meadow where the town itself once stood. It is said that at Eholt, even the ghosts have gone.

The 15.5 kilometre-long Phoenix Branch, abandoned in 1921, climbs steeply up to Phoenix at a 3.4% grade. Although time has taken its toll on pieces of this railbed, it certainly offers a challenge to those willing to tackle it.

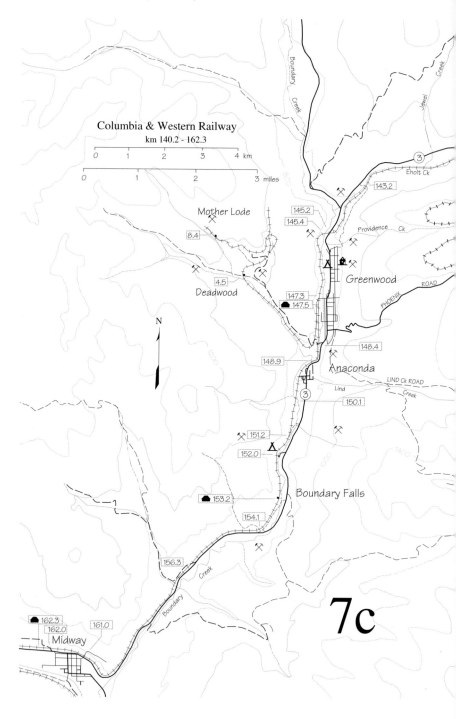

Columbia & Western Railway
km 140.2 - 162.3

7c

134.0   Other branch of the wye.

134.1   Gate
At this point the C&W straddles agricultural land and is cross fenced and gated in numerous places. The majority of gates are easy opening and self closing.

137.9   Highway #3 ⵠ
There are double gates just prior to the highway and a single gate on the other side. The rail bed can have some weed growth on it depending on the time of year. There are a few more gates between here and Greenwood.

139.0   Private access road to Highway #3 ⵠ

143.2   Private access road to Highway #3 ⵠ

145.2   Highway #3 ⵠ ⵝ
The original wooden trestle over the highway was later filled in, with two concrete tunnels for the highway to pass through the fill at ground level. The fill and tunnels have recently been removed, as the concrete tunnels were in disrepair. A highway tunnel dated 1912 was found in the fill and remains intact for heritage interpretive purposes. Although the fill no longer exists, the highway is easily crossed.
   Arno Henning in 1998 painted the flags of the world on the 1912 road tunnel to hide the graffiti on it. It became a millennium project in 2000.

145.4   Boundary Creek
Dated 1912, the same year as the standing highway tunnel, is a large stone arch culvert through which the creek flows under the railway.

146.5   Spur ⵥ

147.3   Deadwood / Mother Load Mine spur—Louisa Street ⵥ ⵠ
At the end of this spur line lay the Mother Lode Mine. Although discovered in 1891, it was not until 1896 that the mine was developed. By the end of 1905, 752,431 tonnes of ore had been shipped to the smelter at Anaconda. In 1913, the glory of the Mother Lode came to an end with a monumentous explosion planned to dislodge further ore, but instead it became hazardous and more expensive to work.
During the increasingly prosperous years of the Mother Lode Mine it was thought that the opportunity existed for a new town near the mine site. So was developed the town of Deadwood. Although there was initial enthusiasm, the population never exceeded 100. The majority of miners and their families lived at the mine site, home for about 400 people.
   This 8.4 kilometre spur is generally passable with a few overgrown sections as it climbs up the Mother Lode Creek Valley.

147.5 Greenwood Station |762 🚂 ♟

🚶 🏕 🏠 🍶 🍴 🍎 (🚲1.0

Greenwood finds its origin back in 1895 when
for the price of $5,000, 81 hectares was pur-
chased and development began. Greenwood
obtained city status in 1897 and quickly became a bustling mining town with a population of 3,000 by 1899. By the end of 1899, 26
hotels were registered as operating in Greenwood with copper being the main reason for
the town's prosperity. It was also in 1899 that
the Columbia & Western Railway reached
Greenwood, reaping the rewards from the
mines in the area. But as with all other surrounding areas, falling demand for ore following World War I was hard on Greenwood. However, the city survived with persistent individuals, and the turning of industry to logging
and millwork. Mining of copper resumed again
for a period after World War II. Unfortunately,
the original station burned down following a
train wreck in 1964.

Today, the mines are all closed and with a
population of 700+ the economy depends
mainly upon logging. Numerous historical
buildings remain from the late 1800s and early
1900s reflecting the affluence of the time. A
heritage tour map can be obtained from the
Greenwood Museum, enabling one to see
Greenwood, Canada's smallest city, as it was
at the turn of the century.

🚂🚃 Greenwood Museum 🚃🚂
214 S. Copper St., 445-6355

148.4 Washington Street ⚓

148.9 Boundary Creek)(41

150.1 Boundary Creek)(21

150.3 Anaconda |735

The smelter at Greenwood was built in 1898
at the mouth of Copper Creek in the town called
Anaconda. During its time, the smelter was
considered the most modern plant in every respect. The smelter began its operations in 1901,

Greenwood

running 24 hours a day. In 1912, production began to slow with decreasing supplies of ore. By 1918 the smelter closed completely. The site was sold to Leon Lotzkar who later gave the site to the city of Greenwood. It is currently known as Lotzkar Park.

Today, you will find many remains of this once active smelter. The smelter smokestack, which was originally made from sheet metal, dates back to 1904 when the metal was replaced with 250,000 bricks and built to the height of 36 metres. You can follow the many walking paths through the mountains of black waste slag that had been loaded into bell-shaped slag cars, then taken by rail to be dumped nearby. Many of the giant hardened black bells that once glowed red in the night can be found within the park. Lotzkar Park can be accessed by turning west on Washington Street, then taking Smelter Road, which follows the Mother Load spur line to the smelter site.

Weeds start to become a major problem after this point. Also, beware that the railbed is ditched at each of the road crossings.

151.2   Road �💧

This road can be used to access Highway #3 to the east in order to get to Boundary Creek Provincal Park, 1 km south on the highway.

152.0   Boundary Creek Provincial Park 𝗫 ▮

This small campsite is right across the creek. To get there, ford the creek or detour on to Highway #3 at km 151.2 or at Boltz Road.

153.2   Boundary Falls Station ┇*706* 🛏 ▮ ⫰ 🚴*1.5*

Placer gold was discovered in Boundary Creek in 1860 and over the next 15 years various claims were worked sporadically. Renewed interest in the area came in 1887 when a rich supply of quartz was discovered near Boundary Falls. By the time the railway arrived in 1900, the small town of Boundary Falls was bustling with activity. A copper smelter and hydro-electric plant were in the plans, all of which thrived up until 1905.

Today Boundary Falls remains a beautiful place to explore. From a viewpoint a short distance from the railway, you can still see in the cliff above the falls the old wooden dam built in 1900, the concrete support and wooden trestle for the wood stove pipe.

154.1   Boltz Road ⚑

156.3   Kerr Road ⚑

161.0   Cemetery Road ⚑

162.0   12th Street ⚑

162.3   Midway Station ┇*580* 🛏 ▮ ⫰ 𝖸 𝗫 🏛 ▮ (

Midway was the division point between the C&W and the KV railways. The station was designated a heritage building and presently serves as part of the Midway Museum. (A map of Midway can be found in the Midway to Penticton section)

Vancouver, Victoria & Eastern
Phoenix Branch – 38.9 kilometres

Eager to get a piece of the rich Phoenix ore hauling pie, the VV&E reached Phoenix in 1904 after overcoming many obstacles thrown in its path by the C&W and the KRVR. But in March 1905, the line started passenger and freight service out of Phoenix. With maximum grades of 2.2%, less than the maximum grade of 3.4% found on the C&W, the VV&E quickly captured the bulk of the ore shipments out of Phoenix. The fall of copper prices in 1919 ended the existence of Phoenix and the railway. The tracks were all pulled up by 1921.

This 38.9 kilometre-long branch of the VV&E loops south around Eagle Mountain, then north up July Creek to circle up Montezuma Hill to Phoenix. The first 11.6 kilometres of this railway winds around the southern edge of Eagle Mountain and is overgrown and impassable. At km 11.6 Danshine Village Road jumps on to the rail bed and follows it to km 16.9. The right-of-way continues past km 16.9 through private property and slowly becomes more overgrown. The next passable section is accessed from Phoenix Road at km 23.2. From here to the missing trestle at Glenside(km 28.5) the rail bed is in excellent condition. Trails now skirt around each of the three missing trestles after Glenside, and the trail winds through the over growth on the rail bed. As this section is discovered and used the trail will improve greatly over time. Past the last missing trestle at km 31.5 finds the rail bed in good condition into Phoenix. A detour up to Marshall Lake and back down Providence Creek Trail will bypass this section with the three missing trestles if required. Links with the C&W Phoenix Branch and B.C. Copper Company Mine spur give's one lots of options to fill a day or two.

km	
0.0	**Copper junction** ⍓
0.4	Kettle River Valley Railway crossing.
1.6	Columbia junction ⍓
1.8	**Weston Station** 🚉
3.2	Copper junction ⍓
5.5	Frame trestle ⵣ174
6.6	Frame trestle ⵣ22
7.0	Reservoir Road ⵟ
7.1	Frame trestle ⵣ12
7.6	Frame trestle ⵣ12

4x4 road connects from highway.

8.7   Frame trestle ⚒ 12

10.9   Spur ⊬

11.4   Spencer Station 🏠

11.6   Danshine Village Road ⊢←⦙
        This road runs atop the original grade to km 16.9.

14.6   Frame trestle ⚒ 107

16.9   Danshine Village Road departs railbed ⊢→⦙
        The rail bed can be followed, though it slowly becomes increasingly over-
        grown. Take Highway #3 to Phoenix Road and reconnect with VV&E at km
        23.2.

18.6   Highway #3 ⅄

22.8   Fisherman Creek—frame trestle ⚒ 30

23.0   Hale Station 🏠 ⅋ ⸾ ⅄

23.2   Phoenix Road ⅄ ⊢←⦙
        The rail bed is passable from the missing trestle at km 22.8 all the way
        around the mountain to Pheniox Road at km 37.8,

25.3   4x4 road
        This 400 metre-long 4x4 road up the hill connects with C&W Phoenix
        Branch at km 4.6.

25.4   Denoro Oro Mine ⚔

25.6   Denoro Station 🏠 ⅋ ⸾ ⊬

25.7   Columbia and Western Railway interchange ⊬
        Taking the spur down will connect you with the C&W Phoenix branch.

28.5   Glenside Station 🏠 ⅋ ⸾

29.1   Glenside Creek—frame trestle ⚒ 205x60 ⅄
        There are only a couple of A bends still standing on the other side of the
        creek. This trestle and the next three are missing, but the rail bed between
        them is passable. Trails have been built around each of the three trestles.
        Also at this point there is a steep 4x4 road up to Marshall Lake.

30.2   Spur ⊬

31.2   Frame trestle ⚒ 51

31.5   Frame trestle ⋊ *128*

33.4   Marshall Lake Ski Trail intersects railbed 🚶‍♂️ 🚴.

34.2   Providence Creek Trail ⊺
            This 4x4 road heads up hill to Marshall Lake.

34.4   Providence Creek ⋊ *90*
            A 4x4 road bypasses the missing trestle over Providence Creek.

37.6   Jordan Station 🚉 ⌡

37.8   Phoenix Road ⊺ ⊢→⌐
            Railbed on the other side of the road quickly becomes lost in the open
            pit mines.

38.8   Granby Victoria Mine spur and wye ⌐ Y

38.9   Phoenix Station 🚉 ⏻ ⌡ Y

Phoenix was a mining town built atop a mountain of copper. At an elevation of 1400 metres, Phoenix was the highest city in Canada. Phoenix was incorporated as a city in 1900 and provided the very best in accommodations and services. By 1911, about 4,000 people lived in Phoenix. There was a hospital, tennis courts, moving pictures, a brewery and 17 saloons that stayed open day and night. There was skating, curling, hockey and skiing. The first professional hockey in British Columbia was played in Phoenix.

For a time Phoenix was the largest producer of copper ore in Canada. However, by 1919 the company closed the mines due to a depleted supply, falling prices and an uncertain demand for copper. Railway service soon slowed and the residents began moving away. By 1920, Phoenix was a ghost town. In 1955, the Granby Company returned to the mountain to develop an open pit mine. Over the next 20 years the pit grew to encompass not only the old mining areas, but all the town site of Phoenix, leaving little to remain from the old pioneer mining era. The station location is lost somewhere in the middle of this large open pit mine.

C&W Phoenix Subdivision
15.6 kilometres

Construction started on the Phoenix Subdivision in 1899 and the last spike was struck on May 21, 1900. Although completed in May, the first load of ore shipped to the Granby Smelter in Grand Forks did not take place until July 11th. With grades approaching 3.4%, Shay engines similar to the one used now by the Kettle Valley Steam Railway were used on the steep grades. In 1905, when the VV&E climbed into Phoenix, it took away the majority of the ore-hauling trade from the C&W because of the easier grades and heavier trains that could be operated on them. The Phoenix mines kept both railways busy until 1919 when post World War I copper prices plummeted. The railway was abandoned and the track removed in 1921.

Cycling this subdivision involves an exploration of the mines of the past. The honeycomb mining techniques and the deep pits remain to be explored. Beware: these mines are dangerous places. Most are very deep, steep-sided pits filled with water. It is easy to fall in to one while wandering through the woods. The rail bed is almost totally intact and is relatively easy to cycle from Eholt to Phoenix. Three minor detours are required. The first is just out of Eholt after crossing Highway #3. A 60 metre-long section of the railbed is totally overgrown and impassable with a bike. The second detour is at Denoro where the frame trestle over the VV&E Phoenix branch is missing, requiring a detour around Oro Denoro mines and up a 4x4 road to regain the rail bed after the missing trestle. The third is at the switchback at Hartford, where the road built upon the old railbed skirts 700 metres around a rock bluff that the railbed made a deep cut through. The railway is somewhat overgrown in this cut, but passable with some difficulty. Once at Phoenix, the rail bed totally disappears within the open pit mines.

Options for riding this section are to make circle routes using the VV&E and Phoenix Road, taking one railway up and the other back down ⛟

0.0   Eholt – Phoenix junction km 134.6 C&W 🚂 ⸝

0.3   Highway #3 ⊢➔⸝
      Fences line both sides of Highway #3. The railbed is difficult to pick up after crossing the highway. It is totally overgrown for the first 60 metres and is impassable by bike. It can be hiked through on foot but not while pushing a bike. There is an old concrete foundation buried in the trees on the east side of the railbed 30 metres past the fence. The railbed can be accessed by bike by taking the rough road just opposite Eholt Road east on Highway #3 and following it to the west. It will connect to the railbed just after the overgrown section.

0.4   4x4 road connects from highway ⊢←⸝
      The railbed is rough in a few spots from here to km 1.1.

1.1   Logging road going down
      Railbed is in excellent shape after this point.

2.0   Logging road going up

2.7   Views of Eholt Valley

3.5   Denoro—B.C. Mines spur ◼ ⇨

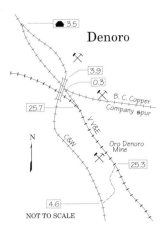

Named B.C. Junction and then Coltern, this station was finally named Denoro when a spur line was built to the Oro Denoro Mine.

The spur departs to the west (right) and the Phoenix branch heads up to the left. Three hundred metres from the spur the missing trestle over the B.C. Mine spur and the VV&E is encountered. A large, loose gravel abutment has to be climbed down to the spur line. This can be avoided by following the spur to the intersection. Beware: this area is littered with deep vertical mine shafts on both sides of the railway.

3.9   Frame trestle ⚒ 70 ➡

This missing trestle spanned the VV&E Phoenix branch and C&W B.C. Copper Company spur. It was under this trestle that the C&W connects with the VV&E. Detour south on VV&E Phoenix branch. Just past Oro Denoro Mine take the 4x4 road 400 metres uphill to reconnect with the C&W.

The Oro Denoro Mine, km 3.5, Phoenix Subdivision.

4.1   Oro Denoro Mine spur

4.2   Oro Denoro loading spur

4.6   4x4 road between C&W and VV&E.

7.9   Silica
Phoenix Road crosses just before Silica.

8.5   Water tower

8.8   Athelston Junction—Reffek spur
This 5.1 kilometre-long spur line ran to B.C. Copper Company's Jackpot Mine. En route, the railway crossed one 49 metre-long frame trestle at km 1.6. The station at the mine was named Reffek after Frederic Keefer, an associate of the B.C. Copper Company. This level spur is passable and is a beautiful cycle through the forest.

9.0   Snowshoe Creek

10.1   Water tower

12.2   Hartford
A 1.5 kilometre-long spur departed here to Winnipeg Mine as the line to Phoenix switched back to head north. The spur now lies under the Lone Star Haul Road.
   The railbed from here to km 13.0 is overgrown and runs through a deep cut with some rockfall. Detour on to Lone Star Haul Road, which at km 13.0 runs atop of the original grade.

13.0   Rawhide spur
The Lone Star Haul Road runs atop the original grade from here to Phoenix.

13.8   Snowshoe spur

14.0   Curlew spur
Just past the open pit mine a section of one of the spurs can be found just uphill from the road.

14.3   Rawhide spur

14.5   Snowshoe spur No. 2.

15.6   Phoenix Station

B. C. Mine Spur
4.0 kilometres

This 4.0 kilometre-long spur departs from the C&W Phoenix branch and heads east to B.C. Copper Company Mine on Thimble Mountain. The spur is a pleasant cycle through cedar forests to the mine remains at the terminus of the spur. A loading chute, donkey engine, log buildings and mine pit can be found. Thimble Mountain Trails, a 14 kilometre-long trail system maintained by the forestry department for hiking, cycling and horseback riding, departs at km 3.5 and at the end of the spur 🚂

0.0   B.C. Mine spur junction. 𝄪

0.3   C&W Phoenix branch crossed over the B.C. Mine spur and the VV&E Phoenix branch on a frame trestle. A 100 metre-long branch connected the VV&E to the C&W at this point The spur turns east toward Thimble Mountain and the branch heads straight up a slight incline to connect to the VV&E.

0.8   Highway #3 ⌖
        The railbed comes to an abrupt break at the ditch for Highway #3. Both sides of Highway #3 have gated fences. Across the highway the railbed is used as a logging road and is in excellent shape. There is a gate just off the highway. The railbed winds it way up through a cedar forest as it looks over Wilgress Lake.

3.5   Thimble Mountain Trail 🚶 🚴
        A registration station with a map of the Thimble Mountain Trail system is found at this trailhead.

3.7   Mine buildings and a loading chute ⚒
        The mine pit can be found up the hill behind the loading chute and donkey engine.

3.8   Road branches to left heading up Thimble Mountain.

4.0   B.C. Copper Company Mine ⚒
        The wooden remains of the loading dock remain.

Log cabin by B.C. Copper Mine.

CLOSING THE CIRCLE

In following an abandoned railway, returning to your point of origin by another route is usually a lot farther and more difficult than re-tracing your tracks. The easiest method of return is by bus, which is available at all of the major centres on route. Cycling between these centres on the highways tends to be just as long as the railway but with grades reaching 7 to 8%. Shoulder width on these roads can vary greatly, and in the summer months, traffic can be very heavy. But for those inclined, closing the circle by bike can add a unique and alluring dimension to a cycling adventure ➤

Here are some possibilities:

Midway to Osoyoos, 274 km (KVR)
• Return trip, 69 km on Highway #3

Osoyoos to Princeton, 171.5 km (KVR)
• Return trip 113 km on Highway #3 and pieces of VV&E.

Princeton to Penticton, 113.4 km (KVR)
• Return trip 112 km on Highways #3, 3A and pieces of VV&E.

Princeton to Hope, 148.4 km (KVR)
• Return trip 133 km on Highway #3. Very hilly.

Hope to Spences Bridge, 162.8 km (KVR and NK&S)
• Return trip 142 km on Highway #1.

Grand Forks to Midway, 51 km (C&W)
• Return trip 69 km on Highway #3.

Grand Forks to Eholt, 28.2 km (C&W)
• Return trip 29.1 km on the C&W Phoenix branch to Denoro, and the VV&E Phoenix branch from Denoro.

Castlegar to Grand Forks, 111.3 km (C&W)
• Return trip 94 km on Highway #3.

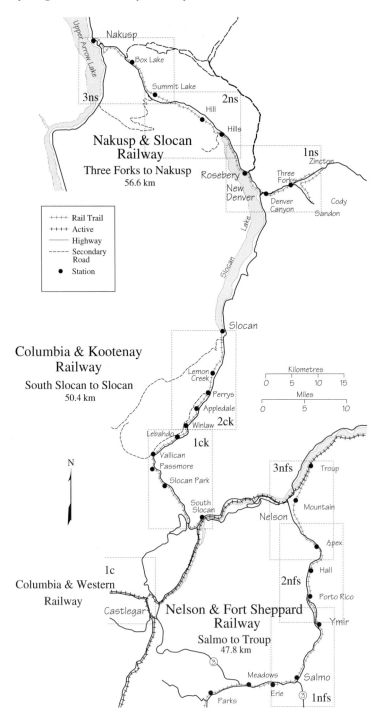

Nakusp

Box Lake

Summit Lake

3ns

Hill

2ns

Hills

Nakusp & Slocan
Railway

Three Forks to Nakusp
56.6 km

Rosebery

1ns

Zincton

Three
Forks

New
Denver

Denver
Canyon

Cody

Sandon

Upper Arrow Lake

+++++ Rail Trail
+++++ Active
——— Highway
- - - - Secondary
Road
● Station

Slocan Lake

Columbia & Kootenay
Railway

South Slocan to Slocan
50.4 km

Slocan

Lemon
Creek

Perrys

Appledale

Winlaw

2ck

Lebahdo

1ck

Vallican

Passmore

Slocan Park

South
Slocan

Nelson

3nfs

Troup

Mountain

Kilometres

0   5   10   15

Miles

0   5   10

N

Apex

Hall

1c

2nfs

Porto Rico

Columbia & Western
Railway

Castlegar

Nelson & Fort Sheppard
Railway

Salmo to Troup
47.8 km

Ymir

Meadows

Erie

Parks

Salmo

1nfs

218

Nelson & Fort Sheppard Railway

Salmo to Nelson

In 1886 Winslow Hall and his brother Oscar Hall and their sons discovered rich deposits of silver on Toad Mountain, just southwest of Nelson. Hugh Nelson, lieutenant-governor of B.C., for whom the city of Nelson is named, convinced both CPR and Daniel Chase Corbin to built railways into Nelson to facilitate the newly discovered riches. CPR was the first in 1891, with the Columbia and Kootenay Railway into Nelson via a water link on the Columbia River.

Daniel Corbin of the Spokane Falls and Northern (SF&N) Railway chartered the Nelson and Fort Sheppard (N&FS) Railway in 1891 and finished construction from Fort Sheppard into Nelson at the end of 1893. In the beginning the railway serviced the mines and provided passenger service to Spokane. In the 1940s passenger use dwindled and was discontinued and the railway mainstay had become the hauling of lumber products to the U.S. market. In 1944 the Great Northern Railway bought the N&FS which in 1970 merged in to the Burlington Northern Railway. The railway was abandonment in 1989. Then in 2001 the B.C. Government purchased the right of way from Troup to just out side Salmo.

The historic town of Salmo provides a pleasant starting point for a day trip on this railbed. The 1930s architecture of the town has been persevered and further enhanced with stone murals adorning the walls of sev-

Salmo Station, km 0.0

Salmo

The trail running along side the Salmo River, km 27.9.

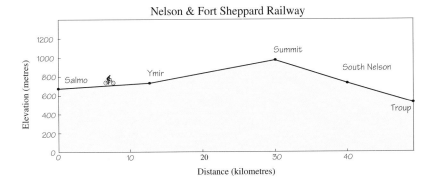

Nelson & Fort Sheppard Railway

eral of the buildings. The murals, by students of Salmo's School of Stone Masonry, depict mining and the wildlife of the Kootenay Area. The rail line is found beside the old railway station across the highway from the Museum. The rail bed to Troup is in great riding condition with a few sandy soft spots caused mainly by ATV using of the trail. The railgrade follows the along side the Salmo River as it climbs at an average one percent grade to Summit at km 30.1. Lots of places along the way to take a cool dip in the river. Along the way the railway passes through Ymir, a former mining town, where you will find the Wild and Wooly Ymir Store that serves great vegetarian and non-vegetarian lunches. After cresting at Summit the trail starts it's decent to Troup first passing Cottonwood Lake Regional Park. It's downhill run follows along side Cottonwood Creek with a fast downhill grade of 2.4 percent.. Soon the railgrade is left high on the mountain side as the creek plunges down to Nelson. Commanding views of the Kootenay Valley and Nelson soon appear. Past Mountain Station, up the hill from Nelson, the railway continues its fast decent to Troup across spectacular trestles overlooking Kootenay Lake. The railgrade ends at Troup where it meets the active CPR line between Creston and Nelson. Unfortunately there is no exit at Troup and the railgrade must be backtracked at least 5.8 kilometres to Elwyn Road in Nelson to exit the railgrade. At one time the home of saloons and silver miners Nelson has become a cosmopolitan oasis in the mountains. A haven now a days for outdoor recreationists Nelson offers wonderful boutiques, eateries and sporting goods stores ▬

km	**Salmo Station** *664*
0.0	As a siding to the new railway originally call Salmon Siding, Salmo began it's existence. With gold and silver mines springing up all around, the wide open valley bottom enticed miners and businesses to locate here. The original railway station is found on the railgrade, right across the highway from the museum. The station received heritage status in 1998.

221

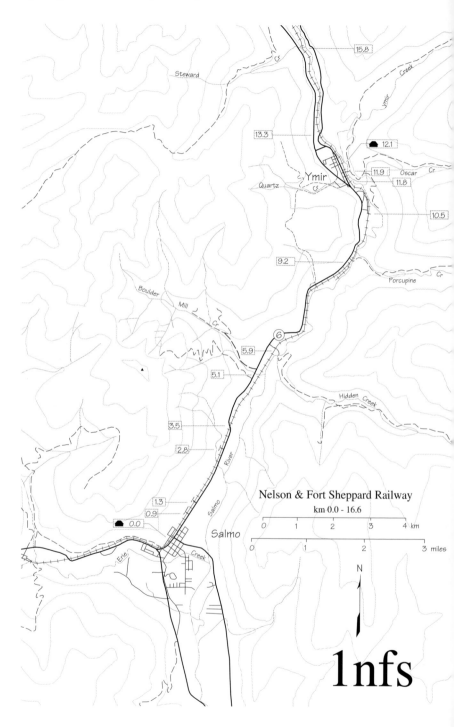

15.8

13.3

12.1

Steward Cr.

Ymir Creek

Oscar Cr.

11.9
11.8

Ymir

Quartz Cr.

10.5

9.2

Porcupine Cr.

Boulder

Mill Cr.

6

5.9

5.1

Hidden Creek

3.5

2.8

Salmo River

Nelson & Fort Sheppard Railway
km 0.0 - 16.6

0 1 2 3 4 km

0 1 2 3 miles

1.3

0.9

0.0

Salmo

Erie Creek

N

1nfs

Although the railgrade is in good cycling condition through Salmo, unfortunately at the time of writing, the railway within the town limits is still owned by Burlington Northern and a short section of the rail grade just north of the town limits is held in private hands. The local trail group, the Nelson Area Trails Society is working on securing these pieces as public lands. Until that time these short sections of railgrade should be respected as private property.

0.9   Potapoff Road 🕆

1.3   Sheloff Road 🕆

2.8   Bonderoff Road 🕆

3.5   Highway #6 🕆
The highway was re alined in 2001 and a trail from the railway grades on both sides of the highway to a cross walk across the highway was built.

5.1   Boulder Mill Creek)(22

5.2   Boulder Mill ⌘

5.9   Boulder Pit Road 🕆

9.0   Pocupine Road 🕆

9.8   Baskins ?

10.5   Wesco Road 🕆

10.6   Quarry Spur ⌁

11.8   Quartz Creek)(12
Just south of the pile trestle over Quartz Creek
is the water tower foundation.

Ymir, km 12.1.

11.9   Wildhorse Creek Road🕆

**12.1   Ymir Station   ⌁734 **

13.3   Porto Rico—Ymir Road 🕆

15.8   Stewart Creek)(6

17.4   Porto Rico—Ymir Road 🕆

15.9   Barrett Creek)(6

16.2   Porto Rico 🚆
Former station named after the mine up Barrett Creek.

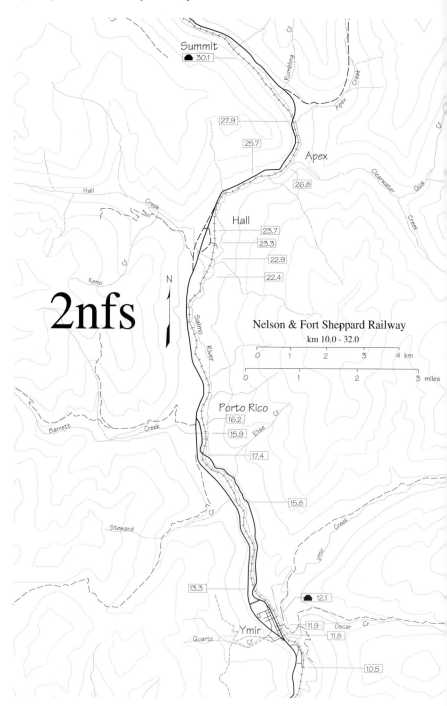

Summit
30.1

27.9

25.7

Apex

26.8

Hall
23.7
23.3
22.9
22.4

2nfs

N

Nelson & Fort Sheppard Railway

km 10.0 - 32.0

| 0 | 1 | 2 | 3 | 4 km |

| 0 | 1 | 2 | 3 miles |

Porto Rico
16.2
15.9
17.4

15.8

13.3

12.1

11.9   Oscar
11.8

Ymir

Quartz

10.5

22.4   Hall Creek)(*25*

22.9   Hall Creek)(*30*

23.3   Riding Club Road †

23.7   Hall ⵏ
Named after the Hall brothers who in 1986 discovered rich silver deposits on Toad Mountain just north west of here. This discovery is what prompted both Daniel Corbin and the CPR to build rail lines into Nelson.

25.7   Washed out culvert.
There is a 4 meter gap in the trail due to a washed out culvert.

26.8   Apex 🏠
A former station

27.9   Highway #6 †

29.1   Summit wye Y

30.1   Summit ∣*960* 🏠 ⵏ ◊ 🚴*2.4*

Cottonwood Regional Park, km 32.6 (Brian Springinotic)

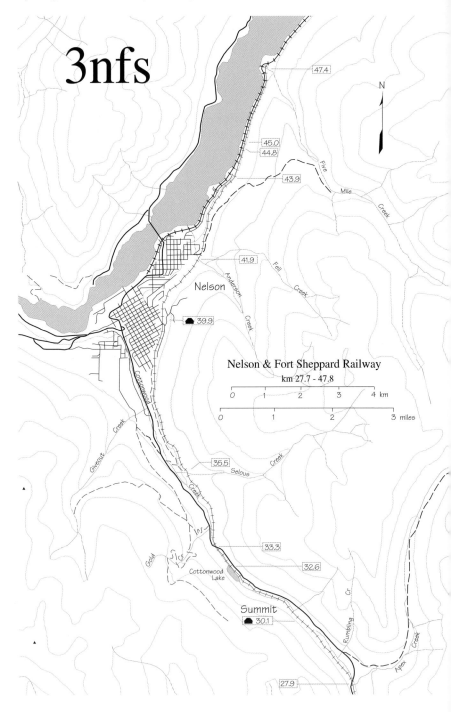

3nfs

47.4

N

45.0
44.8

43.9

Five Mile Creek

41.9

Nelson

Anderson Creek

Fell Creek

39.9

Nelson & Fort Sheppard Railway
km 27.7 - 47.8

Cottonwood Creek

Giveout Creek

35.5

Selous Creek

33.3

32.6

Gold Creek

Cottonwood Lake

Summit

30.1

Rumbling Cr.

Apex Creek

27.9

32.6   Cottonwood Lake Regional Park

33.3   Highway #6

35.5   Selous Creek)(97x9
        Pile trestle

36.5   Dry Ravine)(83x10
        Pile trestle. Although the entire
        length of ties and girders are in place
        on the top, the trestle is missing the
        centre structure of criss-crossing
        timbers for almost a third of its
        length underneath the top ties and
        girders. It is not advisable to cross
        this span. Use the well-beaten path
        beside the trestle.

39.8   Cherry Street

**39.9   Mountain Station—South
        Nelson** ¡727 ♦2.4

Anderson Creek Bridge, km 41.9

41.9   Anderson Creek)(42x9
        Named for Harry Anderson, a mining recorder and constable in Nelson
        between 1887 and 1889.

42.0   Elwyn Road
        Access to Nelson. There is no other exit off the railgrade to Troup. Cy-
        clists heading north of this point will have to return.

43.9   Frame trestle)(131x16
        S-curve frame trestle

44.8   Pile trestle)(164x11

45.0   Frame trestle)(64x11

47.4   Five Mile Creek Bridge 1)(22
        Steel beam bridge

47.5   Five Mile Creek Bridge 2)(18

47.8   Troup Junction ¡538
        Here the railway used the large peninsula of Five Mile Creek to accom-
        modate a loop out in to Kootenay Lake to transfer passengers and freight
        to sternwheelers and to turn trains towards Nelson. The loop out in to
        the lake is gone but the old railgrades on land can still be found that
        show how this intersection use to look.

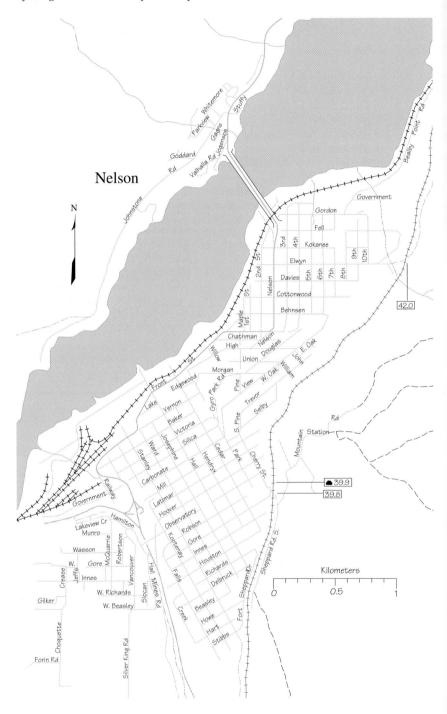

Nelson

N

Columbia & Kootenay Railway

South Slocan to Slocan, 50.4 km

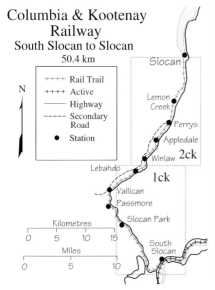

Columbia & Kootenay Railway
South Slocan to Slocan
50.4 km

Legend:
- ++++ Rail Trail
- ++++ Active
- —— Highway
- ----- Secondary Road
- ● Station

N

Slocan
Lemon Creek
Perrys
Appledale
Winlaw   2ck
Lebahdo
1ck
Vallican
Passmore
Slocan Park
South Slocan

Kilometres
0   5   10   15

Miles
0   5   10

Built in 1897 under the charter of the Columbia & Kootenay Railway and Navigation Company (C&K) by the Canadian Pacific Railway (CPR), the railway connected Slocan Junction at South Slocan to Slocan City. This railway allowed ore from the mines around Sandon to find a more direct route to the smelters in Canada and the U.S. Ore would be shipped down from Sandon on the Nakusp & Slocan Railway (N&S) to connect with a rail barge at Rosebery to be ferried to Slocan to continue it's journey south down the C&K. The line was abandon in 1994. In 1998 the CPR donated this section of the C&K to the Trans-Canada Trail Foundation for use as a recreational corridor

Walking along the C&K (Pierre Dupont)

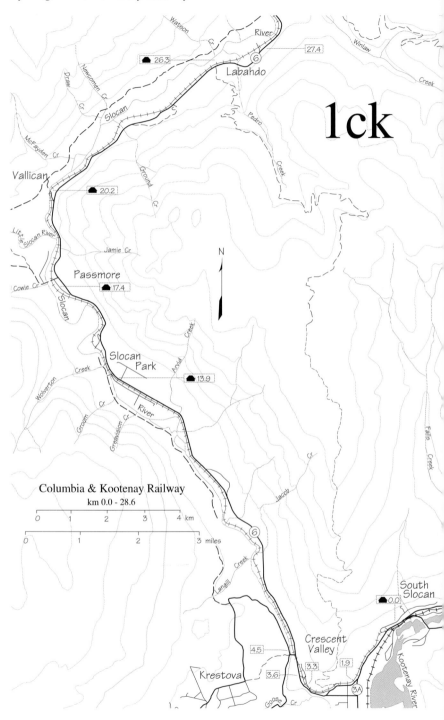

Watson Cr. River

⛰ 26.3

27.4

Winlaw

Creek

Labahdo

(6)

Draw Cr.

Newcomen Cr.

Pedro

Creek

Slocan

1ck

McFayden Cr.

Ground

Creek

Vallican

⛰ 20.2

Cr.

Little Slocan River

Jamie Cr.

N

Cowie Cr.

Passmore

⛰ 17.4

Slocan

Creek

Slocan
Park

Arvid

⛰ 13.9

Wolverton

Creek

Groom Cr.

Greavison Cr.

River

Cr.

Columbia & Kootenay Railway

km 0.0 - 28.6

Jacob

Falls Creek

0   1   2   3   4 km

0   1   2   3 miles

(6)

Langill

Creek

South
Slocan

⛰ 0.0

Crescent
Valley

4.5

3.3   1.9

Krestova

3.6

(3A)

Kootenay River

Goose Cr.

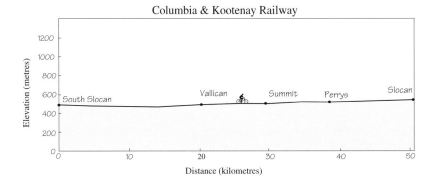

dor. Plans are to transfer this into the increasingly large inventory of rail-trail corridors held by the B.C. government. Until this railway is transferred into the public's hands, permission to cycle the corridor should be obtained from the Trans-Canada Trail Foundation.

The gentle grade of this route follows the flat valley bottom along side the Slocan River for the great majority of it's length. Although there is no official access points yet on the railway, on the south end the easiest access point is at the Mount Sentinel Secondary School. At the north end of the trail access can be gained in Slocan either at the shore of Slocan Lake or where Park Ave crosses the railgrade. There are many other access points along the railgrade as it winds it's way though the many small communities along it's length. Highway #6 runs along side the railgrade for a majority of the route allowing easy access. Although this railway has a very easy grade from end to end the trail surface leaves much to be desired The ballast remains on the railgrade making travel difficult. Some sections are better then others, where the rail bed has received vehicle traffic or is some what over grown the bed is some what stable. Because of this loose surface the railbed is not suitable for heavily ladened bikes. This problem will hopefully be corrected as the local trail group, the Slocan Valley Heritage Trail Society, implements it's management plan in the next couple of years. Check their website for updates on the trail. ◼

The following is a brief description of the trail ◼

km **South Slocan (Slocan Junction)** ¡496 ◼ ┆ ⱶ Ⱳ ⚲0.2

0.0 Junction with the active Canadian Pacific's (CP) Boundary Subdivision, between Nelson and Castlegar. Access to the railway is difficult at this point.

1.9 Mount Sentinel Secondary School ⱶ
Parking lot entrances crosses the C&K making this the easist access point on the south end on this railway.

Morning on the C&K trail, km 24.3.

Lemon Creek Bridge, km 42.5

3.3   Road †

3.6   Road †

4.4   Highway #6/Road †
        The highway was realigned in the fall of 2001 so some disruption of the
        railgrade in this area occurred.

4.5   Crescent Valley ¡487 † 🚲0.1

13.9   Slocan Park ¡477 ⸮ 🚲0.3

14.0   Slocan Valley Road West †

15.0   Old Slocan Park

17.4   Passmore 🏠 ⸮

17.5   Upper Passmore Road †

20.1   Old Vallican Bridge Road †

20.2   Vallican ¡500 ⸮ 🚲0.2
        Flagstop

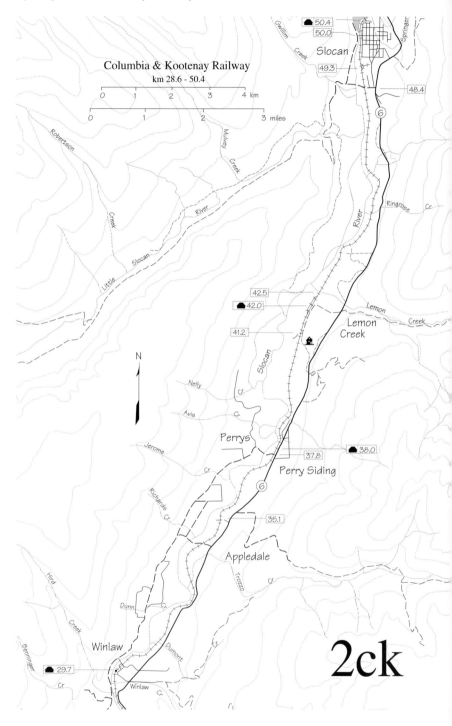

Columbia & Kootenay Railway
km 28.6 - 50.4

2ck

26.2 **Levahdo** ¡510 ⅄ ⚶
Flagstop

27.4 Flipoff Road ⸸

29.7 **Winlaw** ¡512 ⬢ ⌇⚶ 0.3

29.8 Winlaw Bridge Road ⸸

34.6 Nixon Road ⸸

34.3 **Appledale** ¡526 ⅄ ⚶
Flagstop

35.1 Katelnikoff Road ⸸

35.7 **Bridge**)(46

37.8 Perrys Back Road ⸸

38.0 **Perrys** ¡525 ⅄ ⚶ 0.1
This former flagstop was named after the engineer that determined the
route of this railway.

38.9 **Water Tank** ⬙

41.2 Kennedy Road ⸸ ⫽ ⌂ ⋏
Lemon Creek Lodge can be found about 600 metres down the road south
of where the railway crosses Kennedy Road.

42.2 **Lemon Creek** ⬢ ⌇

42.5 **Lemon Creek**)(34

48.4 Gravel Pit Road ⸸

49.3 Slocan City Wye ⅄

50.0 Park Ave—Slocan ⚏ ⌐ ⸸

50.4 **Slocan City** ¡537 ⬢ ⬙ ⌇ ⫽ ⚇ ⌂ ⚇ ⋏

Nakusp & Slocan Railway
Three Forks to Nakusp, 56.6 km

Chartered in 1893 by the Canadian Pacific Railway (CRR) to connect the mining regions in the Slocan and Sandon area to the main line at Revelstoke. Barges connected the line from Revelstoke to Nakusp. From Nakusp the line was originally to be built to Three Forks, relying on the mines in Sandon to transport their ore to the railhead. But the completion of Great Northern's, Kaslo & Sandon Railway (K&S) into the heart of Sandon in 1895 forced the CPR to extend the line up one of the steepest railway grades ever built, within weeks of the K&S arriving. The mines in the area kept both railways busy hauling galena ore rich in silver to smelters in both Canada and the U.S. Problems beset the narrow gauge K&S throughout it's history. Washouts and snowslides assaulted the line continuously until 1912 when the line was sold to the CPR and rerouted and upgraded to standard gauge. The CPR provided service to the mines in Sandon on the N&S line until 1955 when floods washed out numerous sections of the railgrade from Sandon to New Denver. The line from New Denver to Sandon ,including the line to Kaslo, was officially abandoned in 1957, unable to overcome the devastation of the washouts. New Denver to Rosebery was abandoned in 1981 with the rest of the line from Rosebery to Nakusp being abandoned in 1989.

Cable car crossing of Carpenter Creek, km 1.9. (Brian Springinotic)

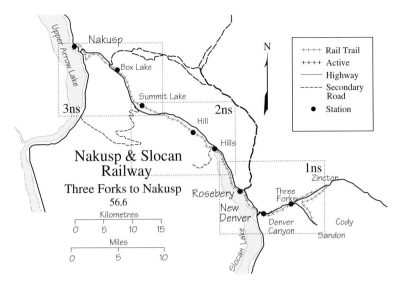

In 1998 a project funded by Human Resources Development Canada, Environment BC's E-Team Program and Forest Renewal B.C. revamped the old railgrade from Three Forks to Rosebery to become the Galena Trail. The railgrade was cleared, rebuilt and bridges constructed or bypasses built. The result is an excellent 13 km cycling trail which includes picnic tables , benches and outhouses. Past Rosebery to Nakusp the rail bed is in good condition over it's length and local trail groups have turned their attention to developing this as a natural extension to the Galena Trail .

The following is a brief description of the trail ▄▄

km	Three Forks ¡793 ▄ ▮ ⫙ 🚐 ⚲62.4
0.0	Named for the three creeks that come together at this point.

The trail head is found just 50 metres up the road to Sandon from Highway 31A. Turn right and follow to the trailhead parking lot. The trail starts with a 300 metre down hill trail to the rail grade.

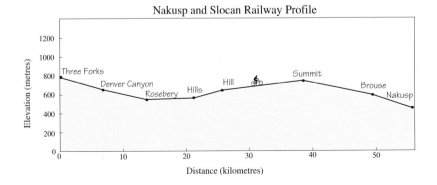

Nakusp and Slocan Railway Profile

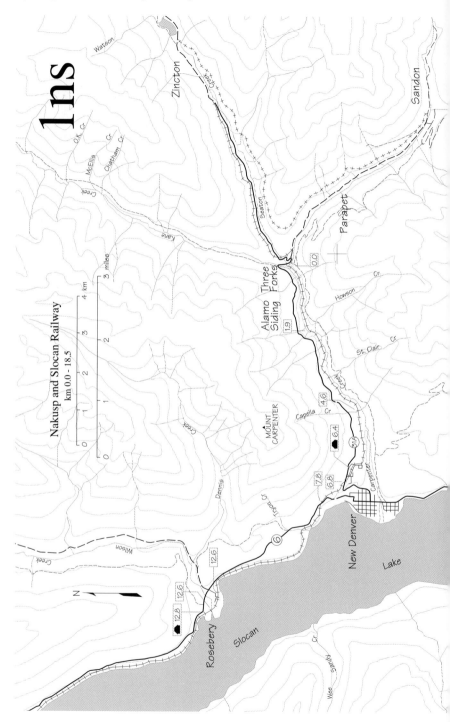

1ns

Nakusp and Slocan Railway
km 0.0 - 18.5

1.8   Alamo Siding

Site of the Alamo Concentrator. At it's height over 200 people lived and worked here, processing the ore from the local mines. Remains of the concentrator, hydroelectric plant and the community that was here can be found littering the hillsides.

1.9   Carpenter Creek ⅄ 88

This missing bridge was a 21 metre deckplate girder span with 37 and 30 metre long timber frame approaches. In 1997 volunteers installed a bike carrying cable car to cross Carpenter Creek. This crossing is the highlight for many on this trail.

Remains of the concentrator at Alamo Siding, km 1.8. (Brian Springinotic)

2.7   Fill

This 74 metre trestle was later filled.

4.3   Frame trestle ⅄ 33

A rideable single track bypasses this missing trestle with a small bridge now crossing the stream.

4.6   Capella Creek ⅄ 74

A new pedestrian bridge has been built on top of the ruins of the original frame trestle

6.0   End of abandoned section 1957.

6.4   Denver Canyon ⅰ*640*　🏠　⸙ ⌐ ▌ 🚲*1.5*

6.7   Denver Siding Road ⊺ 🚐

Just before crossing the road is the local access point for the trail and parking area. To get here from Highway #6 take Highway #31A east through New Denver to Denver Siding Road. Turn south (right) on Denver Siding Road and the trail head can be found a couple hundred metres down the road.

6.8   Highway #31A ⊺

7.8   Highway #6

11.7   Pile trestle)(

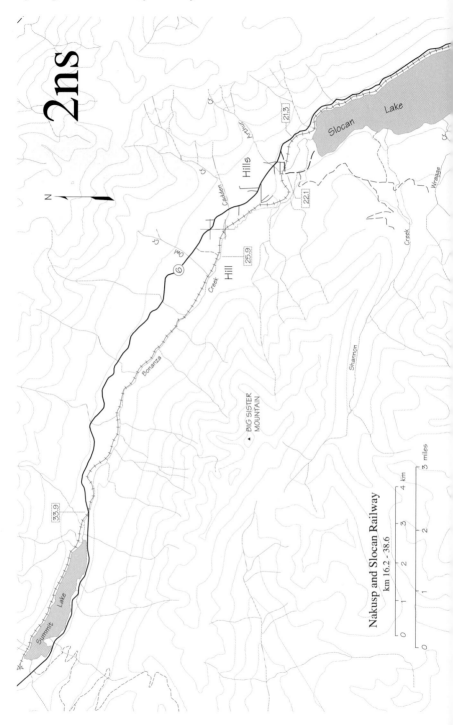

Nakusp and Slocan Railway
km 16.2 - 38.6

Capella Creek Bridge, km 4.6 (Brian Springinotic)

12.2   Derosa Drive—Galena Trail Head (official end of Galena Trail) ↑ ▌🚐
        The north west trail head for the Galena Trail. Here you will find a
        parking lot and trail head with an out house back at about km 12.0..

12.6   Wilson Creek)(30

12.8   Rosebery i542 🚂 ▷ |/ Y 🚴0.2
        Named after the former Prime Minister of Great Britain, the Earl of
        Rosebery. There was a barge slip here which allowed connection to
        Slocan City and the Columbia and Kootenay Railway.

19.6   Water Tank 🛢

21.3   Hills i557 ▷ 🚴2.0

22.1   Road ↑

22.5   Dumont Spur |/

22.3   Arthur Creek—Pile trestle)(14

25.9   Hill i649 ▷ 🚴0.9

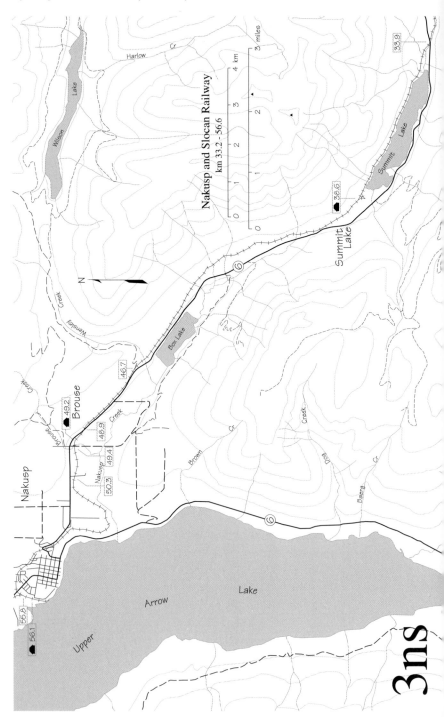

Nakusp and Slocan Railway
km 33.2 - 56.6

3ns

38.6 **Summit Lake** ¡*762* 🏠 ⌇ Υ ⚓*1.5*

This station was situated at the summit of the grade between Nakusp and Rosebery. As such it had a wye for the days of steam engines.

45.4   Trestle)(

46.2   Box Lake Water Tank 🛗

46.7 **Box Lake** 🏠 Υ

48.9   Highway #6 Υ

49.2 **Brouse** ¡*597* 🏠 🛗 ⌇ ⚓*1.9*

49.4   Road Υ

50.3   Road Υ

55.6   Highway #6 Υ

55.8   Canyon Development Spur ⼁

56.1 **Nakusp** ¡*463* 🏠 🛗⌇ Υ

58.6 **Old Nakusp** 🏠

NICOLA, KAMLOOPS & SIMILKAMEEN COAL & RAILWAY COMPANY (NK&S)

Spences Bridge to Nicola, 75.4 kilometres

This route was originally chartered in 1891 by a syndicate that included Hamilton Merritt, for whom the city of Merritt is named. The original charter was for a railway line from the CPR line at Kamloops down through Nicola to Princeton, then on to Penticton. The charter lapsed after financial backing for the railway could not be secured. In 1903, Hamilton Merritt revised the charter, adding to it the run from Spences Bridge to Nicola. By 1905, the CPR needed to access the rich coal reserves of the Nicola Valley, as they had encountered problems with their usual coal supplier on Vancouver Island. In desperation the CPR leased the charter of the NK&S from Hamilton Merritt and immediately started construction on the line in 1905. Fraught with a shortage of ties, the line was not completed until 1907. Amusingly, even once complete, the railway's poor construction had to subsequently be upgraded before it was utilized by paying traffic.

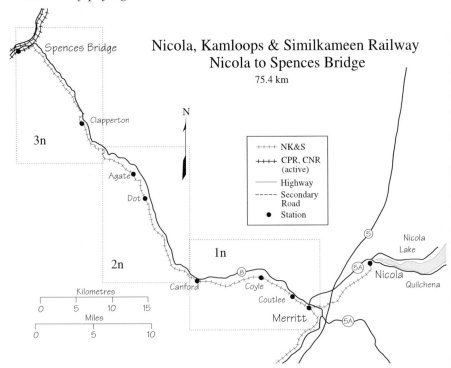

Nicola, Kamloops & Similkameen Railway
Nicola to Spences Bridge
75.4 km

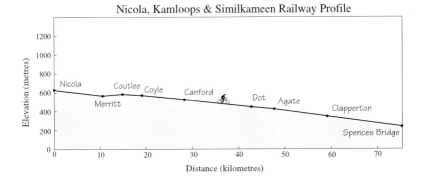

Nicola, Kamloops & Similkameen Railway Profile

This line from Spences Bridge to Nicola became known as CPR's Nicola Branch. In November of 1915, a few months following the opening of the KVR from Midway to Merritt, the CPR transferred the Nicola Branch to the KVR. With the closure of the KVR, this track was subsequently lifted in 1992, along with the remaining track south of Merritt. The B.C. government purchased the right-of-way from CPR in 1995 and the right-of-way running through the three Indian reserves was returned to the reserves.

The easy grade of this railbed entices many cyclists. Weaving through the arid Nicola Valley, the railbed crosses the Nicola River eight times. At km 60.4, the only tunnel on the Nicola branch cuts through Ten Mile Hill, and is noted for its portals made of cut stone. Along the route, the foundations and remains of most of the station houses can still be found. Many of the freight sheds are in service now as storage sheds or livestock shelters. These sheds are usually seen in the fields not far from their original locations. One interesting note is that the eight bridges that span the Nicola River along this route, are of a variety of different designs and construction.

Although the entire length of the branch line is fairly easily cycled, the railgrade is broken up by three Indian Reserves and a ginseng farm. The ginseng farm has taken over the railbed and gated the NK&S that runs through their property near Nicola and accessing the railbed between Merritt and the ginseng farm is difficult. Between Merritt and Spences Bridge the only obstructions are the many gates and gaining permission from the three Indian bands to cross their reserves. Permission from each of the Indian Reserves is required to cycle the rail bed through their property. In the past the Indian bands freely gave permission but privacy issues with some of the members have effectively shut down any access to the rail grade with the reserves.

An historic accommodation can be found overlooking the railway at Spences Bridge. The Steelhead Inn, which was established in 1862, has been beautifully restored with a dining room and Bed and Breakfast. Also interesting side trip from Merritt is to follow along Nicola Lake to the community of Quilchena, 23 kilometres northeast of Merritt on Highway #5A. In 1907, when the line was completed to Nicola, the CPR reaffirmed its commitment to continue the line up the Nicola Valley and

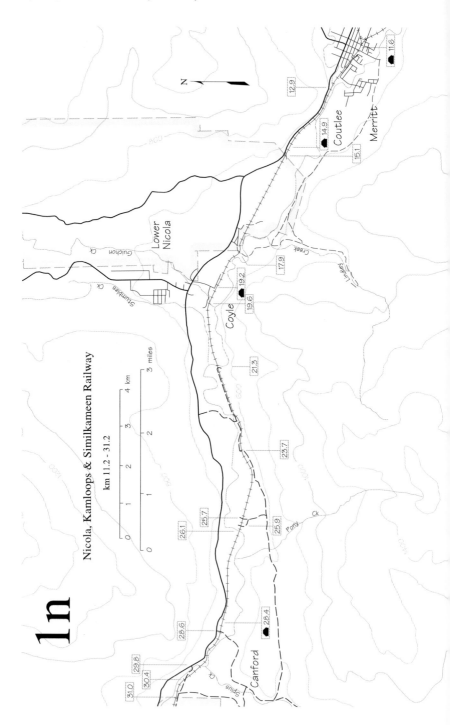

1n

Nicola, Kamloops & Similkameen Railway

km 11.2 - 31.2

then down to Princeton. With this in mind, Joseph Guichon built the Quilchena Hotel in hopes of cashing in on the wealth that the passing railway would bring. Unfortunately, the railway instead headed south from Merritt down the Coldwater Valley. Today, the Quilchena Historic Hotel still operates in all its original glory, and seems to still be waiting for the railway that will never come. ⊨

km

0.0 **Nicola.** |627 ⬤ 🛈 ↓ Υ ⚲

1.3   Ginseng Farms
Unfortunately, the railway line appears to be lost to private interests between here and halfway to Merritt. The railbed is passable between Merritt and the other side of Ginseng Farms.

10.2   Highway #5
The railway crosses under the highway through a culvert with no access to the highway.

11.3   Kettle Valley Railway junction ⊬

11.6 **Merritt** |567 ⬤ 🛈 ↓ ⊬ Υ Δ 🏛 ⋒ 🛈 ⟨ ⚲
A number of streets in Merritt cross the right-of-way giving access to the NK&S. From Merritt to Spences Bridge the railbed is in excellent shape. The dry nature of the Nicola Valley has inhibited the growth of weeds, and the sparse population of this area has fortunately created very little disruption to the railbed. The station in Merritt has been moved and can be found sitting in a field by Canford.

12.9   Nicola River—through plate girder span)(26

14.9 **Coutlee.** |583 ⬤ ↓ ⚲0.1

15.1   Nicola Mameet Indian Reserve boundary—Billwiller Road ↑ ┼→¦
The railbed through the Indian Reserve is private property (km 15.1–17.9). This is private property and must be respected as such.. Venturing on to the reserve is at your own risk. Contact the Lower Nicola Band Administration Office for more information.

17.9   Exiting Nicola Mameet Indian Reserve.

18.0   Road. ↑
Although this road is outside the Indian reservation boundary to get to requires going though the reserve community to access it.

19.2 **Coyle.** |570 ⬤ ⊬ ⚲0.5 ⟵¦

19.6   Guichon Creek—half deck plate girder span)(21

21.3   Nicola River—pony truss)(34

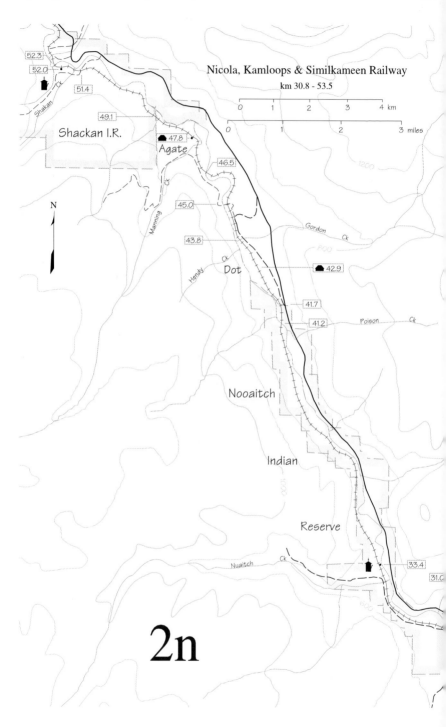

Nicola, Kamloops & Similkameen Railway
km 30.8 - 53.5

Shackan I.R.

Agate

Dot

Nooaitch

Indian

Reserve

2n

For nearly the entire length of this rail line you'll cycle an excellent railbed and enjoy the dramatic scenery of the Nicola River valley.

23.7 Sunshine Village Road ⟙

25.7 Graham Road ⟙

25.9 Thornkonson Road ⟙

26.1 Nicola River—pony truss)(34

28.4 Canford. ⌐525 🏠 |⁄ 🚴0.5

28.6 Sunshine Village Road ⟙

29.8 Nicola River—double through truss)(50

29.9 Canford spur |⁄

30.4 Petit Creek Road ⟙ ⊢→⁚
      Access to Highway #8 to detour around reserve.

30.7 Washout
      This washout will require hiking down to the river bed and backup the other side.

31.0 Nooaitch Indian Reserve
      A gate across the railbed defines the western boundary of the reserve. This is private property and should be respected as such. Venturing on to it is at your own risk. Contact the Nooaitch Indian Band Administration office for more information.

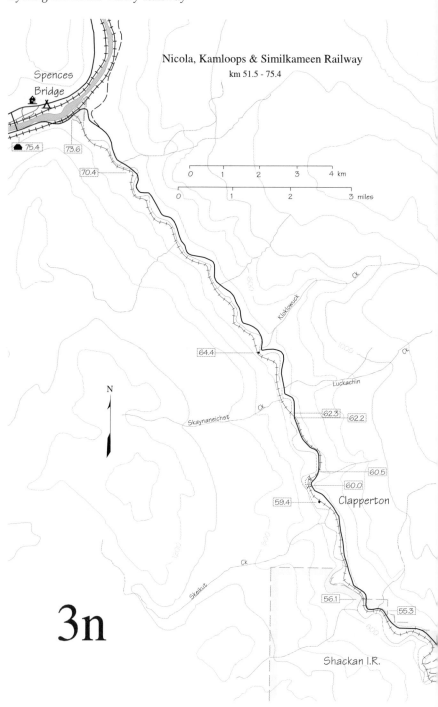

Nicola, Kamloops & Similkameen Railway
km 51.5 - 75.4

Spences Bridge

75.4
73.6
70.4

64.4

Klok!owuck Ck

Luckachin

62.3 62.2

Skaynaneichst Ck

60.5
60.0
59.4 Clapperton

Skelkut Ck

56.1
55.3

Shackan I.R.

N

3n

33.4   Water tower 🯄

41.2   Nicola River)(50

41.7   End of Nooaitch Indian Reserve—pile trestle)(18 ⌐←⌐
A gate just before the trestle defines the northern boundary of the reserve. There is a dirt road access just off the road at this point

42.9   Dot. i447 🏠 ⌐ 🚲0.5

43.8   Gordon Creek—pile trestle)(18

45.0   Manning Creek Forestry Service Road ⌐ ⌐→⌐
Gates line both sides of the road. Last exit before Shackan Indian Reserve.

46.5   Nicola River—through truss)(48

47.8   Agate. i424 🏠 🚲0.8

49.1   Shackan Indian Reserve boundary—gate
A gate across the railbed defines the western boundary of the reserve. This is private property and must be respected as such. Venturing through the reserve is at one's own risk. Contact the Shackan Band Administration for more information.

51.4   Chief Anthony Joe Bridge Road ⌐

52.0   Water tower 🯄

52.3   Nicola River—half deck plate girder)(50

53.5   14 Mile Ranch Road ⌐

55.3   Highway #8 ⌐
Highway #8 has been shifted onto the original railbed for 500 metres, as both the railway and the highway are pushed against a canyon wall by the Nicola River.

56.1   End of Shackan Indian Reserve—gate ⌐←⌐
A few hundred metres past the reserve boundary there are multiple access points as the highway and the railgrade run along side each other. There are six more gates between here and Clapperton Tunnel.

59.3   Clapperton. i348 🏠 ⌐ 🚲0.7

59.5   Fence

Clapperton Tunnel, km 60.0, is noted for its portals made of cut stone.

60.0   Tunnel 🔲99

This 99 metre-long curved tunnel runs through Ten Mile Hill. Unique to this tunnel are the portals built of cut stone.

60.5   Highway #8 ⊤

62.2   Highway #8 ⊤

62.3   Nicola River—deck plate girder and deck truss.)(50

64.4   Water tower 🚰

70.8   Highway #8 access,

This is only access point to Highway #8 between km 62.3 and 73.6.

73.6   Highway #3 ⊤

75.4   Spences Bridge ℹ240 🚂 🚰) ⫽ Y ⛺ 🏠 🍴 ☕ 🍶

Just prior to Spences Bridge, the NK&S parallels alongside the CPR main line. Spences Bridge shows the signs of a once more prominent railway centre. The scars of many more sidings and a wye can be seen etched into the landscape. Located at the end of the line is the historic Steelhead Inn, restaurant and hotel, established in 1862.

VANCOUVER, VICTORIA AND EASTERN RAILWAY (VV&E)
Midway to Princeton, 218.5 kilometres

The VV&E was chartered in 1896 by William Templeton, Mayor of Vancouver, as the railway to bring the riches of the Kootenays to Vancouver, a coast-to-Kootenay line. Not a spike was driven along this imaginary railway until it was taken over by J. J. Hill in 1901. As a direct competitor of the KVR, the VV&E struggled through the mountain ranges of southern B.C. and northern Washington from Midway to Brookmere. In fact, the VV&E was the first railway to reach Princeton from Midway, via Oroville, Keremeos and Hedley. It was subsequently built onward to Brookmere.

Some sections of the VV&E corridor between Midway and Oroville have unfortunately deteriorated past the point of being cycleable and much of it is privately owned. The majority of the VV&E corridor from Oroville to Princeton is not truly cyclable, but the highway follows its path closely or is on top of the grade. However, there are also sections of the railway that still call out to be ridden and explored.

Midway to Oroville

From Midway to the U.S. Border just south of Bridesville two sections of the railgrade are left to explore. The first is from Midway to the 260 metre-long tunnel, at km 9.9. The Midway Dump Road now runs atop the original VV&E grade for 9.1 kilometres. At km 5.0 is the disputed parcel of land that resulted in the Battle of Midway. Departing the road at km 9.1 the tunnel can be found 0.7 kilometres farther down the VV&E grade. The tunnel it's self is on private property but the rail grade on the other side is again on public lands. Past the tunnel the right-of-way is so overgrown with trees that even travel on foot is difficult. One kilometre of bushwhacking past the tunnel, the missing trestle over Myers Creek makes further travel impossible

The second section is the 8.5 km long section between km 25.7 and km 34.2. This section is accessed from the Rock Mountain Forest Service Road at km 28.1.

The only major section on the U.S. side not lost to orchards, private interests, or overgrown in sagebrush is the 15 kilometres that now runs under Nine Mile Road from Circle City to Molson. Although the distance between Oroville and Molson is only 16.9 kilometres, 37 kilometres of track was needed to assault the 850 metre elevation gain with grades near 2.4%. Circle City, about halfway between Oroville and Molson, was named after the large loop that was needed to gain the elevation required to get to Molson. This loop is now a large scar in a farmer's field. Along Nine Mile Road there are many plaques in memory of the railway and the towns that the VV&E affected.

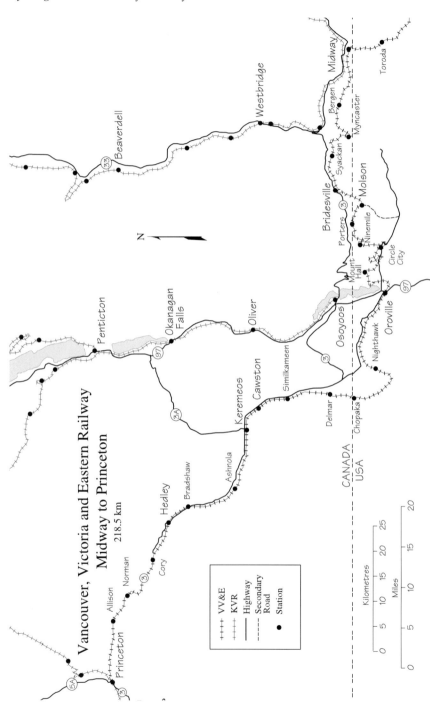

Vancouver, Victoria and Eastern Railway
Midway to Princeton
218.5 km

VV&E
KVR
Highway
Secondary Road
Station

At the near ghost town of Molson, the evidence of the VV&E is still clearly visible. The broad expanse of land for the many sidings, the wye and the station foundation are clearly evident in the middle of town. Located at the southern corner of Molson is an outdoor museum with many preserved and restored buildings of an earlier period of time. To get to Circle City from Oroville, take the Oroville/Cheesaw Road to Nine Mile Road. At the Nine Mile Road intersection, the VV&E grade crosses the Oroville/Cheesaw Road twice as it makes a lazy loop up the side of the hill. You will notice that the trestles are missing, as with most of the trestles on the VV&E.

Oroville to Princeton

There exists no other notable section on the U.S. side of the border that has not been reclaimed by nature or is now in private hands, other then a small section used locally in the town site of Oroville, .

Back on Canadian side of the border two more sections can be ridden. The first is the 5.4 km section, now part of Asnola Road, from the covered "Red Bridge" west of Keremeos to km 161.3 The "Red Bridge" was built in 1907, and is one of a very few still intact. This spot is also the location of the local swimming beach.

The second section runs from the missing bridge over the Similkameen River just out side Hedley at km 181.9 to the town of Princeton. 31 kilometres of this section is now under Highway #3. The remainder is a gravel road that runs back from the intersection with Highway #3 to the missing bridge. Hedley is an old gold mining town that flourished with the help of the railway. Today, you find walking tours available of the historic sites and buildings, and you still see remnants of the workings of a mine still clinging to the mountainside ▄▄

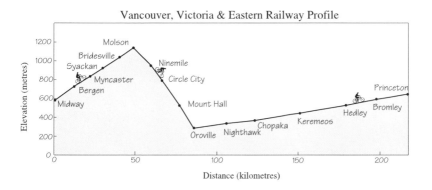

Vancouver, Victoria & Eastern Railway Profile

Molson, km 49.3, was a thriving railway centre in the early 1900s. Today, the memories live on in the "Ye Old Molson" outdoor museum.

Easy cycling and peaceful surroundings make this section between Bridesville and Myncaster a perfect destination for a lazy afternoon, approximately km 34.0.

km   **Midway** 🚋 ⬆ ⌗ ⛺ ♨ ⛩ ⬥
0.0
     The rail bed is passable from Midway to the tunnel at km 9.9, following
     the Midway Dump Road for the most part.

6.5   Hooligan siding ⌗
     Named for the "Battle of Midway," which occurred here when the VV&E
     drove tracks across a piece of property owned by the CPR.

9.9   Tunnel ⬛*274*
     Past the tunnel, the rail bed is impassable to bicycles but can be hiked
     to km 11.5.

10.3   Roberts spur 🚋 ⌇

11.5   Myers Creek ⋇*181*
     Although the rail bed is passable after Myers Creek, there is no way to
     bypass this missing bridge.

13.6   **Bergen** 🚋 ⬥ ⌗

13.9   Kettle Provincial Forest Boundary.
     The railgrade past this point is privately held to km 15.9.

15.0   Tunnel ⬛*35*

15.2   Myers Creek ⸙ ⋇*151*
     A private 4x4 access road from Rock Creek intersects the railway.

15.9   Kettle Provincal Forest Boundary.
     The railgrade is on public lands to km 17.5. There are no public access
     roads to this section.

16.8   Tunnel ⬛*34*

17.5   Kettle Provincal Forest Boundary.
     The railgrade past this point is privately held to km 25.7

21.1   Bridge)(*55*
     Still standing but not for long. It is not advisable to cross on this bridge.

21.8   Myers Creek—horseshoe trestle ⋇*249x27*
     The apex of this huge trestle came within six metres of the interna-
     tional border. The trestle and tracks were removed in 1936. Only the
     fill approaches remain. Myncaster Road crosses underneath the west
     approach.

22.2   Myncaster spur ⅃

This spur line heads south across the border for a few hundred metres to a grain elevator at Bolster Washington. It was intended to run to Cheesaw about eight kilometres south of here.

22.7   Myncaster 🚃 ⛪ ⌐

At Myncaster there was a station, water tank, customs house and post office.

25.0   Tunnel ▣*107*

The entrances of this tunnel are almost covered by rock slides.

25.7   Kettle Provincal Forest Boundary.

The railgrade is on public lands to km 34.2. The only public access to this section of rail grade is by the Rocky Mountain Forest Service Road which crosses at km 28.1.

28.1   Rock Mountain Forest Service Road ⅄

The VV&E crosses a paved road from Rock Creek. From this intersection the railbed to the west is utilized as a forest service road.

30.6   Syackan 🚃 ⌐

34.2   Kettle Provincal Forest Boundary.

The majority of the railgrade past this point to the Molson is privately held.

34.5   Collapsed Bridge ⋇

35.1   Dumont ⅃

35.5   McCoy Creek ⅄ ⋇

The VV&E crossed over McCoy Creek Road and McCoy Creek on this missing trestle.

37.9   Bridesville Road ⅄

West of this road, the railway becomes discontinuous and troublesome as it makes it's way to Bridesville.

41.3   Bridesville 🚃 ⛪

The VV&E loops up and around this small community. For a short section the railbed is under Highway #3 as it passes by the town and the station site. Past Bridesville, the VV&E passes though private farmland and is plowed under in spots, overgrown in others and not passable.

46.2   International border

49.3 Molson 🏠 🏢 ⌇ ⌇ ⌐

Molson was a major railway centre, sporting numerous sidings, spurs and a wye. Today the scars on the landscape around Molson still tell the story of those early days when the railway was an important part of this community. Heading north out of Molson, Nine Mile Road runs atop the original railbed until the Oroville/Cheesaw Road intersection.

57.3 Porters 🏠

60.7 Ninemile 🏠

The railway follows the first of many loops as it starts its descent to Oroville. The road departs the rail bed briefly as the VV&E carves out a couple of large loops as it descends the hillside. At the bottom of the loops the two reconnect.

67.3 Circle City 🏠

Past Circle City, Nine Mile Road departs from the VV&E and connects to the Oroville/Cheesaw Road. The rail bed continues as a rough over-grown scar in the arid landscape. Cycling is not possible past this point. There are a couple of discontinuous sections between here and Oroville that can be cycled, but accessing them is difficult.

78.4 Mount Hull 🏠

84.2   Oroville/Cheesaw Road ⌁

86.3   Great Northern junction ⌇ ⅄

87.7 Oroville 🏠 🏢 ⌇ ⛺ 🏛 ⛱ 🏢 ℂ

95.7   Tunnel ▣

105.9 Nighthawk 🏠

114.5 Ruby Mines 🏠

124.1 Chopaka 🏠 ⌇

124.2 International border

From the international border to Cawston, the VV&E spends the major-ity of its length within the boundaries of three Indian reservations.

126.8 Sneuhumption Creek ⨝ *34*

128.4 Delmar 🏠

130.8 Similkameen River ⨝ *185*

This "Red Bridge" in Keremeos dates back to 1907 and the days when the Great Northern Railway dominated this area.

132.6 Bridge ⚒ *36*

133.6 Similkameen River ⚒ *63*

133.7 Similkameen River ⚒ *257x11*

134.4 Bridge ⚒ *51*

139.7 Similkameen 🏠 ⸙

145.0 Cawston 🏠 ⸙ 🚻 ☕
From Cawston to Keremeos the rail bed follows alongside the highway.

147.7 Spur ⸙

151.6 Keremeos 🏠 ⛽ ⸙ ⛺ 🏛 🛖 🚻 ☕

155.9 Similkameen River)(*287*
This through timber truss-covered bridge is still in use today as the Ashnola Road Bridge. The Ashnola Road is built upon the original grade until km 161.3. From km 161.3 to the missing bridge over the Ashnola River, the grade is marginally passable but is within the Asnola Indian Reserve.

161.3   Ashnola Road leaves railgrade.- Asnola Indian Reserve

162.1   Ashnola River ⚓ *70*

162.2   Ashnola 🏠

167.1   Similkameen River ⚓ *208*

172.4   Bradshaw 🏠
Past Bradshaw, sections of this right-of-way can be seen running along side the highway.

173.6   Highway #3 ⛾

179.6   Highway #3 ⛾

179.8   Hedley 🏠 🏕 ⑂ ⑁ ⛺ 🏛 ⛩ 🔋 (

180.1   Hedley Creek ⚓ *239*

181.9   Similkameen River ⚓ *280*

186.2   Henri Creek ⚓ *44*

186.8   Highway #3 ⛾
Just before Cory, Highway #3 crosses the Similkameen River and turns on to the VV&E right-of-way, following it to Princeton. At this junction, the VV&E can be followed back to the missing bridge over the Similkameen River at km 181.9. This section of the right-of-way is in good shape and is used as a local road.

188.1   Cory 🏠 ⑁

189.1   Smith Creek ⚓ *34*

198.9   Bromley 🏠 ⑂

201.6   Wolf Creek ⚓ *42*

204.4   Spring Creek ⚓ *26*

206.6   Norman 🏠 ⑂

210.0   Short spur ⑁

214.2   Allison 🏠

Laying track on the KVR into Princeton in 1915. VV&E bridge into Princeton can be seen in the background. (Princeton Museum)

215.2 Portland Cement Plant spur ⱱ

This spur runs 2.6 kilometres to the Portland Cement Plant. Past the cement plant the spur crosses the KVR Princeton Subdivision at km 109.2. Because it was abandoned so many years ago, it is difficult to find.

217.4 Spur ⱱ

217.6 Similkameen River Ⱨ

217.7 Kettle Valley Railway junction ⱱ

218.5 Princeton 🏠 🏚 ⱱ ⱱ ⛺ 🏛 ⛩ 🍴 (

Groups Involved with Rail-Trail Conversion

Outdoor Recreation Council of B.C.
334-1367 West Broadway
Vancouver, B.C. V6H 4A9
p 604-737-3058
f 604-737-3666
orc@intergate.ca
www.orcbc.ca/

Boundary Rails-to-Trails Society
c/o Chris Moslin
Grand Forks, B.C.
p 250-442-2620
email: cmoslin@sunshinecable.com

Okanagan-Similkameen Parks Society
Box 787, Summerland, B.C.
V0H 1Z0
p 250-494-8996 f 250-494-1415
sloan@vip.net

International Bicycling & Hiking Society
c/o John Bremmer
Box 5, Oliver, B.C. V0H 1T0
p/f 250-498-4781

Princeton-Brookmere Rails-to-Trails Society
Box 2A, Comp. 3
Tulameen, B.C. V0X 2L0
Princeton, B.C.
p 250-295-6572

Summerland Trans Canada Trail Society
c/o Joyce Parsons
RR 3, S43A, C65
Sumerland, B.C. V0H 1Z0
f 250-494-3022
d&jparsons@telus.net

Kettle Valley Steam Railway
18404 Bathville Road,
Summerland, B.C.
p 250-494-8422
    1-877-494-8424
kvr@telus.net
www.kettlevalleyrail.org

Trans Canada Trail Corporation
6104 Sherbrooke West
Montreal, P.Q. H4A 1Y3
p 1-800-465-3636

KVR Woodwackers
c/o Naramata Parks & Rec
Commision Box 224,
Naramata, B.C. V0H 1N0

Myra Canyon Trestle Restoration Society
PBC Box 611,
Kelowna, B.C. V1Y 7P2

Wine Country Walkways Society
Box 22041
Penticton, B.C. V2A 8L1

B.C. Ministry of Parks
Southern Interior Regional Office
101 - 1050 West Columbia Street
Kamloops, B.C. V2C 1L4
p 250-828-4501

Canadian Rails to Greenways Network
p 1-888-822-2848
www.goforgreen.ca/Greenways/
info@goforgreen.ca

Slocan Valley Heritage Trail Society
Box 22, Winlaw, B.C. V0G 2J0
svhts@telus.net
www.slocan-valley.org

Greenwood Heritage Society-Museum/Archives/Tourism (The Greenwood Museum) Ernie R Hennig Director
214 S. Copper
Greenwood, B.C. V0H 1J0
p/f 250-445-6355
museumgwd@direct.ca
www.greenwoodheritage.B.C..ca

Trails B.C. Southwest Region
Contact: Léon Lebrun
www.trailsbc.ca/southwest_region/
sw_home.asp
southwest@trailsbc.ca

Nicola Valley Explorers Society
P.O. Box 1499
Merritt, B.C. V1K 1B8
nvexplorers@uniserve.com

Accommodations

There are many accommodations available along the KVR route. Picnicking, camping and lodging facilities are all conveniently located. The following list is not meant to be a recommendation of any particular facility, but to provide a guide to those facilities that are on or readily accessed from the KVR right-of-way. We have not listed the numerous facilities that are available in the larger centres such as Penticton. We recommend obtaining a B.C. Accommodation Guide available from B.C. Travel Infocentres or Tourism British Columbia, Legislature Buildings, Victoria, B.C. V8V 1X4, 1-800-663-6000, 604-387-1642, or checking out the provided web site addresses.

If phoning any facility in British Columbia, note that the area code is now 250, except for the lower mainland, which is 604, i.e. Vancouver and Hope.

Carmi Subdivision (Midway to Penticton)

Midway Motor Inn (km 0.0)
622 Palmerston Street, Midway. Not in operation at time of writing.

🏠🍴 Kettle River Inn & Saloon (km 0.0)
Located across from Kettle River and community campground in Midway. Originally the old Thomet Hotel built in 1900.
p 250-449-2288

⅄ Frank Carpenter Memorial Park (km 0.0)
Located on Kettle River in Midway—Florence Street and 5th Avenue. Community campground, washrooms, showers coming soon.
p 250-449-2222

⅄Jim Blaine Campground (km 16.1)
Community campground, sports and picnic area, flush toilets, showers, water, picnic tables.

🏠🍴The Rock Creek Hotel & Prospector Pub (km 18.8)
Junction Highway #3 & #33 in Rock Creek. The oldest continuous operating pub in B.C.
p 250-446-2474

🏠🍴Edelweiss Inn & Motel (km 18.8)
Highway #3, Rock Creek.
p 250-446-2400

⅄Kettle River Provincial Park (km 25.2)
Campground situated in a ponderosa pine forest, flush toilets, showers, water, picnic tables, pay phone.

⅄Little Dipper Campground (km 43.2)
Rhone (Westbridge),
p/f 250-446-2213
ldcamp@wkpowerlink.com

Beaverdell
www.beaverdell.com

🏠🍴 Beaverdell Hotel (km 68.1)
Oldest operating heritage hotel in British Columbia, sleeping units, shared baths, dining and pub. Highway #33, Beaverdell.
p 250-484-5513

🏠🍴 Tamarack Lodge (km 68.1)
Highway #33, Beaverdell.
p   250-484-5616

🏠 Brian Collins Cabins
5839 Highway # 33, Beaverdell
p 250-484-5121
brico2@hotmail.com

⅄🏠Zacks Campground and Rooms
Beaverdell
p 250-484-5532
zack2852@hotmail.com

⅄Arlington Lakes Campground (km 98.2)
Primitive but scenic campsite in the trees on the southwest shore of the southernmost Arlington Lake. Pit toilets, picnic tables.

🏠⅄ Idabel Lake Resort
(turn off at km 117.1) Idabel Lake, 4.2 kilometres from KVR.
p 250-762-1421

⅄Hydraulic Lake Campsite (km 120.8)
Ministry of Forests campsite, pit toilets, picnic tables.

🏠⛺🍴 McCulloch Lake Resort and Campground (km 121.2)
9995 McCulloch Road, Kelowna B.C.
Radio Phone: 250-491-8804
f 250-862-7834
www.members.cnx.net/mcculloch/

Kelowna
(Myra Forest Service Road km 135.2, Little White Forest Service Road, km 148.8, or Gillard Creek Forest Service Road, km 159.1)
www.kelownachamber.org

🏠⛺🍴 Chute Lake Resort (km 171.4)
Large lodge in antique decor with sleeping rooms overlooking Chute Lake, rustic log cabins (linen extra) and campground, showers, flush toilets, laundry, licensed restaurant/ coffee shop, meals may be ordered from the regular menu, dinner is by reservation.
c/o RR#1, Site 16, Comp 16, Naramata V0H 1N0
p 250-493-3535

Naramata and Area
(turn off at km 200.3)

🏠 Vine Vista Family B & B
910 Orchard Lane, Naramata, (Gulch Road at North Naramata Road) Pool, Hot Tub, Bike Rentals, Tours.
p 250-496-5222
info@kettlevalleytrail.com
www.kettlevalleytrail.com

🏠 Lavender Lane Guesthouse (km 202.2)
3005 Debeck Road (East)
Naramata, B.C.
p 250-496-5740
leechman@telus.net
http://www.bctravel.com/ lavenderlane

🏠 Casa Blanca B&B
1109 Sutherland Rd.
p 250-492-1072
f 250-492-1074
vshupp@home.com
www.geton.com/casablanca

🏠 Fox Ben Vineyard Guesthouse
2615 Winifred Rd.
p 250-496-5750
f 250-496-5750

🏠 Lavender Lane Guesthouse
3005 Debeck Rd., Naramata V0H 1N0
p 250-496-5740
f 250-496-5741
leechman@telus.net
www.bbcanada.com/lavenderlane

🏠 Paradise Cove Guest House
3129 Hayman Rd.
p 250-496-5896
f 250-496-5896
www.bctravel.com/pcove
buchanan@vip.net

🏠 Apple Tom & Wild Rudy's Orchard Bed & Breakfast
1056 Naramata Rd.
p 250-487-2188
appletom@canoemail.com

🏠 Sandy Beach Lodge & Resort
4275 Mill Rd.
p 250-496-5765
f 250-496-5765
www.sandybeachresort.com
sandybeachresort@home.com

🏠 Shimmering Lake B&B
1015 Hyde Rd.
p 250-496-5050
f 250-496-5051
wmmeyer@telus.net
www.bbcanada.com/shimmeringlake

🏠 Butternut Ridge B&B
1086 Three Mile Rd., Penticton B.C.
p 250-490-3640
f 250-490-3670
butternut@img.net
www.bbcanada.com/butternutridge

🏠 BC Motel
365 Robinson Avenue
p 250-496-5482
f 250-496-5482

🏠 Village Motel
244 Robinson Avenue
p 250-496-5535
f 250-496-5744
www.villagemotel.com
info@villagemotel.com

🏠 Naramata Heritage Inn & Spa
3625 - 1st Street, Box 130
Naramata, B.C. V0H 1N0
p 250-496-6808
f 250-496-5001
innkeeper@naramatahotel.com
www.naramatainn.com

Paradise Cove Bed & Breakfast
RR1, S2, C31
Naramata, B.C. V0H 1N0
p 250-496-5896
f 250-496-5896
buchanan@vip.net
pcove@bctravel.com/okanagan/
paradisecove

Sandy Beach Lodge & Resort
P.O. Box 8
Naramata, B.C. V0H 1N0
p 250-496-5765
f 250-496-5765
sandybeachresort@vip.net
www.sandybeachresort.com

Shimmering Lake B & B
1015 Hyde Rd.
Naramata, B.C. V0H 1N0
p 250-496-5050
f 250-496-5051
wmmeyer@telus.net
www.bbcanada.com/
shimmeringlake

Butternut Ridge Bed & Breakfast
1086 Three Mile Rd.
p 250-490-3640
f 250-490-3670
   1-877-990-3650
butternut@img.net
www.bbcanada.com/butternutridge

Whistlestop Farm
1175 Chapman Road
p 250-770-8897
lorraine_taylor@hotmail.com
www.bbcanada.com/whistlestop

Canyon Falls Bed & Breakfast
1490 Smethurst Place
Naramata, B.C. V0H 1N0
p 250-496-0007
canyonfalls@home.com
www.canyonfallsbb.com

Penticton (km 215.0)
Numerous camping and lodging
accommodations.
51 Hotels/motels
27 B&Bs
7 campgrounds
Check www.penticton.org

Hostelling International-Penticton
464 Ellis Street, Penticton
p 250-492-3992
f 250-492-8755
bike tools/alarmed bike storage/
private & shared rooms.
penticton@hihostels.bc.ca
www.hihostels.com

Osoyoos Subdivision (Penticton to Osoyoos)

Banbury Green RV Park (km 8.4)
Pine Drive, Penticton, B.C.
Tents welcome, showers, phone,
laundry, flush toilets.
p 250-497-5221.

Okanagan Ponderosa Point Resorts
319 Ponderosa Avenue
Kaleden, B.C.
p 250-497-5354
f 250-497-5312
thepoint@telus.net
www3.telus.ca/thepoint

Bears Den B&B
189 Linden Avenue
Kaleden, B.C.
p 250-497-6721
f 250-497-6453
stay@bearsdenbb.com
www.bearsdenbb.com

Deer Path Lookout B&B
Kaleden, B.C. V0H 1K0
p 250-497-8999
f 250-497-8949
   1-877-497-8999
jarcher@img.net
www.deerpathlookout.bc.ca

Eden House Bed & Breakfast
104 Arlayne Road
Kaleden, B.C. V0H 1K0
p 250-497-8382
f 250-497-8535
   1-888-497-3336
edenhouse@telus.net
www.edenhouse.ca

Grape Arbour Bed And Breakfast
Kaleden, B.C. V0H 1K0
p 250-497-6610
f 250-497-6609
   1-800-644-7177
grape@vip.net
www.bb.canada.com/2594.html

⌂Three Gates Farm
Kaleden, B.C. V0H 1K0
p 250-497-6889
f 250-497-6889
threegates@img.net

⌂Sage Pine B&B
153 Cedar Ave., Kaleden, B.C.
p 250-497-6382

⌂Smith & Wife B & B
230 Ponderosa Ave., Kaleden, B.C.
p 250-497-5536

Okanagan Falls (km 17.1)
Numerous camping and lodging
accommodations.

⌂ La Villa Motel
5029 7th Ave.
p 250-497-6936

⌂ Okanagan Falls Hotel
1046 Main Street, P.O. Box 598
p 250-497-5768
f 250-497-8690

⌂ South Shore Motel
620 Cedar Street Box 9
p 250-497-5789

⌂ Casa Espana
Okanagan Falls,
p 250-497-6002
f 250-497-6009
casa@vip.net
www.bctravel.com/okanagan/
casaespana.html

⌂Willow House B & B
1136 Willow Street, OK Falls
p 250-497-5148

⌂Grey Sage B&B
Highway #97, OK Falls
p 250-497-8138

⚊ Vaseux Lake Provincial Park

(Highway #97 detour route)
Highway #97, four kilometres south of
Okanagan Falls
p 250-494-0321

⚊ Vaseux Lake Campground

(Highway #97 detour route)
Highway #97, Vaseux Lake, Oliver, B.C.
p 250-498-4234.

⌂ Vaseux Lake Lodge
9710 Sundial Road
p 250-498-0516
info@vaseuxlakelodge.com
www.vaseuxlakelodge.com

Oliver (km 36.5)
Numerous camping and lodging
accommodations.

⌂Fritzville B & B
34032 Highway #97, St.,
p 250-498-3645.

⌂AnneMarie's B & B
34427 - 97 St.
p 250-498-0131

⌂Orchard Ridge Guest House
12346 - 318th Ave.
p 250-498-4786

⌂The Log House B & B
30864 Highway #97, Oliver, B.C.
p 250-498-0414

⌂Mirror Lake Guesthouse
9551 - 306 Ave. and Highway #97,
Oliver, B.C.
p 250-495-7959.

⌂Wildflower B & B
Oliver, B.C.
p 250-498-4326.

Osoyoos (km 58.1)
Numerous camping and lodging
accommodations.Check:
www.osoyooschamber.bc.ca
for listings.

Princeton Subdivision
(Penticton to Brookmere)

Summerland (km 15.3)
Numerous camping and lodging
accommodations. Check:
www.summerlandchamber.bc.ca, for
further listings.

⌂Beachside Operates day-to-day
15811 North Lakeshore Drive
p 250-494-8977

⌂F & F Ikeda
12514 Barnes Street
p 250-494-1993

⌂Heritage House circa 1907
11919 Jubilee Road
p 250-494-0288
f 250-494-0024
m.walker9399@telus.net

⌂Lakeview
6915 Solly Road
p 250-494-8556

⌂Laur-O-Winn House
16423 Kean Street
p 250-494-1973
www.pixsell.bc.ca/bcbbd/3/
3000387.htm

⌂Okanagan Lakeview
11591 Front Bench Road
p 250-494-9856
oklakebb@vip.net
www: bbcanada.com/2624.html

⌂Orchard Pines Bed & Breakfast
16575 Logie Road
p 250-494-1626

⌂Past Times Inn
14612 Garnet Avenue
p 250-494-9919

⌂Solly House
6313 Solly Road
p 250-494-8032

⌂Somerset Place
12007 Trayler Place
p 250-494-1644

⌂Summerview
3792 Gartrell Road
p 250-494-1914

⌂Wildhorse Mountain Ranch B & B
25808 Wildhorse Road
Summerland, B.C. V0H 1Z0
p 250-494-0506
f 250-494-0507
stknecht@vip.net
www.wildhorsemountainranch.com

⌂Summerview B & B
Summerland, B.C. V0H 1Z0
p 250-494-1914
summer@vip.net
www.bbcanada.com/2159.html

⌂The Twisty Hazel
P.O. Box 503
13808 Spencer Avenue
p 250-494-3175

⌂The West Summerland Station
7190 South Victoria Road
p 250-494-7578

⌂Wild House Mountain Ranch B & B
25808 Wild Horse Road
p 250-494-0506

⌂Windmill Bed & Breakfast
21606 Highway #97 N.
p 250-494-9302

⋀ Cedarbrook Campground
5011 Highway #97
p 250-494-0911

⋀ Illahie Beach Campground/RV Park
7919 Highway #97
p 250-494-0800

⋀ Peach Orchard Campground
6321 Peach Orchard Road
p 250-494-9649
Off season phone: 250-494-1859

⌂ Creekside Cottages
15216 Lakeshore Drive
p 250-494-9394

⌂ Pleasant View Motel & RV Park
13608 Highway #97
p 250-494-7406
   1-800-801-5469.

⌂ Rosedale Motel
14001 Rosedale Avenue
p 250-494-6431
www.rosedalemotel.com
enquiries@rosedalemotel.com

⌂ Summerland Motel
Corner of Highway #97 & Tait St.
p 250-494-4444
   1-877-245-4406

⋀ Kettle Valley Campgrounds
Don and Joyce Parsons, Owners
p 250-494-4130
f 250-494-3022
d&jparsons@telus.net

⋀ Thirsk Lake Campsite (km 55)
Ministry of Forests campsite on the
shore of Thirsk Lake.

⌂Osprey Lake Lodge B & B
p 250-295-6866
   1-877-295-6866

⋀ Stan & Gail's Place, (km 65.3)
Bankier, B.C.
p 250-295-6898

(km 65.3) Private campsite on Link Lake.
gdickson@nethop.net
www.geocities.com/linkladyca/linklake.html

⚊ Chain Lake Campsite (km 71.1)
Ministry of Forests campsite on the shore of Chain Lake.

⚊ Jellicoe Station Inn B & B (km 71.0, 72.9)
p 250-295-0160

⚊ Friesian Ranch
p 250-295-3160
friesian@nethop.net
www.friesianranch.com

⚊ ⚊ Princeton Castle Resort (km 109.4)
Highway #40, Princeton, B.C.
p 250-295-6250
info@castleresort.com
www.castleresort.com

Princeton
Check: town.princeton.bc.ca/ for additional listings

⚊ Woodside Inn B & B
141 W. China Creek Road, Princeton
p 250-295-3554
   1-800-880-0822.

⚊ Coalmont Hotel (km 132.3)
Built in 1912, newly restored with antique decor. Five sleeping units, shared baths, public dining area, and pub.
p 250-295-6066

⚊ Granite Creek Campground (km 132.3)
Ministry of Forests campsite located at the original site of Granite City.

⚊ ⚊ Trading Post General Store and Restaurant. (km 138.7)
Tulameen, B.C.
p 250-295-6478

⚊ Otter Sleep Inn (km 138.7)
Otter Avenue, Tulameen, B.C.
p 250-295-7494
p 250-295-6449

⚊ Tulameen Retreat B & B (km 138.8)
Tulameen, B.C.
p 250-295-7005
tulameenretreat@nethop.net

⚊ Otter Lake Provincial Park (km 139.1)
Large park on the opposite shore of Otter Lake.

⚊ Stillwaters Lakeside B & B
Tulameen, B.C.
p/f 250-295-3728
Lakeside cabins, mobile on-site catering
p 250-295-3009
stillwaters@nethop.net
www.stillwatersbb.com

⚊ Buckhorn Ranch Cabins (km 146)
Trail Rides (horses) Tulameen, B.C.
p 250-295 7168

⚊ Burt Sharkey's Horse Motel (km 168.5)
c/o Kershar, Smiles
N. Otter Valley Road
Box 2A, Comp 2, Tulameen, B.C.

⚊ ⚊ Coley Creek Lodge Brookmere
   1-888-724-7799
p 604-463-7588
Cabins, camping, showers, laundary.
wMethot@bigfoot.com
Terry_Methot@bc.sympatico.ca
www.coleycreeklodge.com

Merritt/Nicola Subdivision (Brookmere to Merritt/ Nicola to Spences Bridge)

⚊ Quilchena Hotel
Quilchena, B.C.
p 250-378-2611

Merritt (km 47.3 Merritt Sub km 11.6, Nicola Sub)
Numerous camping and lodging accommodations. Check:
www.city.merritt.bc.ca

A.P. Guest Ranch
Highway #5A—Merrit-Princeton Highway
p 250-378-6520

⚊ Winding River Guest Ranch
Torgerson Rd., Merrit, B.C.
p 250-378-6534

⚊ Guichon Creek Outdoor Adventures
322 Guichon Ave., Lower Nicola
Near "KVR's" Nicola Subdivision
p 250-378-2065
bike rentals, guided tours

♨Grant Ranches Ltd.
Aberdeen Rd., Lower Nicola
p 250-378-9865

♨ Aberdeen Inn & Pub
318 Aberdeen, Lower Nicola
p 250-378-2868

♨ Steelhead Inn (km 75.4—Nicola Sub)
Fourteen units: 1862 historic hotel
located at the end of the Nicola line.
Box 100, Spences Bridge, V0K 2L0
p 250-458-2398.

♨ Quarter Circle J Motel
Riverview Avenue, Spences Bridge
p 250-458-2223

Spences Bridge
Motels, campgrounds and the local
pub are all located in the town on the
north side of the Thompson River.

Coquihalla Subdivision (Brookmere to Hope)

♨ ⅄ Coquihalla Lakes Lodge and Campsite (km 28.9)
Exit 228 Coquihalla Highway
p 250-378-2096
    1 877 978-2096
lakes@coquihalla.com
www.coquihalla.com

⅄ Othello Tunnels Campground (km 78.7)
67851 Othello Road
p 604-869-9448

⅄ Coquihalla Campsite (km 85.7)
800 Kawkawa Lake Road, Hope, B.C.
p 604-869-7119

Hope (km 87.4)
Numerous camping and lodging
accommodations. Check:
www.hopechamber.bc.ca for listings.

Columbia & Western Railway (Castlegar to Midway)

Castlegar (km 0.0)
Numerous camping and hotel
accommodations.

♨Mountain Retreat Guest House
Castlegar, B.C.
p 250-365-9396

♨ Best Western Fireside Inn
1810-8th Ave
p 250-365-2128

♨ Castlegar Motel
Raspberry Village
p 250-365-3333

⅄ Castlegar R V Park Campground
1725 Mannix
p 250-365-2337

♨ Cozy Pines Motel
2118 Crestview Cr.
p 250-365-5613

♨ Days Inn Castlegar
651-18th St.
p 250-365-2700

♨ Flamingo Motel
1660 Columbia Ave.
p 250-365-7978

♨ Marlane Hotel
330 Columbia Ave.
p 250-365-2626

⅄ Kootenay River Kampground
651 Rosedale
p 250-365-5604

♨ Monte Carlo Motor Inn
1935 Columbia Ave.
p 250-365-2177

♨ Mountain Retreat Guest House
1542 Mountain Pass Ck.
p 250-365-8386

♨ Twin Rivers Motel
1485 Columbia Ave.
p 250-365-6900

♨Robson Homestead B & B
3671 Broadwater Rd.
p 250-365-2374

♨Hope's End Plantation
887 Waterloo Rd.
Castlegar, B.C.
p 250-365-3206

♨Blue Berry Hill B & B
145 Fairview Dr., Castlegar, B.C.
p 250- 365-5583

♨The Greenhouse B & B
Syringa Creek Park, Castlegar, B.C.
p 250- 365-2696

Chistina Lake (exit C&W from Fife km 82.2 or Santa Rosa Road km 86.8)

Numerous lodging accomodations in Christina Lake. Check for additional listings; www.christinalake.com

♨ Blue Mountain Lodge
p 250-447-6356

♨ Λ Camp Beverly Hills Cottages & Campground
p 250-447-9277

♨ Harmony Farms
p 250-447-6444

♨ Lakeview Motel
p 250-447- 9358

♨ New Horizon Motel
p 250-447-9312

♨ Parklane Motel & RV Park
p 250-447-9385

♨ Λ Schulli Resort
p 250-447-9269

♨ Sunflower Inn B & B
p 250-447-6201

♨ Λ Totem Motel & R.V. Park
p 250-447-9322

Λ Cascade Cove RV Park & Campground
p 250-447-6662

♨ Christina Lakeside Resort
p 250-447-9213

Λ Christina Pines Campground
p 250-447-9587

♨ Royal Inn B & B
1 Chase Rd.
Christina Lake, B.C.
p 250-447-9090

♨ Ruby's Garden B & B
94 Holmes Rd., Christina Lake, B.C.
p 250-447-6693

Λ Cascade Cove Campground (km 90.1)
1290 River Road, Christina Lake, junction of Highway #3 & U.S. 395
p 250-447-6163

Λ Country Hideaway RV Park & Campground (exit C&W from km 105.4)
Manly Meadows Road
p 250-442-2341

Λ Riviera RV Park & Campground
Highway #3—two kilometres east of Grand Forks
p 250-442-2158

Grand Forks (km 111.3)

Numerous lodging accommodations in town.

Λ Grand Forks Municipal Park & Campground
Twenty-eight sites: flush toilets, showers, firepits, river swimming, near downtown shopping area, sandy beach and playground. Located two blocks south of Highway #3 on 5th Street.
p 250-442-2833

♨ The White House B & B
1350-73 Ave., Grand Forks, B.C.
p 250-442-8481

♨ The Powell House B & B
981 Central Ave., Grand Forks, B.C.
p 250-442-5737

♨ The Dewdney Trail B & B
3555 Sion Frontage Rd., Grand Forks, B.C.
p 250-442-5757

♨ The Orchard B & B
5615 Spencer Rd., Grand Forks, B.C.
p 250-442-8583

Greenwood (km 147.8)

Check :www.city.greenwood.bc.ca for additional listings

♨ Λ Greenwood Motel & Campground
256 North Copper St.
p 250-445-6363

♨ Evening Star Motel
798 North Government St.
Greenwood, B.C.
p 250-445-6733

♨ The Forshow House B & B
197 Kimberly Ave. S.
Greenwood, B.C.
p 250-445-2208

Λ Boundary Creek Provincial Park (km 152.0)
Eighteen sites: camping, pit toilets, located on the east side of Boundary Creek. The creek is easily forded at the campsite or you can exit the

railway at km 154.1 on Boltz Road, then continue along the highway to the campground.
p 250-825-4421

⚎ Boundary Falls Ranch and Campground
Forty sites: Eight kilometres west of Greenwood on Highway #3.
p 250-445-6578

Midway (km 162.3)
For accommodations refer to the KVR Carmi Subdivision (Midway to Penticton).

Nelson & Fort Sheppard Railway (Salmo to Troup)

⚏ Pine Springs Motel
5125 Highway #3, Salmo, B.C.
p 250-357-9660

⚏ Reno Motel
123 Railway, Salmo, B.C.
p 250-357-9937

⚏ Sal Crest Motel
110 Motel, Salmo, B.C.
p 250-357-9557

⚏ Salmo Hotel
101 4th St., Salmo, B.C.
p 250-357-9414

⚏ Selkirk Motel
Highway 3, Salmo, B.C.
p 250-357-2346

⚏ Silver Dollar Hotel
115 - 4th St., Salmo, B.C.
p 250-357-9666

⚏ Ymir Hotel (km 11.9)
7104 1st Ave., Ymi, B.C.
p 250-357-9611

⚏ Cedarwood Cottage
15 min. south of Nelson on Hwy #6
p/f 250-352-0147

⚏ Nelson (km 39.8)
Numerous camping and lodging accommodations. Check: www.discoverNelson.com, for additional listings.

⚏ Dancing Bear Inn (Hostel)
A171 Baker St.
p 250-352-7573
dbear@netidea.com

⚏ Flying Squirrel International Hostel
198 Baker St., Nelson, B.C.
p 250-352 7285
  1 866 755 RIDE
info@flyingsquirrelhostel.com

⚏ Alpine Motel
1120 Hall Mines Rd.
p 250-352-5501
  1-888-356-2233
alpine@alpine-motel.com

⚏ Best Western Baker Street Inn
153 Baker Street
p 250-352-3525
info@bwbakerstreetinn.com

⚏ Duhamal Store and Motel
6235 Greenwood
p 250-825-4645

⚏ Heritage Inn
422 Vernon Street
p 250-352-5331
info@heritageinn.org

⚏ Lakeside Motel
805 Nelson Ave.
p 250-352-3185

⚏ North Shore Inn
687 Highway #3A
p 250-352-6606

⚏ New Grand Hotel
615 Vernon Street Nelson
p 250-352-7211

⚏ Prestige Lakeside Resort and Convention Centre
701 Lakeside Dr.
p 250-352-7222
nelson@prestigeinn.com

⚏ Viking Lakeview Motel
1301 Front St.
p 250-352-3595

⚏ Villa Motel
655 Highway #3A North
p 250-352-5515

⚏ Willow Bay Motel
2615 Highway #3A North
p 250-825-9421

⚏ Big Louie's Beach House
4596 Highway #3A North
p 250-825-4100

Anka's Garden View Retreat Bed and Breakfast
2115 Fort Sheppard Dr.
p 250-352-5907
  1-866-937-7700
gardenbb@telus.net

Blue Heron Beach House
5590 Highway #3A, Nelson, B.C.
p 250-229-4471
blueheronbeachhouse@telus.net

By the Brook Guest House
2348 Boyer Rd., Nelson, B.C.
p 250-825-0144
bythebrook@telus.

Casa Blanca B & B
724 Second St.
p 250-354-4431

Dandelion B & B
519 Carbonate St.
p 250-505-5466
lion@netidea.com

The Dragon Fly Inn
1016 Hall Mines
p 250-354-1128
  1-866-354-1128
dragnfly@netidea.com

Emory House B & B
811 Vernon St.
p 250-352-7007

The Five Gables Inn
3531 Keiran North
p 250-825-3419

Gingerbread House
820 Cottonwood St.
p 250-354-1192
  1-877-2-ginger
GingerbreadBB@aol.com

The Grand B & B
1413 Front St.
p 250-505-5005
  1-800-670-4955

Greystone Cottage B & B
1319 Josephine St.
p 250-354-4587

Inn The Garden B & B
408 Victoria St.
p 250-352-3226
  1-800-596-2337

Mountain View B & B
2181 Taylor Dr.
p 250-825-4674
nelmed@netidea.com

Nelson Guest House
2109 Ft. Sheppard
p 250-354-0198

Redfern House
102 - 402 Baker
p 250-352-1854

Robson House
624 Robson
p 250-352-2448

Sen Tosa B & B
402 Observatory St.
p 250-354-1993

Silver King Hideaway
1605 Robertson St.
p 250-354-4340

Sunflower B & B
324 Observatory St.
p 250-354-1850
margaret_hornby@hotmail.com

Taghum Beach B & B
3289 Granite Rd.
p 250-352-0362
  1-866-260-2200
taghumbeach@telus.net

Willow Point Lodge
2211 Taylor Dr.
p 250-825-9411
  1-800-949-2211
willowpl@uniserve.com

Whitewater Inn
4666 Whitewater Rd.
p 250-352-9150

Columbia & Kootenay Railway (South Slocan to Slocan)

Cathedral Lakes Lodge
Slocan Park,
p 250-226-7560
  1-888-255-4453
info@cathedral-lakes-lodge.com
www.cathedral-lakes-lodge.com

Cedar Creek Guest House (km 29.7)
Winlaw, B.C.
p 250-226-7891

Slocan (km 50.0)

Slocan Inn & Restaurant
912 Slocan, B.C.
p 250-355-2223
Restaurant 250-355-2600

⚓ Slocan Motel
801 Harold, B.C.
p 250-355-2344

⚕ Springer Creek RV Park & Campground
Slocan, B.C.
p 250-355-2226

⚓⚕ Karibu Park Cabins and Camping
5730 Cedar Creek Road, Winlaw,
B.C.
p 250-226-7306
f 250-226-7306
   1-888-452-7428
Karibu@netidea.com

**⚓⚕⫸ Lemon Creek Lodge, Restaurant &
Campground**
7680 Kennedy Road, Lemon Creek
   1-877-907-0809
www.lemoncreeklodge.com

⚓⫸Haus Lemon Creek
P.O.Box 329, Slocan, B.C.
p 250-355-2536
hauslemon@netidea.com

Nakusp & Slocan Railway (Three Forks to Nakusp)

⚓⫸Mistaya Country Inn B & B
Silverton, B.C.
p 250-358-7787
f 250-358-7787
www.bctravel.net/mistaya/

⚓⫸Sweet Dreams Guesthouse
P.O. Box 177 New Denver, B.C.
702 Eldorado, New Denver, B.C.
p 250-358-2415
f 250-358-2556
jbus@wkpowerlink.com

⚓ Silverton Resort
Silverton, B.C.
p 250-358-7157
f 250-358-7157

⚓ Blue Sky Resort
8021 Lower Galena Farm Road,
Silverton, B.C.
p 250-358-2362
blueskyresory@telus.net

⚓⫸Three Maples B & B
710 Arthur, B.C.
p 250-355-2586

New Denver (km 6.8)

⚓⫸Mistaya Country Inn B & B
Highway #6 New Denver, B.C.
p 250-358-7787
mistayaresort@netidea.com

⚓ Valhalla Inn
416 5th Ave., New Denver, B.C.
p 250-358-7771

Canyon Court Motel
937 Highway #23, Nakusp, B.C.
p 250-265-3737

⚓⫸Country B & B
1012 Highway #6, Nakusp, B.C.
p 250-265-4448

⚓⫸Country Hills B&B
Highway #6, Nakusp, B.C.
p 250-265-3004

⚓⫸Cozy Cabin B&B
228 First Ave., Nakusp
(250) 265-3049

⚓ Huckleberry Inn
Hotspring Rd., Nakusp, B.C.
p 250-265-4544

⚓ Kuskanax Lodge
515 Broadway, Nakusp, B.C.
p 250-265-3618

⚓ Leland Hotel
96 4th Ave. SW, Nakusp, B.C.
p 250-265-4221
pub 265-3314

⚕ Nakusp Hot Springs Campground
92 - 6th Ave. NW, Nakusp, B.C.
p 250-265-4528

⚓ Rock Island Resort
3774 Rock Island Rd.., Nakusp, B.C.
p 250-265-0040

⚓ Selkirk Inn
210 - 6th Ave., Nakusp, B.C.
p 250-265-3666

⚓⫸Three Island Resort
Summit Rd., Nakusp, B.C.
p 250-265-3023

Tour Operators

Great Explorations
#305 - 1510 West 1st Ave.
Vancouver, B.C. V6J 4S3
p 604-730-1247
f 604-738-7655
info@great-explorations.com
www.great-explorations.com

Vista Treks
Kettle Valley Trail Tours & Shuttle
Bike Rentals
Craig Henderson
Box 186, Naramata, B.C. V0H 1N0
p 250-496-5220
f 250-496-5422
craig@kettlevalleytrail.com
www.kettlevalleytrail.com

Monashee Adventure Tours
1591 Highland Dr., North Kelowna
p 250-762-9253
  1-888-762-9253
info@monasheeadventuretours.com
www.monasheeadventuretours.com

Tulameen Adventure Tours
Bicycle Shuttle
Tulameen
p/f 250-295-6681

Tykes Can Tour
p 250-762-9216
  1-888-211-9043
tykescantour@home.com
www.welcometokelowna.com/
tykescantour/

West Canada Bike Tours
Vermittlungsagentur Europa
Natours
Untere Eschstrasse 15
D-49179 Ostercappeln
Telefon: (49) 05473-922929
Fax: (49) 05473-8219
agenturwcbt@natours.de
www.kanada-bike.com

Company of Adventurers
Guichon Creek Outdoor Adventures
Bike rentals and guided tours.
322 Guichon Avenue, Lower Nicola
p 250-378-2065

Okanagan Bicycle Tours
11059 Eva Road, Winfield
p 250-766-4086
  1-800-991-3233

Wildways Adventures Sports Tours
1925 Highway #3, Christina Lake
p/f 250-447-6561
  1-800-663-6561

Canadian Trails Adventure Tours
One week and longer tours.
Suite 153, 162-2025 Corydon Ave,
Winnipeg, Manitoba
  1-800-668-2453
canadiantrails@email.msn.com
www.canadiantrails.com

The Great Canadian Adventure Company
300, 10190 104 Street, Edmonton,
Alberta
1-888-285-1676
info@adventures.com
www.adventures.com

Landowners

Trans Canada Trail Corporation
6104 Sherbrooke West
Montreal, P.Q. H4A 1Y3
  1-800-465-3636

Penticton Indian Band Administration
Westhill Dr., Penticton, B.C.
p 250-493-0048

Coldwater Indian Band
2249 Quilchena, Merritt, B.C.
p 250-378-6174
f 250-378-5351

Lower Nicola Band Administration Office
#73 Shulus, Highway #8,
Lower Nicola, B.C.
p 250-378-5157

Nooaitch Band Administration
p 250-378-6141

Shakan Band Administration
2090 Coutlee, Merritt, B.C.
p 250-378-5410

Topographical Maps

Map Suppliers
Nanaimo Maps & Charts
8 Church Street
Nanaimo, BC V9R 5H4
1-800-665-2513 Fax 754-2313

Map Town
640 - 6 Ave SW
Calgary, AB T2P 0S4
Tel (403) 266-2241
Fax (403) 266-2356

1:250,000
Kettle Valley Railway
92 H Hope
82 E Penticton

C&W Railway
82 E Penticton
82 F Nelson
NK&S Railway
92 H Hope
92 I Ashcroft

N&FS and C&K Railway
82 F Nelson

N&RS Railway
82 F Nelson
82 K Lardeau

VV&E Railway
92 H Hope
82 E Penticton
NM 11-10 Okanagan

1:50,000
Midway to Penticton
82 E/2 Greenwood
82 E/3 Osoyoos
82 E/6 Beaverdell
82 E/11 Wilkinson Creek
82 E/14 Kelowna
82 E/12 Summerland
82 E/5 Penticton
82 E/4 Keremeos

Penticton to Princeton
82 E/12 Summerland
92 H/9 Bandeir
92 H/8 Hedley
92 H/7 Princeton

Princeton to Brookmere
92 H/7 Princeton
92 H/10 Tulameen
92 H/15 Aspen Grove

Brookmere to Merritt
92 H/15 Aspen Grove
92 I/2 Merritt

Brookmere to Hope
92 H/15 Aspen Grove
92 H/14 Boston Bar
92 H/11 Spuzzum
92 H/6 Hope

C&W Railway
82 F/5 Castlegar
82 E/8 Deer Park

82 E/1 Grand Forks
82E/2 Greenwood

NK&S Railway
92 I/2 Merritt
92 I/3 Prospect Creek
92 I/6 Spences Bridge

N&FS Railway
82 F/3 Salmo
82 F/6 Nelson
82 F/11 Kokanee Peak

C&K Railway
82 F/5 Castlegar
82 F/12 Passmore
82 F/14 Slocan

N&S Railway
82 F/14 Slocan
82 K/3 Rosebery
82 K/4 Nakusp

VV&E Railway
92 H/7 Princeton
92 H/8 Hedley
92 H/1 Ashnola River
92 E/4 Keremeos
82 E/3 Osoyoos
82 E/2 Greenwood

USA Maps (VV&E Railway)

1:25,000	7 x 15' Series
48119 - H1-T	M-025
48119 - H3-T	M-025
48119 - H5-T	M-025

Services

Following is a list of some services you may find useful when cycling or planning your trip. This is not a comprehensive list or a recommendation of any particular facility.

Bicycle Services

Sun Country Cycle
533 Main Street, Penticton
p 250-493-0686

The Bike Barn
300 Westminster Avenue, Penticton
p 250-492-4140

Kettle Valley Bike Rentals
3005 Debeck Road (East), Naramata
p 250-496-5740
leechman@telus.net
www.kettlevalleybikerentals.pentiction.net

High Country Sports
10120 Main, Summerland
p 250-494-5050

Kelowna Cycle
2949 Pandosy, Kelowna
p 250-762-0660

Ry-Dan Sports
2049 Quilchena Ave., Merritt
p 250-378-3939

Backroads Bike Shop
Nicola Ave. & 5th Street, Tulameen
p 250-295-3735

Backroads Bike Shop
308 Bridge St., Princeton
p 250-295 3722
backroadsbikeshop@hotmail.com
backroads.vitualave.net

Wildways Adventure Sports & Tours
Johnson Road & Highway #3,
Christina Lake
p 250-447-6561
   1-800-663-6561

Chain Reaction Bike and Board
5th St. and Market Ave. Grand Forks
p 250-442-0118
After hour repairs 250-442-8561

Entertainment

Kettle Valley Brakemen
Folksy band with a great live performance, stories and songs of the KVR. CD's and performance information contact:
Jack Godwin
C/O General Delivery,Naramata, B.C.
V0H 1N0
p 250-496-5401
question@kvbrakemen.com
www.kvbrakemen.com

Airlines

Air Canada/Air BC (Penticton)
250-492-2165
Air Canada/Air BC (within B.C.)
1-800-663-3721
Air Canada/Air BC (from USA)
1-800-663-8868
Westjet Airlines
1-800-538-5696
Airlines provide daily service to Castlegar, Penticton and Kelowna.

Greyhound Bus Lines

1-800-663-8868
Penticton   250-492-2606
Provides bus service to most towns en route.

Via Rail

From Canada   1-800-561-8630
From USA   1-800-561-3949
Provides rail service to Edmonton, Jasper, Kamloops, Boston Bar, Ashcroft, Hope and Vancouver.

Car Rentals

Avis Rent-A-Car   250-493-8133
Budget Rent-A-Car   250-493-0212
Tilden Rent-A-Car   250-493-7288

Travel Infocentres

Midway	250-449-2614
Rock Creek	250-446-2455
Penticton	250-493-4055
	fax 250-492-6119
Oliver	250-498-6321
	fax 250-498-3156
Osoyoos	250-495-7142
	fax 250-495-6161
Summerland	250-494-2686
	fax 250-494-4039
Princeton	250-295-3103
	fax 250-295-3255
Merritt	250-378-2281
	fax 250-378-6485
Hope	604-869-2021
	fax 604-869-2160
Castlegar	250-365-6313
	fax 250-365-5778
Christina Lake	250-447-6161
Grand Forks	250-442-2833
Greenwood	250-445-6777
Nelson	250-352-3433
	fax 250-352-6355

B.C. Wine Institute (Kelowna)
1-800-661-2294, 250-762-4887
Okanagan Wine Tours
250-490-9898
Weather Forecasts (Penticton)
250-492–6991

Grocery Stores

Castlegar, Christina Lake, Grand Forks, Greenwood, Midway, Rock Creek, Westbridge, Beaverdell, Penticton, Kaleden, Okanagan Falls, Oliver, Osoyoos, Summerland, Osprey Lake (3 Lakes General Store), Princeton, Tulameen, Hope, Nicola, Merritt, Lower Nicola, Spences Bridge, Salmo, Ymir, Nelson, Slocan Park, Slocan, New Denver, Nakusp.

Laundromats

Castlegar: Bel-Air Laundry, 632-18th Street, 250-365-5145

Christina Lake: Christina Lake Laundry, 19 West Lake, 250-447-6422

Grand Forks: Sunshine Valley Laundromat, 7344-3rd Street, 250-442-2315

Greenwood: Motherload Laundry, corner of Gold St.(Highway #3) and Washington St., 250-445-6763

Chute Lake: coin laundry at Chute Lake Resort

Penticton: The Laundry Basket, 976 W. Eckhardt Ave., 250-493-7899

Osoyoos: Lakeview Plaza Laundry, 8401-93 St., 250-495-7577

   Pete's Laundry, 7301-62 Ave., 250-495-3295

Princeton: 148 Bridge St. & Halliford Ave., 250-295-7542

Tulameen: corner of 2nd Street & Otter Road

Merritt: laundry/showers, across from Coldwater Hotel on Quilchena Ave.

   Clean Gene's coin laundry, 2749 - Nicola Ave. (east end of avenue)

Hope: coin laundry located in Midtown Mall

Nelson: Esso Village Coin-op Laundry 524 Nelson Ave, 250-352-3534

   The Laundry Mat 323 Nelson Ave, 250-352-1233

   Plaza Laundromat 616 Front Street, 250-352-6077

Emergency Medical Services

1-800-461-9911

In case of any emergency, dial this phone number and a dispatcher will best assist you in obtaining the emergency service you require.

Hospitals are located at Castlegar, Grand Forks, Penticton, Oliver, Summerland, Princeton, Merritt, Hope, Nelson, and Nakusp.

Museums

Greenwood Heritage Society-Museum/Archives/Tourism
Ernie R Hennig Director
214 S. Copper
Greenwood, B.C. V0H 1J0
p 250-445-6355
museumgwd@direct.ca
www.greenwoodheritage.bc.ca

Boundary Museum
7370-5th St.
Grank Forks, B.C. VOH 1HO
p/f 250-442-3737

Nakusp & District Museum
92 6th Ave. NW
Nakusp, B.C. V0G 1R0
p 250-265-0015

Salmo Museum
100 4th St.
Salmo, B.C. V0G 1Z0
p 250-357-2200

Nelson Museum
402 Anderson St.
Nelson, B.C. V1L 3Y3
p 250-352-9813
f 250-352-9810

Castlegar & District Heritage Society
400 13th Ave.
Castlegar, B.C.V1N 1G2
p 250-365-6440

Midway Village Of - Kettle River Museum
661 8th Ave.
Midway, B.C. V0H 1M0
p 250-449-2614
f 250-449-2614

Silvery Slocan Historical Society Museum
202 6th Ave.
New Denver B.C. V0G 1S0
p 250-358-2201
f 250-358-2656

Princeton & District Pioneer Museum
167 Vermilion Ave.
Princeton, B.C. V0X 1W0
p 250-295-7588

Hope Museum
919 Water
Hope, B.C. V0X 1L0
p 604-869-7322

Nicola Valley Archives Association
P.O. Box 1262 Stn. Mai
Merritt, B.C. V1K 1B8
p 250-378-4145
f 250-378-4145

Suggested References

Barlee, N. L., *Gold Creeks and Ghost Towns*. Canada West Magazine, Box 995, Summerland, Western Heritage Supply, Box 208, Burnaby 1, Nov. 1980

Basque, Garnet, *Ghost Towns & Mining Camps of the Boundary Country*, Sunfire Publications Ltd., Langley 1992

Blake, Don, *Blakeburn, From Dust to Dust*

Boundary Historical Society

4th Report 1964, 5th Report 1967, 9th Report 1983, 10th Report 1985, 12th Report 1992

Joe Smuin, *Canadian Pacific's Kettle Valley Railway*, British Railway Modellers of North America, 5124 - 33rd St., N.W., Calgary AB T2L 1V4

McCulloch, Andrew, *A History of the Kettle Valley Railway*

Okanagan Historical Society, 13th Report 1950, 25th Report

Turner, Robert D. & Wilkie, David S., *The Skyline Limited: The Kaslo & Slocan Railway*, Sono Nis Press, Victoria, 1994

Sanford, Barrie, *McCulloch's Wonder*, Whitecap Books, Vancouver 1989

Sanford, Barrie, *Steel Rails and Iron Men*, Whitecap Books, Vancouver 1990

Shewchuck, Murphy, *Backroads Explorer Vol. 2: Similkameen and South Okanagan*, Hancock House, Surrey, 1988

Shewchuck, Murphy, *Coquihalla Country*, Sonotek Publishing, Merritt, 1990

Turnbull, Elise G., *Ghost Towns and Drowned Towns of the West Kootenay*, Heritage House Publishing Company Ltd., Surrey 1988

Turner, Robert D., *Steam on the Kettle Valley,* Sono Nis Press, Victoria 1995

White, John, *Driving the Kettle Valley Railway, Field Maps and Notes,* John White 1996, 344 Oxford Drive, Port Moody, BC V3H 1T2, (604) 936-2367 email jwhite@planeteer.com

Wisnicki, Mike, *Over the Hill, A Guide to Mountain Bike Rides in the Grand Forks Area*, Ground Forks Publications, Grand Forks 1994

Web Sites

Check out the **author's** web site for updates and changes.
www.planet.eon.net/~dan/

Check out **Rocky Mountain Books'** site for more outdoor recreation guides.
www.rmbooks.com